IMPOSING STANDARDS

A volume in the series
Cornell Studies in Money

Edited by Eric Helleiner and Jonathan Kirshner

A list of titles in this series is available at cornellpress.cornell.edu

IMPOSING STANDARDS

The North-South Dimension
to Global Tax Politics

Martin Hearson

CORNELL UNIVERSITY PRESS   ITHACA AND LONDON

Thanks to generous funding from the Economic and Social Research Council and
UK Aid, along with the Bill and Melinda Gates Foundation, the ebook editions of
this book are available as open access volumes through the Cornell Open initiative.

First published 2021 by Cornell University Press

Library of Congress Cataloging-in-Publication Data

Names: Hearson, Martin, author.
Title: Imposing standards : the north-south dimension to global tax politics /
    Martin Hearson.
Description: Ithaca [New York] : Cornell University Press, 2021. | Series: Cornell
    studies in money | Includes bibliographical references and index.
Identifiers: LCCN 2020038497 (print) | LCCN 2020038498 (ebook) |
    ISBN 9781501755989 (paperback) | ISBN 9781501756009 (pdf) |
    ISBN 9781501755996 (epub)
Subjects: LCSH: International business enterprises—Taxation—Developing
    countries. | Double taxation—Developing countries—Treaties. | Investments,
    Foreign—Developing countries. | Taxation—Law and legislation—Developing
    countries. | Globalization—Economic aspects. | Developing countries—Foreign
    economic relations—Developed countries. | Developed countries—
    Foreign economic relations—Developing countries.
Classification: LCC HD2753 ,H43 2021 (print) | LCC HD2753 (ebook) |
    DDC 336.2009172/4—dc23
LC record available at https://lccn.loc.gov/2020038497
LC ebook record available at https://lccn.loc.gov/2020038498

Contents

Acknowledgments

Thanks to all at ActionAid, Tax Justice Network Africa, the International Relations Department of the London School of Economics, the International Centre for Tax and Development at the Institute of Development Studies, and Cornell University Press. In particular, thanks to Hugh Ault, Leonardo Baccini, Eduardo Baistrocchi, Lucy Barnes, André Broome, Nelly Busingye, Pamela Chisanga, Rasmus Corlin Christensen, Alison Christians, Jeff Chwieroth, Lee Corrick, Andrew Delatolla, Michael Durst, Marian Feist, Judith Freedman, Diego Gonzalez-Bendiksen, Nadia Harrison, Roger Malcolm Haydon, May Hen, Nora Honkaniemi, Jalia Kangave, Anders Larsen, Michael Lennard, Lukas Linsi, Jan Loeprick, Rhiannon McCluskey, Lovisa Moller, Mick Moore, James Morrison, Alvin Mosioma, Savior Mwambwa, Kryticous Patrick Nshindano, Daisy Ogembo, Ronen Palan, Sol Picciotto, Lauge Poulsen, Wilson Prichard, Daniel Schade, Roberto Schatan, Len Seabrooke, Heather Self, Deeksha Sharma, Jason Sharman, David Spencer, Todd Tucker, John Vella, Heidi Wang-Kaeding, Duncan Wigan, Steve Woolcock, Joanne Yao, Matti Ylonen, and all those who participated in research interviews.

Thanks to Rachel for putting up with all the traveling without much complaint. Of course, she didn't have to wait for a telegram to find out when I would be home.

Tax paid for this research. It was made possible by funding from the Economic and Social Research Council and UK Aid, as well as from the Bill and Melinda Gates Foundation.

Abbreviations

ATAF	African Tax Administration Forum
ASEAN	Association of Southeast Asian Nations
BEPS	base erosion and profit shifting
BIT	bilateral investment treaty
CAN	Community of Andean Nations
CBI	Confederation of British Industry
CFA	Committee on Fiscal Affairs
COMESA	Common Market of Eastern and Southern Africa
CPP	Cambodian People's Party
CTPA	Centre for Tax Policy and Administration
DTA	double taxation agreement ("tax treaty")
DTI	Department of Trade and Industry
DTT	double taxation treaty ("tax treaty")
EAC	East African Community
ECOSOC	Economic and Social Council (of the UN)
EEC	European Economic Community
FCO	Foreign and Commonwealth Office
FDI	foreign direct investment
FTA	free trade agreement
GATT	general agreement on tariffs and trade
GDP	gross domestic product
GDT	General Department of Taxation
ICC	International Chambers of Commerce
IMF	International Monetary Fund
MFA	Ministry of Foreign Affairs
MMD	Movement for Multi-party Democracy
NGO	nongovernmental organization
OEEC	Organisation for European Economic Co-operation
OECD	Organisation for Economic Co-operation and Development
PE	permanent establishment
RTZ	Rio Tinto Zinc
SADC	Southern African Development Community
TIEA	tax information exchange agreement
TJNA	Tax Justice Network Africa

UN	United Nations
UNCTAD	United Nations Conference on Trade and Development
UNICE	Union des Industries de la Communauté Européenne
VAT	value-added tax
VBF	Vietnam Business Forum
WTO	World Trade Organization
ZRA	Zambia Revenue Authority

IMPOSING STANDARDS

PROLOGUE

The research for this book took an unexpectedly personal turn as I arranged fieldwork in Africa. A Kenyan organization, Tax Justice Network Africa (TJNA), had agreed to cover my travel costs through a consultancy fee. Kenya imposes a 20 percent tax on service fees paid to providers based abroad, but I was glad to learn that I would have to pay only 12.5 percent, thanks to a four-decades-old treaty between Kenya and the United Kingdom (UK). This saved me (and cost Kenya) a few hundred pounds. In total, British multinational companies have invested over a billion dollars in Kenya, earning over $100 million per year from this investment.[1] When they bring those earnings back home, they also benefit from reduced tax rates thanks to the Kenya-UK treaty.

As I emailed the digitally signed contract back to Nairobi, I realized that the treaty in question had been concluded in a building just opposite my office at the London School of Economics. Somerset House was the headquarters of the Inland Revenue for much of the nineteenth and twentieth centuries. As with all tax treaties, the design of the Kenya-UK treaty can be traced back to a model convention negotiated among the major powers when Kenya was still under British colonial rule. The "London Draft" of 1946, as it is universally known, was also concluded at Somerset House. It seems fitting that this grandiose building had previously been the headquarters of the Navy Board, the administration of Britain's maritime force at the peak of its empire.

Throughout the twentieth century, Inland Revenue officials at Somerset House worked to create a set of postcolonial power structures that would cement British capital's enduring ability to profit from the former empire and further afield. A global network of over three thousand bilateral treaties shields multinational companies from millions of dollars of tax payments on their foreign activities. They are all descendants of the London Draft, produced by the League of Nations' Fiscal Committee. Britain exerted a strong influence on the committee, in recognition of what one committee member called its status as a "great economy."[2] It now has more bilateral tax treaties than any other country, and many of those in force today were negotiated in that very same building.

Historical records show that the particular clause from which I benefited nearly ended the negotiations. In January 1972, a British negotiator in Nairobi sent a telegram to his colleagues back at Somerset House. "Talks with Kenya have broken down," he wrote, "over treatment of management fees and royalties. The Keanyans [sic] have pressed me to obtain confirmation from the Board that the UK cannot agree to a 20% withholding tax."[3] Kenya wanted to replace a treaty inherited at independence with one that would give it more rights, including the right to impose a 20 percent tax on gross fees paid by Kenyan companies to British managers and consultants. It would be a withholding tax, deducted by the payer in the same way that personal income tax is usually deducted from an employee's salary. The UK had never agreed to this before, taking the view that such payments should be taxable only in the UK.

Kenya was focused and determined, choosing to terminate the old colonial agreement in order to put pressure on the UK to relent on its point of principle. A meeting with business representatives in Somerset House in March 1972 appears to have been instrumental in the British climbdown, with the minutes recording how "the general feeling of the meeting was that it was necessary to hold out for a low rate on royalties, but that management fees could be treated differently."[4] Kenyan and British officials eventually initialed a treaty permitting Kenya to tax management and consultancy fees paid to the UK, but only at rates up to 12.5 percent.[5] For over forty years, this would be the lowest cap that Kenya had agreed to in any treaty.

The British did not give up without a fight and in a tense exchange during the Nairobi talks, a Kenyan negotiator asserted that "the UK wanted to make UK management cheaper in the Kenyan market than Swedish management."[6] Sweden, along with Norway and Denmark, had already agreed to the 20 percent rate, which meant that Scandinavian firms would have needed to charge 20 percent more than their British counterparts for the same post-tax return had the UK got the zero rate that it sought.

The final sentence of the January 1972 telegram illustrates how times have changed between the negotiation of the treaty and its impact on my own tax liability. "I would be grateful if you could get a message to my wife that I will probably not be home until Wednesday," wrote the British negotiator, giving a home telephone number.[7] In contrast, thanks to the excellent mobile internet coverage across Africa and Asia today, my wife had no such uncertainty to endure. It seems unlikely that either side in 1972 could have been thinking of a world dominated by email, WhatsApp, Zoom, and Skype.

Today, as trade in services becomes a larger share of the global economy, lower-income countries'[8] right to tax service fees paid to providers overseas is one of the biggest North-South flashpoints in global tax politics. The UK, for example, has changed its mind again. The service fees clause became a routine concession for decades after Kenya broke the mold, but since the turn of the twentieth century it has become a red line in negotiations. During interviews for this book I heard of at least three UK negotiations in which this had led to a stalemate.

The UK is on one side of a global conflict. In 2013, after years of protracted discussions and several knife-edge votes, a United Nations (UN) committee voted to amend its model bilateral treaty to introduce a clause permitting withholding taxes on technical service fees like that in the Kenya-UK treaty. The UN model is supposed to articulate a suitable compromise for negotiations between lower-income and higher-income countries, and the more influential equivalent published by the Organisation for Economic Co-operation and Development (OECD) continues to outlaw withholding taxes on service fees. In practice, lower-income countries have rarely obtained anything like the new UN clause in their bilateral tax treaties, even though most levy such taxes in their domestic laws.

Just as neither TJNA nor I considered the UK-Kenya tax treaty until after we had decided to work together, evidence suggests that tax treaties may only rarely influence multinational companies' investment decisions. If that is the case, lower-income countries have little to show for the revenue sacrifices they must make to obtain them. Some have started to reconsider individual tax treaties or even their whole networks, and organizations as diverse as African civil society groups and the International Monetary Fund (IMF) have adopted a critical stance. From 2012 to 2020, Mongolia, Argentina, Rwanda, Senegal, Malawi, and Zambia have repudiated a total of 11 tax treaties, apparently due to fears that they were open to abuse or overly generous. Back in Nairobi, the fieldwork I had conducted with TJNA supported its legal challenge to Kenya's treaty with Mauritius, which culminated in 2019 when the treaty was struck down by the High Court.

The rate at which lower-income countries are signing new tax treaties, however, shows no sign of declining. Kenya, for example, has already negotiated a new agreement with Mauritius. This book is an attempt to understand the inconsistency between fifty years of negotiations that have resulted in thousands of tax treaties binding lower-income countries into an international regime, on the one hand, and the evidence that this regime may cost them more than they gain, on the other.

THE PROBLEM WITH TAX TREATIES

> African countries have been brainwashed into thinking that they need [tax] treaties. But they don't.
>
> —Tax treaty negotiator, African country

Stories of tax-dodging corporate giants make headlines on a weekly basis. Nonetheless, governments manage to collect over US\$2 trillion in corporate income tax each year, much of it from big multinational businesses.[1] This book is about the rules governments have negotiated to divide the tax base among themselves: how they are designed to work, rather than how they are circumvented by unscrupulous companies and individuals.[2] As a long tradition of legal scholarship argues, those rules, written by a club of higher-income countries, deny lower-income countries a fair share.[3] Tax is hardly unique in this regard, and the past two decades have seen backlashes against institutions of global economic governance that exhibit such a bias, including the IMF, the World Trade Organization (WTO), and the network of bilateral investment treaties (BITs).[4] There are now some signs of organized discontent in the international tax regime, but its long-standing resilience, while other lopsided regimes have faltered, makes it an interesting case in the broader story of global economic governance.

The key mechanism depriving lower-income countries of tax revenues is something they have signed up for—and in which they continue to participate—entirely voluntarily: a network of bilateral treaties, and the international standards that those treaties encode into hard law. Tax treaties cover 82 percent of the world's foreign direct investment (FDI) stocks, including 81 percent of the FDI in lower-income countries.[5] They set limits on when, and in some cases at what rate, signatories can tax cross-border economic activity, primarily imposing restrictions on the host countries of FDI. Many legal scholars are skeptical of the benefits. According to Tsilly Dagan, the main effect of these tax treaties is "regressive redistribution—to the benefit of the developed countries at the expense of the developing ones."[6] Kim Brooks and Richard Krever agree that "the success of the high-income states in negotiating ever more treaties has come at the expense of the tax revenue bases of low-income countries."[7] If this is the case, why have lower-income countries been willing to sign more than a thousand of these treaties?

The vast majority of literature—policy and academic—sees tax treaties as instruments through which lower-income countries compete for inward investment. A cross-country study of the reasons countries sign tax treaties, conducted by Fabian Barthel and Eric Neumayer in 2012, found that countries were more likely to sign up when their competitors for foreign investment had already done so.[8] This conclusion appears to be borne out in policy discourse too. For example, investment promotion literature from countries including Kenya and Zimbabwe highlights tax treaties as important factors that should attract investors.[9] In budget speeches introducing tax treaties to Uganda's parliament, successive finance ministers have explained that their purpose was "to protect taxpayers against double taxation, and to ensure that the tax system does not discourage direct foreign investment" and "to reduce tax impediments to cross border trade and investment."[10] A study conducted by the Ministry of Finance of Peru states that "these conventions create a favourable environment for investment. In signing a double taxation convention, a country is sending a positive signal to foreign investment and offering investors security with respect to the elements negotiated."[11]

There are a number of problems with this: there is little evidence that tax treaties have a positive impact on investment in lower-income countries; I found conflicting views among those involved in the treaty-making process in lower-income countries as to the purpose of tax treaties, with many of those who negotiate treaties skeptical that they attract investment; capital-exporting countries are frequently the ones initiating and driving negotiations, not lower-income countries; and the tax competition literature does not tell us why lower-income countries typically give away far more in negotiations than they need to in order to secure an agreement.

To the extent that tax competition is a fact, then, it is a social fact. What matters is how it is understood by different actors. In this book, I characterize two competing narratives among those involved in making tax treaties. A tax competition motivation, based on the unsubstantiated claim that treaties will attract investment, is shared among those who are less familiar with the technical details. This includes politicians, nonspecialist civil servants, and business executives who lobby them. Treaties are seen as a trade-off between investment promotion and revenue raising, although the fiscal costs, which are hard to estimate, are not always given much weight in the assessment.

The narrative among tax treaty specialists, both in government and in business, is different. Often socialized into a transnational policy community, their detailed technical knowledge comes as part of a package, developed and refined among experts from OECD countries. A powerful logic of appropriateness pervades this community: the OECD's model tax treaty is the acceptable way to tax multinational companies. Its bias against lower-income countries was never agreed to by those countries at a political level; instead, it is justified in technical terms as more economically efficient. Proponents of this view accept that companies' investment decisions may well be influenced by the presence or absence of a particular treaty, and a country with a wide treaty network may be expected to have more cross-border investment. The main mechanism through which this should occur, they suggest, is the convergence on OECD standards set out in the treaty, not the creation of tax-rate-based distortions. Tax professionals in advisory firms and multinational companies share with civil servants the objective of disseminating OECD standards. If they want to be part of this expert community, there is little room for those from lower-income countries to challenge such a long-standing consensus, even where it exhibits a strong bias against them.

For half a century, higher-income countries have taken advantage of these two narratives, together with capacity constraints and imperfect rationality in lower-income countries, to negotiate hundreds of treaties that constrain the taxing rights of lower-income countries unnecessarily. All along, but rarely acknowledged, the *higher-income* countries have been in competition with each other to give their multinational investors a competitive edge by securing the most advantageous tax treaties. Yet the tax costs of this competition endure for a long time in the lower-income countries with which they sign. Almost three hundred African tax treaties, well over half those in force, are more than two decades old, meaning that they were signed in the last century.

The closest analogy to this situation is BITs. Like tax treaties, they are country-specific tax incentives with questionable effectiveness at promoting investment, which have nonetheless proliferated throughout the Global South. Literature on BITs recognizes that to understand lower-income countries' decisions to conclude, we must acknowledge that policymakers' rationality is "bounded."[12] BITs, it is argued, were at first perceived by lower-income countries as a cost-free means to signal political and economic ties with others, and to attract investment. Little attention was paid to the potential downsides. It was only years after they were signed that investors began to use their dispute settlement clauses, and even then lower-income countries did not immediately learn from each other's experiences, although they did become much more reluctant to sign them.[13]

Tax treaties are a more difficult case to explain than BITs, because their costs to signatory governments are immediate, predictable, and significant. There has been no slowdown in tax treaty negotiation, as there has been for BITs, but some lower-income countries have begun to question the costs and benefits of their tax treaty networks. Indonesia, Senegal, South Africa, Rwanda, Argentina, Mongolia, Zambia, and Malawi are among those that have canceled or renegotiated tax treaties, while others, such as Uganda, have undertaken reviews.[14] Civil society groups have begun to mount campaigns against particular tax treaties, culminating in TJNA's lawsuit in Kenya.[15] Even the IMF now cautions lower-income countries that they "would be well-advised to sign treaties only with considerable caution."[16]

Aside from questioning the existence of treaties per se, there is a steady drumbeat of concern that the tax treaty system has too great a bias toward the interests of capital-exporting "residence" countries and against capital-importing "source" countries. According to a press release by a group of finance ministers from francophone lower-income countries, "The global tax system is stacked in favour of paying taxes in the headquarters countries of transnational companies, rather than in the countries where raw materials are produced. International tax and investment treaties need to be revised to give preference to paying tax in 'source' countries."[17] The African Tax Administration Forum (ATAF), a membership organization for revenue authorities, notes that "Africa is still beset by serious issues such as . . . tax treaties with no appropriate tax allocation rights between source and residence taxation and thus susceptible to abuse."[18] An official statement from the Indian government concurs: "The OECD principles have evolved from the perspective of only developed countries since they were prepared by the OECD countries, and many issues relating to developing countries have not been taken into consideration. This has resulted in serious curtailment of the taxing powers of the developing countries in relation to international transactions."[19]

Bilateral tax treaties differ from BITs in that they are drafted in a highly multilateralized context. Each one is derived directly or indirectly from a model formulated and promoted by the OECD, which inherited this role from the League of Nations. That model, naturally, embodies the interests of OECD countries, a club of capital-rich higher-income nations. Alternatives exist, in particular the UN model bilateral treaty, which makes some modest changes to the OECD model in the interests of lower-income countries. Yet it is the OECD model that predominates, even in tax treaties signed by pairs of lower-income countries.[20] Put simply, lower-income countries have given up large chunks of their tax bases by signing these treaties, with few certain gains to show as a result. This book is an attempt to understand why.

It is a substantively important question affecting the livelihoods of hundreds of millions of people. Today, on average, OECD member states collect taxes amounting to 34 percent of gross domestic product (GDP), while in Africa the equivalent figure is half that amount.[21] This reflects a lower level of taxable capacity within their economies, and the availability of "rent" income from natural resource extraction and overseas aid.[22] On the other hand, corporate tax revenue is twice as important to African governments as it is to OECD governments as a share of total revenue raised, and tends to come disproportionately from multinational investors.[23] Lower-income countries' decisions over the taxation of inward investment are thus crucially important to the provision of public services and ultimately to their development prospects.

What Are Tax Treaties?

The global network of over three thousand bilateral tax treaties is the "hard law" foundation of the international tax regime: its DNA. Enforceable in domestic courts and—increasingly—through a bespoke system of international arbitration, tax treaties take precedence over domestic law in most countries.[24] This foundational role has two quite different elements. On the one hand, tax treaties are explicitly political, each one the outcome of a bilateral negotiation between two countries that carves up the right to tax the cross-border economic activity between them. The language of "taxing rights" commonly used in discussions about tax treaties reflects the sacrifice of sovereignty that they entail,[25] and goes some way to explaining why states have only been willing to enter into binding agreements at the bilateral level, where they have more control over the content.[26]

On the other hand, most of that content is a cookie-cutter replication of one of the multilateral models, largely deriving from the OECD model.[27] Just as DNA is organized into chromosomes, all tax treaties follow the same structure of articles, and the most significant variation within many of those articles comes down to just a few words. Nonetheless, the invariant text also constrains countries' taxing rights and is the product of a century of multilateral negotiations. Furthermore, beyond the treaty text itself, the models also incorporate detailed commentaries and associated standards that courts will use when interpreting treaty articles based on them. Thus, the statement that tax treaties are the regime's hard-law foundation also means that they convert a corpus of multilateral soft law into binding, enforceable hard law.

The formal function of tax treaties, reflected in the more commonly used term "double taxation agreement" (DTA) and the formal titles of most treaties, is to promote trade and investment by reducing the potential that companies operating in the two countries will be taxed twice on the same income. For example, the introduction to the model tax treaty developed by the United Nations Committee of Experts on International Cooperation in Tax Matters ("the UN model"), which is intended as a template for lower-income countries to use in negotiations, states: "Broadly, the general objectives of bilateral tax treaties therefore include the protection of taxpayers against double taxation with a view to improving the flow of international trade and investment and the transfer of technology."[28] Similarly, the introduction to the OECD Model Tax Convention on Income and on Capital ("the OECD model") describes its main purpose as "to clarify, standardise, and confirm the fiscal situation of taxpayers who are engaged in commercial, industrial, financial, or any other activities in other countries through the application by all countries of common solutions to identical cases of double taxation."[29]

When a taxpayer has a potential tax liability in more than one state, the taxpayer will face double taxation if each state claims the right to tax it. States can leave double taxation intact, but this may create an onerous burden on taxpayers that deters cross-border trade and investment. As Tsilly Dagan shows, capital-exporting states have a greater incentive to relieve double taxation unilaterally, but they prefer a more coordinated approach. This is because, as well as more comprehensively resolving the problem, cooperation transfers some of the cost of double taxation relief from the capital-exporting state to the capital-importing state. Both the political and technical roles played by tax treaties are achieved primarily by limiting taxation in capital-importing states: the bilateral negotiation affects how much of the fiscal cost will be borne by the host state, but so does the adoption of supposedly technocratic concepts and standards embedded in the model treaties.

Table 1.1 summarizes some of the main restrictions on taxing rights that tax treaties impose. As can be seen, a large proportion of the treaty is designed to restrict the host country's taxing rights over foreign investors. Broadly speaking, it does this in three ways. First, it sets activity thresholds for a foreign company's activity in the host country, although the length of time, extent of presence, and type of activity that form these thresholds can vary. Below these thresholds the host country cannot tax a foreign company or individual at all, and the treaty therefore shifts the balance of taxing rights away from the host country by an amount that depends on the specific threshold. For example, Mongolia's tax treaty with China, signed in 1991, prevents it from taxing Chinese companies' construction sites within its borders (of which there are many) unless they are present for eighteen months. In practice this exempts many Chinese construction projects from Mongolian tax.

Second, in some instances tax treaties allocate the right to tax in a binary way. Income such as royalties, pensions, and many types of capital gains may be taxable only by the home country once the treaty comes into force, again shifting the balance of taxing rights in its favor. For example, where a company in the host country pays out pensions to its former employees who now reside in the treaty

TABLE 1.1. Selected provisions of tax treaties and their effects

ARTICLE	TAX(ES) CONCERNED	EFFECT
5	Corporate income tax	**Permanent establishment.** Prescribes that states can tax a foreign company only if its activity within their borders meets the thresholds set out under the treaty definition of "permanent establishment" (PE). Typically these thresholds include a minimum amount of physical presence over a minimum length of time, and a list of business activities that do or do not count as a PE.
7	Corporate income tax	**Business profits.** Sets out how the profits made by a foreign business should be calculated for the purpose of taxation by the state in which it is operating. The state can only take into account profits that it is permitted to by this article, and it must allow the taxable profits to be reduced by any expenses specified in this article.
10–12	Withholding taxes	**Withholding tax limits.** In addition to profit taxes, states often levy taxes on overseas payments made by companies, such as interest payments, royalties, and dividends. These clauses specify the types of payments on which a country can levy withholding taxes, and the maximum rates at which they can be levied. The maximum rates are usually set lower than the statutory rates in the capital-importing country, as a key concession making the treaty advantageous to the capital-exporting country.
13	Capital gains tax	**Capital gains tax.** The country in which a foreign investor realizes a capital gain can tax it only in the circumstances set out in this clause. This may include that a shareholding being sold must constitute a minimum threshold (so that the host country can tax gains only on direct investment and not on portfolio investment).
21	Others	**Other forms of taxation.** Generally this states that only the home country has the right to levy taxes on its residents that are not explicitly mentioned in the treaty.
23	All	**Relief of double taxation.** All previous articles limit the capital importer's taxing rights. This article is the quid pro quo, under which the capital exporter agrees either that its resident taxpayers will receive credits against their tax bills for equivalent taxes paid in the treaty partner or that it will exempt income and capital in the treaty partner from taxation altogether.
25	All	**Mutual agreement procedure.** Where the provisions of the treaty are interpreted differently such that a taxpayer still incurs double taxation, this provides for a mechanism through which the countries can try to resolve the dispute. Some treaties signed since the mid-2000s include taxpayer-initiated binding arbitration within this clause.
26	All	**Exchange of information.** Obliges and provides a legal authority for states to cooperate with each other when investigating taxpayers with affairs in both countries.

partner (typically former expatriate employees of a multinational firm who have worked for a subsidiary in the host country), many treaties prohibit the host country from taxing those payments.[30] In Uganda, a dispute between the tax authority and telecommunications multinational Zain relates to the Uganda-Netherlands tax treaty, which prevents Uganda from levying capital gains tax on certain types of gains made by Dutch residents, including the sale of holding companies.[31]

Third, in some instances tax treaties set a maximum tax rate on cross-border transactions that the host state must not exceed. Lower-income countries commonly levy withholding taxes on dividends, interest payments, royalties, and service fees, and the maximum rates imposed by tax treaties are probably their most visible and high-profile aspects. For example, the Philippines imposes taxes of up to 30 percent on dividend payments abroad and 20 percent on interest payments, but some of its tax treaties have the effect of reducing these rates to 5 percent and 0 percent, respectively. According to analysis by Petr Janský and Marek Šedivý, these reductions cost the Philippines—the biggest loser from a sample of fourteen lower-income countries—revenue amounting to US$509 million (0.17% of GDP) in 2015.[32]

In return for these restrictions on taxation in the host country, the signatories also agree to bear the cost of eliminating any remaining double taxation incurred by their own residents, where they are the home country, by making allowances for taxes paid in the treaty partner when calculating their tax liability. This is usually done through a combination of credits for tax paid abroad and exempting income earned in the treaty partner altogether. From the 1970s to the 1990s, it was common to include a "tax-sparing" clause, in which the home country agreed to honor any tax incentives its firms were granted by the treaty partner, by giving them credits as if they had paid taxes in full. This practice, which created costs for capital-exporting countries, fell out of fashion with the publication of an OECD report, *Tax Sparing: A Reconsideration*, which argues that these provisions were vulnerable to tax avoidance, and encouraged investors to repatriate profits rather than invest them in the lower-income country.[33]

If the flows of investment and people between the two treaty partners are broadly equal, changes to the balance of taxing rights resulting from the treaty may affect the incentives for taxpayers to move or invest between the signatories. They will not, however, have a significant impact on the overall distribution of taxing rights between the two countries. This is because each country is simultaneously a home and host country with respect to different investors, and so will gain and lose in roughly equal proportion from the restrictions on host or home country taxing rights. But when a treaty is concluded between two countries whose capital stocks are not equal, the settlement will have distributional consequences.

The same applies at the system level: a country with a broadly balanced capital account may face a net fiscal loss from one treaty but gain from others; where a country is overwhelmingly a capital importer—as lower-income countries are, almost by definition—the sum total of imbalances across its treaties can be considerable.

The negotiated content of the treaty may be more or less advantageous to the capital-exporting country depending on the level of the permanent establishment (PE) threshold, the allocation of the binary provisions, and the maximum withholding tax rates set. But it is normally the case that even treaties that are comparatively favorable to the capital-importing country still place significant restrictions on their taxing rights relative to domestic legislation. For example, for Uganda, accepting the concept of PE, regardless of how broadly it is defined, is a restriction relative to a domestic tax framework that does not include the concept.[34] This illustrates the power of the model treaties, drafted over decades by tax experts from higher-income countries, which have these concepts baked in. It also illustrates that the real impact of tax treaties is often not to alleviate double taxation but to transfer some of the cost of doing so from the capital-exporting country to the capital importer, or to reduce the overall effective tax rate of investors operating across the two countries.

The First Puzzle: Why Sign at All?

Tax treaties can be expensive for lower-income countries, costing them significant amounts of tax revenue. Sebastian Beer and Jan Loeprick of the IMF estimate that each additional tax treaty concluded by an African country is associated with a 5 percent reduction in its corporate tax revenues.[35] If governments' policy preferences are "rational," these costs should be justified in some way by the likely benefits, either in terms of aggregate national welfare or in terms of more parochial benefits for the individuals who determine those preferences. The strong version of this book's underlying contention is that such a rational justification rarely exists, making most decisions to conclude a tax treaty puzzling.

A hypothetical rational policymaker would have little trouble finding work in the policy and academic law literature that might give them pause for thought. For forty years, legal scholarship has debated the extent to which the sacrifice of taxing rights by a lower-income country in signing a tax treaty is justified by its impact on the tax treatment of inward investment.[36] Critical legal scholars have argued that tax treaties place too much of the burden of relieving double taxation on lower-income countries, or that the entire rationale is "a myth" or "aid in reverse—from poor to rich countries," because, rather than relieving double taxation, tax treaties between higher-income and lower-income countries merely shift the burden of doing so from the former to the latter.[37] This is because the credit or exemption provisions in treaties that limit the home country's right to tax its own residents—the quid pro quo for the restrictions in the host country— are largely unnecessary. Most major capital-exporting countries relieve double taxation incurred by their investors, either by giving credits against their tax bill for tax paid abroad or increasingly by exempting foreign profits from tax alto- gether.[38] Indeed, Tsilly Dagan demonstrates using game theory that, absent a treaty, the Pareto optimal outcome for a home country will always be to take unilateral steps to relieve double taxation incurred by its multinationals that invest abroad.[39] For capital-importing lower-income countries, then, the best strategy should be to sit tight.

Authors who believe that tax treaties can nonetheless attract investment in lower-income countries make the following points.[40] First, not all capital- exporting countries relieve double taxation unilaterally in all circumstances, and so there may be a strong argument for a tax treaty in these cases. Second, although in other instances there may not be what Dagan refers to as "heroic" double taxation, there would still remain instances in which companies are caught out, because each country's tax code defines a particular transaction differently. Treaties help resolve this both by standardizing many definitions and by providing taxpayers with an avenue through which to initiate dispute settlement between the treaty partners. Third, an important benefit to businesses from tax treaties is that they create stability. A tax treaty is effectively a tool to deliver a credible commitment that many aspects of the tax treatment of an investment will not change in a way that is dramatically worse for the investor—for example, a large hike in withholding taxes.

Finally, it is also argued that tax treaties create a more favorable treatment for investors because they reduce taxes that are a direct cost to businesses. This oc- curs if income is already exempt from tax in the home country or if the home tax rate is lower than the host tax rate on the income concerned. In simple terms, if both countries tax corporate profits at the same rate, a business will be indiffer- ent to which country is granted the taxing rights in the tax treaty, since it will pay the same in either case. But if the home country does not tax profits earned over- seas, or its tax rate is much lower than that of the host country, then investors stand to benefit significantly from a treaty that ensures they are taxed only in their home state. This makes investments in the host country a more attractive proposition. It is one reason why investment is often channeled through hub jurisdictions, which combine low effective tax rates with wide networks of treaties that allocate them—rather than to host countries—to the lion's share of taxing rights.[41]

Eduardo Baistrocchi adds that Dagan's result does not hold when multiple lower-income countries are competing for inward investment. In this situation they are in a prisoner's dilemma, and once one host country has signed a tax treaty with a given capital exporter, the optimal solution for the others is to follow suit.[42] This competition model also applies if tax treaties are reducing direct costs to investors, as opposed to eliminating double taxation—here tax treaties may be tools of tax competition in the same manner as statutory tax rates, in which case lower-income countries face a collective action problem.

Perhaps more pertinent is the empirical question: Do tax treaties increase investment in lower-income countries? Unfortunately, the economic evidence is not much clearer cut. For every published study that finds a positive association between tax treaties and investment in lower-income countries, there is another that does not. When a comprehensive collection of studies was published in 2009, some even found a negative association.[43] Since then, some studies using aggregate investment statistics have found a positive impact from tax treaties in lower-income countries,[44] while others have found none.[45] The quality and coverage of such data are notoriously poor in the case of lower-income countries, and there are considerable methodological challenges. In particular, it is difficult to distinguish between new investment resulting from a treaty and investment diverted or routed from elsewhere to take advantage of its terms.

Two promising avenues are company-level microdata in place of aggregate investment data, and network analysis techniques. Papers using data on the foreign affiliates of Swedish, German, US, and Austrian multinationals have all found positive effects in certain circumstances.[46] Unfortunately, coverage of lower-income countries is still patchy, such that only the Swedish study has sufficient coverage of sub-Saharan countries to be able to apply its results to that region: the effect it found was also small.[47] A second innovation is network analysis, which allows researchers to control for treaty shopping. Several studies using this technique appear to point in a more positive direction.[48] It is too soon, however, to make any conclusive statements about if, when, and how tax treaties might affect investment in lower-income countries.

A final note about the evidence base concerns tax-sparing clauses, which are added to some tax treaties signed by lower-income countries to give a stronger effect to tax incentives granted by the lower-income country to multinationals from the home country. The OECD asserts that "investment decisions taken by international investors resident in credit countries are rarely dependent on or even influenced by the existence or absence of tax sparing provisions in treaties."[49] In spite of this, several studies have found positive and significant effects of tax-sparing provisions on investment in lower-income countries, independent of the presence of a tax treaty per se.[50]

What would a policymaker in a lower-income country, seeking to rationally analyze all the evidence available, conclude? Certainly, the sweeping statements about the benefits of tax treaties to lower-income countries often seen in policy literature seem hard to sustain. In all probability, any effect of a tax treaty on investment depends on the characteristics of the two signatories' tax systems, on the presence or absence of specific clauses, on whether the treaty contains effective protection against treaty shopping, and on the treaties concluded by a country's competitors. The research question lower-income countries need answered, then, is not "Do tax treaties attract investment?" but "In what circumstances might a tax treaty attract investment, and on what terms?" Yet such qualifications are absent from policy discourse and, as the evidence in this book will show, from policymakers' descriptions of their own considerations. It thus seems unlikely that the prevalent view, that tax treaties have a blanket investment-promoting effect that outweighs the cost of foregone revenue, is based on a rational assessment of the strength of the available economic or legal evidence.

The Second Puzzle: Why Sign Away So Much?

Even if we do not accept the strong contention that the benefits of any tax treaty are unlikely to exceed the costs, a puzzle still remains: those costs are frequently much greater than they need to be. Within the parameters set by the model treaties, there is considerable variation in tax treaties' content, which may affect their impact on investment flows and on tax revenues. Even if we accept that tax treaties have some investment-promoting effect, data showing the way in which they have been negotiated by lower-income countries demonstrate the systematic sacrifice of far more taxing rights than would have been necessary to reach agreement, creating revenue losses that surely tip the cost-benefit calculation into the red. It is hard to conceptualize this as a rational pattern of negotiations.

The UN model treaty is generally regarded as a better compromise between the costs and benefits for lower-income countries than the OECD model treaty,[51] although, as Oladiwura Ayeyemi Eyitayo-Oyesode argues, it is "only a modest improvement on the OECD rules."[52] Where the two models vary, it is almost always because the UN model allocates greater taxing rights to the capital-importing country. But some research has demonstrated that the outcome of tax treaty negotiations between higher-income and lower-income countries are generally closer to the OECD model than to the UN model. Where UN model clauses differ significantly from those of the OECD model, in areas such as the PE definition and capital gains tax, they often appear in only a minority of treaties signed by lower-income countries.[53] The UN model clauses are found relatively more frequently in treaties between two non-OECD countries than in treaties signed by one OECD country and one non-OECD country. This suggests that lower-income countries seek, but fail to secure, more expansive taxing rights in negotiations with OECD countries, where the division of taxing rights really matters.

A few papers have looked for patterns within the negotiated content of tax treaties. Kim Brooks observes that Australia has tended to be more generous in the terms of its tax treaties with lower-income countries than Canada, and that the latter has become less generous over time.[54] Charles Irish suggests that the prevalence of African tax treaties with Nordic countries and West Germany in the 1970s was a result of these countries' openness to negotiate and to conclude treaties on preferential terms. These countries "do recognise the necessity of greater taxation at source and are willing to enter into tax agreements favourable to developing countries."[55] Veronika Dauer and Richard Krever find marked differences between countries in Africa and Asia, noting that "as a group, these African countries appear not to have been as successful as Asian countries in retaining taxing rights."[56] Jinyan Li finds that China has changed its preference in negotiations, from preferring clauses that expanded its taxing rights as a capital importer to preferring clauses that expand its taxing rights as a capital exporter.[57] Eduardo Baistrocchi adds that China was initially willing to accept treaties on OECD members' terms, despite the costs it incurred as a capital-importing country, in order to signal that it was open to investment.[58]

Do these patterns imply rational negotiation strategies? One question in particular is how the stock of FDI between countries shapes the content of treaties. Broadly speaking, we would expect countries to defend their source taxing rights much more when they are overwhelmingly in the position of capital importer, since the costs of a one-sided treaty will be higher. As Honey Lynn Goldberg suggests, "Treaty partners having unequal income flows will allocate jurisdiction to tax so as to achieve a more even balance between the two extremes."[59] Three studies have considered the asymmetry in the FDI relationship between the two negotiating countries and the withholding rates in those treaties.[60] Each found that, as Goldberg predicted, withholding tax rates are higher where the asymmetry in the FDI relationship between treaty partners is higher, shielding countries that are overwhelmingly capital importers from some revenue losses. Looking at the content of tax treaties as a whole, rather than only withholding taxes, I found the precise opposite. Treaties tend to impose greater restrictions on lower-income countries' source taxing rights when the distribution of FDI between signatories is more one-sided, suggesting that, when lower-income countries need investment more, they are more willing to give taxing rights away.[61] This is consistent with descriptive studies finding that, when negotiating with higher-income countries, lower-income countries are quite unsuccessful at obtaining the versions of clauses that they seem to prefer when negotiating treaties with each other.[62] Clearly, FDI asymmetry may point to a power asymmetry in negotiations, but there is more to the variation than that. For example, I also found that lower-income countries secure a greater share of the taxing rights as they gain experience in negotiating and applying treaties.

Beyond Domestic Politics . . .

Most international relations literature on global tax governance, in common with that on economics, assumes that signing tax treaties is a rational course of action for lower-income countries, and concerns itself little with the terms on which they do so. In general, it accepts the double taxation problem as fact in modeling the negotiation of tax treaties, assuming that states' first order of preference is to resolve this problem, while their second-order preference is to maximize their share of the tax base.[63] Some studies modify this by focusing on competition between capital-importing states, which may alter their preferences, creating a more intense preference for signing a treaty despite the loss of the tax base that it entails.[64] All of this literature struggles once we question the rationality of concluding tax treaties on the terms that lower-income countries have done. Perhaps we need to look more closely at what motivates the political leaders who ultimately sign tax treaties. After all, "the state is not an actor but a representative institution constantly subject to capture and recapture, construction and reconstruction by coalitions of social actors."[65]

Consider the classic model in which democratic political leaders' economic policy preferences are shaped by the aggregation of two constituencies' preferences: voters, who are affected through general welfare effects and want the provision of public goods, and interest groups such as businesses and trade unions, which seek private benefits for their members and can influence policy through campaign contributions.[66] This model is unhelpful for tax treaties, because it is hard to ascertain any effect in either direction, especially given the manifest lack of any strong pressure from either voters or interest groups.

Pressure from voters could in principle go either way. A prevailing public belief that tax treaties will attract inward investment may encourage governments in democracies, especially those of the left, to seek to conclude them in order to create jobs.[67] There is no evidence that political partisanship affects a government's enthusiasm for tax treaties in this way, or that democracies are more likely to conclude them. While other tax instruments provide politicians with opportunities for credit claiming, regardless of their effectiveness,[68] no such possibilities are provided by an instrument that few voters are aware of. Indeed, a median voter effect may push a government in the opposite direction, because tax treaties reduce the tax liabilities of foreign multinationals, compromise the government's ability to redistribute wealth and provide public services, and undermine efforts to force foreign multinationals to pay their "fair share" of tax.

There is a similar ambiguity with respect to domestic interest groups. Capitalists and other wealthy individuals in a lower-income country's elite may benefit from the opportunities for "round tripping," a form of tax avoidance, created by some treaties.[69] A good example of this is India's treaty with Mauritius, which for many years was abused by Indian nationals who routed their domestic investments via Mauritius to make use of an exemption from Indian capital gains tax that was intended for foreign investors, not Indian residents.[70] Catherine Ngina Mutava points to instances of "political-motivated" treaties driven by diplomatic rather than economic motivations.[71] Although such concerns have clearly been a part of some tax treaty dynamics, the bulk of discussion about tax treaties in lower-income countries is focused on the benefits they may provide to foreign multinational companies rather than any selective benefits they may offer elites. It is also hard to see such advantages in the majority of tax treaties, which are with higher-tax countries rather than tax havens.

In practice, elites may have more reasons to oppose the conclusion of tax treaties. For domestic businesses, a tax treaty is in effect a reduction in the tax burden facing their foreign-owned competitors, placing the domestic firms at a competitive disadvantage. Those evading tax may also be concerned about the revenue authority gaining information on any wealth they have deposited in the treaty partner, through the information exchange provisions of tax treaties. Some studies have even found a negative impact of tax treaties on investment flows, which they attribute to this dynamic.[72] With a few exceptions, however, the jurisdictions that act as tax-friendly investment conduits for multinational firms are not the same as those that act as havens for illicit wealth, so any conflict between direct investment promotion and offshore evasion may again be limited to a small number of treaties.[73]

The exception to this story is lobbying on behalf of multinational firms, which clearly stand to gain from tax treaties. The interviews and archival research in this book suggest that lobbying is largely a phenomenon of the Global North, and most effective when directed not toward politicians but toward specialist bureaucrats. In contrast, multinationals' local affiliates in lower-income countries direct requests via their embassies to their home governments, not directly to host governments.

There is, in sum, little evidence for organized interest group pressure for the conclusion of tax treaties in lower-income countries, just as there is almost no political or public debate about them in democracies. It is therefore just as likely that political actors may block the ratification of tax treaties, as we will see in chapter 6. When the negotiators interviewed for this research commented on their country's politicians, it was indeed predominantly along the lines that they had slowed down the ratification process.

. . . Beyond Bureaucratic Capacity

It was an admission of past mistakes by a civil servant that originally motivated this research project. While I was researching tax planning by a multinational company in Ghana, a tax policy official told me that his country had lost out in tax treaty negotiations through poor preparation and had not fully taken into account the way treaties could allow certain jurisdictions to act as conduits for tax avoidance.[74]

Empirical legal research often highlights deficits in the knowledge, capacity, and ideas of those making the decisions. As early as 1974, Charles Irish, reflecting on his experience in Zambia, bemoaned lower-income countries' "unawareness of the adverse nature of double taxation agreements" and "unquestioned acceptance of the status quo."[75] Lower-income countries, he wrote, "have or believe they have a relatively weak bargaining position," while higher-income countries "have a propensity to take advantage" of them.[76] Tsilly Dagan suggested that the tax treaties myth concealed "much more cynical goals, particularly redistributing tax revenues from the poorer to the richer signatory countries."[77]

Doubts about the quality of lower-income countries' tax treaty policymaking are expressed in even more forthright terms by lawyers from those countries themselves. Festus Aukunobera, the author of a chapter on Uganda in a volume on different countries' approaches to treaty negotiation, argues that "tax administration and tax policy officials in Uganda are not sufficiently trained in the area of tax treaties and international taxation. As a result, Uganda has a weak tax treaty negotiation team that concludes treaties more intensively reflecting the position of the other contracting state."[78] His Colombian counterpart, Natalia Quinones—who subsequently became a negotiator for her country—describes in her chapter how a decision by the Uribe government in 2004 to adopt a policy of "attracting investment at any price" led to poorly prepared negotiations that resulted in an outcome that was less favorable to Colombia than might otherwise have resulted.[79] In a study based on interviews with negotiators from seven African countries, Catherine Ngina Mutava observed that few had clear negotiation policies in place, and as a result they were "slowly ceding their taxing rights over income earned within their jurisdiction."[80]

An important clarification is needed up front, as I introduce these observations about the level of understanding and preparation among negotiators from lower-income countries. It is not hard to find intelligent, astute, and well-informed negotiators from lower-income countries, whose meticulousness and tenacity are acknowledged by their opposite numbers. What is at issue here is the structural constraints in which they operate: a relative lack of experience and training combined with bureaucratic and political pressures that reduce their room to maneuver. ATAF, a body representing revenue authorities, emphasizes that "Africa is still faced with, among others, inadequate resources and level of expertise in international tax policy as well as clashes with other political priorities like inequality, climate change, unemployment and security that constrain their ability to influence decision-making on global tax issues."[81]

In general terms, we expect that bureaucratic capacity and the quality of state institutions have a strong bearing on the capacity to raise revenue, especially where domestic interest groups and global capital markets exert a downward pressure.[82] As the case studies in this book illustrate, it is certainly the case that a weaker, less specialized tax bureaucracy is not as able to provide evidence-based advice to its political leaders, leaving them more exposed to the influence of ideas, interest groups, and foreign governments. The creation of a stronger, specialist international tax unit within the bureaucracy can lead to a more focused, critical approach to the exogenous pressures to make tax treaties. It may also endogenize those pressures, creating an institutional logic of tax treaty making, not least through a group of civil servants with a vested interest in maintaining an active tax treaty negotiation program.

This is not, however, a question of bureaucratic capacity per se but something more idiosyncratic. Tax treaty policy is a small, specialist function, a niche within a niche. Negotiations are frequently led by just one individual, or at most by a handful of staff, operating in obscurity with little scrutiny. Much therefore depends on the knowledge and experience of this individual or group of people, as well as quite specific resourcing decisions concerning the number of people in such a team. Comparing the UK with the United States, for example, or Cambodia with Vietnam illustrates that the size and competence of the tax treaty negotiating team does not necessarily correlate with the size and capability of the state apparatus, even that pertaining to taxation. For this reason, the focus of this book is precisely on the knowledge and experience of a handful of officials, as well as on how they are constrained within a system of checks and balances.

The Argument

International tax is not unfairly seen as complex and obscure. A partner at a law firm once described it to me as a specialism that other tax lawyers and accountants, already the pointiest headed in their professions, consider arcane and nerdy.[83] Because of this obscurity, many participants in policy debates must necessarily act without a comprehensive understanding of the available information, especially those in capacity-constrained contexts, which are more likely to be found in lower-income countries. This gives considerable power to actors whose authoritative command of technical knowledge is recognized, allowing them to shape others' preferences. We must therefore analyze the actions of those involved in tax treaty making through a framework of bounded rationality, the notion that policymakers rely on cognitive shortcuts to filter the available information.[84]

Political (Nonspecialist) Actors

The role of tax treaties is constructed differently by different actors, along two axes: Global North to Global South, and dependent on a person's level of technical knowledge. For this reason, chapters 3 and 4 discuss nonspecialist and tax specialist actors separately. Consider first the former group, including most civil servants, politicians, and business executives. Here, the tax treaties myth prevails: treaties are black boxes that stimulate investment flows across borders by resolving a generalized problem of double taxation—or more simply still, by lowering the effective tax rate on cross-border investment. In this view, tax treaties act rather like a geographically specific tax incentive, a tool of tax competition.[85] It should be noted that these pressures are largely indirect and anticipated, as tax treaties are simply too low salience among voters or special interest groups to become deeply politicized.

Looked at along a North-South axis, tax competition works both ways. From the perspective of the government of capital-importing country A, the absence of a treaty with capital-exporting country X will disadvantage it in competing for investment, especially if its competitors B and C have tax treaties with X. This is the framing that underpins studies of tax treaty dissemination found in international relations literature.[86] The government of X, however, may also be concerned that its outward-investing multinationals are disadvantaged when competing in country A, compared with their competitors from Y and Z, countries that already have treaties with A. The ideas that drive tax competition, which may differ from legal and economic facts, act in both directions: while we commonly focus on competition for *inward* investment, countries also compete for *outward* investment opportunities.

The International Tax Community

Let us now turn to the transnational community of tax treaty negotiators and administrators, tax lawyers and advisers, and those working on cross-border taxation within multinational firms. In this book I use the concept of "transnational policy community," which consists of public and private officials with shared educational or professional backgrounds, mutual affinity, and widely accepted principles and which operates as a club.[87] Because the international tax community has always bridged the public and private sectors, this framing is more appropriate than the widely used concept of an "epistemic community" of private individuals that acts as an exogenous influence on government bureaucracies.[88]

Members of the international tax community are endowed with considerable specialist technical knowledge that is ordered within socially constructed frames and embodied in the OECD model tax treaty, which codifies its members' view of the *right way of doing international tax*. The project of concluding more and more bilateral tax treaties is primarily a means of protecting multinational companies from taxation that might occur in the *wrong* way—that is, in ways that deviate from OECD standards. Such standardization is partially consistent with the emphasis on double taxation in tax treaty discourse, since that is one potential consequence of inconsistent tax rules among countries. But it is only one, alongside others such as excessive, complex, unpredictable, and economically inefficient taxation, and more recently "double nontaxation," when inconsistent rules and inadequate cooperation permit tax avoidance and evasion.

Convergence with OECD standards is not mutually exclusive with a logic of tax competition, since the bilateral character of the tax treaty regime means that multinational firms operating between countries with a treaty are likely to gain selective benefits from these protections. But it is not the same as the tax treaties myth. Indeed, many members of the international tax community on both sides of the North-South divide see tax treaties as a means of reducing the costs for investors after they have decided to invest, not as a means to encourage them to invest in the first place. Such motivations may be guided less by a logic of consequences whereby the fiscal costs to the lower-income country are justified by the investment gains, and more by a logic of appropriateness, wherein it would be undesirable for an investor to face difficulties because of the lack of a treaty.

Civil servants who have learned specialist technical knowledge about tax treaties as they join the international tax community also hold different ideas than other actors at a national level who do not have the same specialist training. As they understand the technical detail of tax treaties better, officials become increasingly aware of their costs, and of the limited evidence that they will attract inward investment. Often, they become more persuasive critics of the status quo that disadvantages their country, and stronger negotiators as a result. But as they learn how the international tax community conceptualizes tax treaties, many also come to regard tax treaties' true role as lying outside any immediate increase in investment. They move from a logic of consequences to one of appropriateness, and their preferences for treaty partners and treaty content shift. The nature and extent of officials' learning can therefore shape the extent to which they support or oppose particular treaties.

Business Power and the Politics of Knowledge

The technical and nontechnical mechanisms do not exist in isolation from each other; they interact at a national level. Scholarship examining the national political economy of international tax rules is limited to only a few examples,[89] and the prevailing, state-centric view considers national preferences to be a function of the aggregate welfare implications and interest group politics concerned with the tax-driven effects of investment promotion and revenue raising.[90] Because transnational corporate capital has a clear interest in reduced taxation, and there is no organized lobby against it, states are expected to have a first-order preference for stimulating trade and investment by concluding tax treaties that eliminate double taxation, and a second-order one for sacrificing as little tax revenue as possible when doing so.[91] Because this framing entails a number of assumptions that are hard to sustain, at least for lower-income countries, I consider political actors' analysis of their own incentives to be filtered through the heuristic of the tax treaties myth.

In contrast, members of a transnational policy community take for granted certain focal points, which may lead them to different preferences in the domestic context than those of political actors, even if they share the same end goals. If community members have sufficient instrumental power, the national preferences arrived at by governments may differ from those that might be arrived at simply through analyzing the presumed interests of domestic stakeholder groups, even once we take into account the heuristics used by political actors. My analysis of control over the process of making treaties focuses on veto points.[92] This power may result from formal bureaucratic and political responsibilities, but technical specialists may also hold a de facto veto created by the complex technical content and obscure terminology associated with tax treaties, which forces nonspecialist actors to defer to them.[93]

Even the power of transnational capital is mediated through ideas. The tax treaties myth is an idea that supports an agenda in the interests of higher-income countries, although not, in general, one of "regressive redistribution" of tax revenue between states as posited by Dagan. Because the benefits accrue primarily to multinational firms themselves, rather than to the governments of the capital-exporting countries in which they reside, the narrative of this book is consistent with a business power perspective.[94] To be sure, multinational firms possess significant instrumental and structural power. They lobby their home governments for tax treaties and make numerous inputs into transnational policy processes. Structural power is built into the tax treaties myth, since it leads policymakers in lower-income countries, who have not been lobbied, to fear that investment may be withheld or withdrawn without a treaty. For the most part, these mechanisms operate in a "quiet politics" environment unencumbered by public attention.[95]

Instrumental and structural power are most effective, however, when aligned with discursive power: the social construction of the tax treaties myth driving tax competition, and shared understandings within a transnational policy community whose members include multinationals' tax executives, as well as lawyers and accountants that service them. As some of the cases in this book will illustrate, the narrow interests of a transnational company in a certain country at a given time may be at odds with the long-term project of the international tax community. The fault line can run through the middle of business lobby groups. When discursive power pushes in a different direction than instrumental and structural power, the former tends to be more influential unless political pressure can be brought to bear on entrenched specialist bureaucrats.

Past Legacies and Institutions

This book is necessarily a historical narrative. Treaties are not negotiated in a vacuum but within an institutional framework built up over a century. It is clear from the evidence in this book that, as historical institutionalism argues, institutions built in the past condition states' options for cooperation in the present day.[96] Already in the 1920s, northern countries in the League of Nations began to gain a first-mover advantage, deciding on the terms of cooperation in ways that privileged the interests of capital-rich countries over capital-poor countries. When representatives of lower-income countries were invited to join them, they questioned those decisions but were overruled. In the 1950s and 1960s, as the OECD became the institutional home of international tax cooperation, it built on the League of Nations work from the perspective of its capital-rich members. Ever since lower-income countries began to negotiate tax treaties from the late 1960s onward, they have had little option but to fall in line with the OECD, and the only alternatives to have gained traction have been compatible with (that is, based on) the OECD approach.[97]

As for formal rules and legal instruments, so also for the international tax community and its shared norms. The complex, decentralized, and imprecise design of international tax rules created the need for a large number of professionals to apply them, as well as the reliance on shared understandings of how to interpret those rules.[98] To gain acceptance to that community, new entrants must comply with these norms, making it a challenging task to argue for any significant change from the inside.[99]

At the level of individual countries, past negotiations have an enduring impact on possibilities in the present. While a government may safely be able to say no to a treaty offered to it on bad terms, the calculation is different when such a treaty is already in effect, perhaps signed many decades ago. When terminating, overriding, or renegotiating an international agreement designed to offer stability to investors, there may be diplomatic and economic repercussions. Direct renegotiations do not start from a blank slate but from the agreement already concluded between two states. More importantly, past precedent shapes the conduct of new negotiations, and good negotiators will do their research. Countries can use this strategically, obtaining precedents from easier negotiations to bolster their positions in tougher ones to follow; conversely, today's negotiators will find their mistakes—and those made by their predecessors—used against them.

Evidence Base

To build the argument throughout this book, I use evidence from interviews, participant observation in international meetings, and official documentation. In total, the book draws on seventy-five interviews with ninety-one stakeholders in the tax-treaty-making process, listed in the appendix. Of these stakeholders, most were or had been national civil servants involved in setting tax treaty policy, negotiating tax treaties (many were their country's lead negotiator), or administering tax treaties (the umbrella term "tax treaty officials" is used for all three types of civil servants). The sample also included twenty-seven individuals currently working in the private sector, primarily for business lobby groups and tax advisory firms, and eight international organization staff.[100] The sample includes individuals from thirty different countries, including the case study countries.

The interview sampling was a combination of convenience and purpose. Most of the interviews were conducted at meetings convened by the United Nations Committee of Experts on International Cooperation in Tax Matters ("UN Tax Committee"), but these were supplemented with some in-country interviews during incidental travel. In addition to the three contemporary case studies—Cambodia, Vietnam, and Zambia—in-country interviews were conducted in Uganda, Kenya, Denmark, South Africa, and the United States. A multistakeholder focus group was also conducted at a tax conference in Nairobi in 2013, involving local businesses, tax advisers, revenue authority officials, and academics. The sampling strategy was designed to obtain a cross-section of countries by income and region. At the request of numerous interviewees, countries and names have been kept confidential.

Over thirty days of participant observation at international meetings, including hundreds of informal conversations, supplemented the interview data. These are also listed in the appendix. In particular, meetings of the UN Tax Committee are gatherings of dozens of tax treaty officials that last over several days. During formal proceedings, the twenty-five committee members speak in a personal capacity, while country observers speak on behalf of their country, and a small number of representatives from nongovernmental organizations (NGOs), the private sector, and academia also participate as observers.[101] The meetings were an opportunity to observe the formal statements made by participants during the committee's deliberations, as well as the informal discussions during breaks and social functions. Comments made by committee members, however, cannot be attributed.

A degree of triangulation was also possible within the interview methodology. Triangulation techniques included speaking independently with negotiators who had experience across the table from each other, speaking with more than one official from the same country, and using field visits to focus on interviews with stakeholders who did not participate in international tax meetings, in particular in finance ministries and the private sector. It was also possible to triangulate between interview and observation data and other sources of information on the negotiating experience or practices of countries.

Written documentation was drawn from a number of different sources. Official statements were taken from written documents on government websites, parliamentary transcripts, and a number of archives, which also yielded internal discussions for historical sources. The UK National Archives, discussed in more detail in chapter 5, were an important source. Meeting agendas and minutes, as well as input documents, could be found in the online archives of the OECD/ OEEC and the United Nations, supplemented by a visit to the OECD archives and by copies of documents held in the British archives. In addition, the Public

Library of US Diplomacy maintains a database of US diplomatic cables, includ-ing both a historical archive from the 1970s and leaked cables.[102] Searches of the cables for "tax treaty" and "double taxation" yielded 232 results, mostly cables recording discussions between finance ministers or officials and US diplomats.

A final source of data for this book is a new data set of more than two thousand tax treaties signed by lower-income countries, which allows for a more powerful comparative analysis than has been conducted in any prior study.[103] Each treaty is coded for twenty-eight points of variation, of which twenty-four reflect the protection for source taxing rights in the treaty. I constructed an index of overall source taxing rights, an average of these twenty-four provisions for each treaty. This gives a very broad assessment of each treaty, enabling a broad-brush comparative analysis between countries and over time. For example, there is a widening gap in the way that lower-income countries negotiate with each other, and the way that OECD member states negotiate with them. Figure 1.1 shows the negotiated content of tax treaties signed by lower-income countries, dividing their negotiating partners into two groups: OECD members and the G77 group of lower-income countries. Although there is some fluctuation over the long term, the gap has been widening over the past fifteen years.

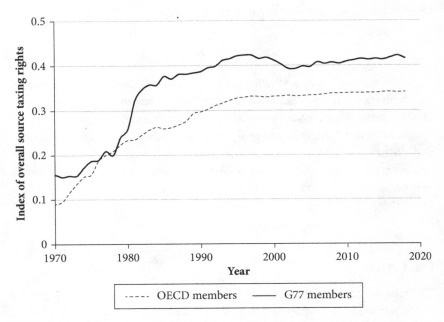

FIGURE 1.1. Overall source taxing rights in lower-income countries' tax treaties, cumulative, by treaty partner

Source: Martin Hearson, "Tax Treaties Explorer," 2020, http://treaties.tax.

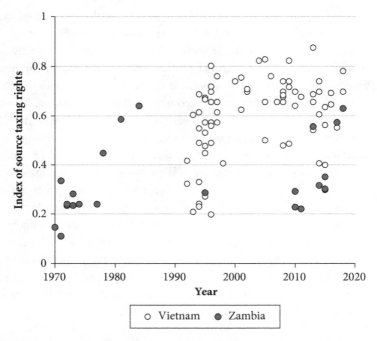

FIGURE 1.2. Overall source taxing rights in Vietnam's and Zambia's tax treaties

Source: Hearson, "Tax Treaties Explorer."

Analysis using this data set allows me to go beyond previous quantitative research on tax treaties that has focused largely on withholding tax rates. Figure 1.2 illustrates this, showing how the index of overall source taxing rights can be used to study a country's negotiating history. It compares the treaties signed by Zambia and Vietnam. When Vietnam began negotiating, it signed some very residence-based treaties, subsequently concluding agreements that were more source-based. Zambia has been through the same process, twice: in the 1970s–80s and again in the 2010s.

Outline

The book is structured in two parts. Chapters 2–4 make the argument in general terms, beginning with chapter 2, which gives a historical perspective on lower-income countries' involvement in the international tax regime. It shows how, from the 1920s onward, higher-income countries dominated the development of the model tax treaties, first at the League of Nations and then at the OECD. While it is true that the design of institutions of cooperation reflected the preferences of the states for which the need for those institutions was most pressing, it is also clear that they used their first-mover advantage and economic strength to lock down the institutional design that now exhibits a bias in their favor. This pattern was not limited to the tax treaty regime and can be seen more broadly in the development of lower-income countries' tax systems, which have always been influenced by their position as rule takers and recipients of technical assistance.

Chapters 3 and 4 bring the analysis up to the present day, using interview, observation, and documentary evidence to characterize the mechanisms through which lower-income countries have been encouraged to conclude tax treaties. Chapter 3 focuses on actors who influence international tax policy but are not specialists, such as business executives, senior civil servants, and politicians. To do so, it emphasizes how such individuals act using bounded rationality, applying cognitive heuristics to process information. Interview and documentary evidence in this chapter show that decisions by lower-income countries to open tax treaty negotiations have at times been motivated by competition for inward investment, but that this is often hard to explain based on a model of purely rational legal and economic analysis of their likely impact. The chapter then turns the tables, demonstrating a strong evidence base that it is often *higher-income* countries that seek tax treaties with lower-income countries, in order to enhance the competitive position of their own multinationals.

The emphasis in chapter 4 is on the transnational tax policy community, whose members are at the heart of the international tax regime and of bilateral tax treaty negotiations. Through interviews and participant observation at international meetings, it demonstrates that community members share a set of ideas about tax treaties that differs from the ideas held by nonspecialist actors. They favor tax treaties not because of any immediate impact on investment flows but because they disseminate a set of standards that embody an acceptable and responsible way to tax multinational companies. The chapter argues that community influence can happen through "teaching" civil servants and through the influential position acquired by community members through their mastery of complex, interdisciplinary technical knowledge. Nonetheless, technical knowledge is a prerequisite for good negotiating outcomes.

The second half of the book consists of three case study chapters. The UK, discussed in chapter 5, is an archetypal case, a country heavily implicated in the international tax regime and, during the 1970s, a prolific negotiator with lower-income countries. Archival evidence allows the detailed tracing of individual negotiations and substantiates the arguments of the first part of the book: negotiations were driven by the UK, to provide a competitive edge to its multinational investors; different conceptualizations of the benefits of treaties existed in the expert and nonexpert communities, leading to conflicting preferences, with the expert community controlling the negotiating process.

In chapter 6, archival evidence and field interviews allow for a comparison between Zambia's negotiations during the 1970s and the 2000s. In the earlier period of negotiations, negotiators lacked the technical capacity to understand the agreements they were signing, but believed tax treaties would attract investment. They were insulated from the tax costs at first by the government's large income from the mining sector. As a result, they signed away excessive amounts of taxing rights to higher-income countries. By the 2000s, learning from the international tax community gave officials a much greater understanding and a more precise set of objectives from treaty negotiations, including renegotiations, premised on community norms. They were unable to gain domestic political support for this negotiation program in an environment of falling mining revenues, until the 2011 election brought about an alignment of bureaucratic and political priorities.

Field interviews contrast Vietnam and Cambodia in chapter 7. The former is a hugely prolific tax treaty negotiator that, like Zambia, made some negotiating errors in its early days. Subsequently, it came to be known as a tenacious and expert negotiator, but the errors made in its earlier negotiations combined with an insistence on concluding as many treaties as possible continue to prove costly. Cambodia, in contrast, is a negative case. It came very late to tax treaty negotiation and then approached it cautiously. This was in part because of its limited state capacity, but mostly because a lack of corporate tax revenue increased the salience of the revenue costs in policymakers' minds, creating a strong skepticism toward tax treaties. The result has been a small number of well-negotiated treaties.

The book ends with a discussion, which draws on the preceding evidence as well as additional interviews and observation, of how the development of the tax treaty regime might encourage a rethinking of present-day challenges. If the North-South dimension is not surfaced as an important axis of conflict between states, the tools of tax cooperation will continue to deprive lower-income countries of revenue, even though they are being recast as weapons to help all states in the fight against tax avoidance and evasion. Lower-income countries should not continue to negotiate if they lack the capacity to do so with their eyes fully open, and must beware "capacity-building" efforts by states and international organizations with a vested interest in the present system. Expert knowledge about international tax is far from neutral.

A HISTORY OF LOWER-INCOME COUNTRIES IN (AND OUT OF) GLOBAL TAX GOVERNANCE

Actually if I had a choice I would scrap all double taxation treaties, because that was really a concept put there by developed countries to help their multinational companies.

—Former tax treaty negotiator and Commissioner of Internal Revenue, Asian country

While the tax treaties that are the focus of this book range from those signed in the 2010s to some that are fifty years old, the models on which they are all based date from earlier still. It was in the 1920s and 1930s that the basic design of the international tax regime was laid out, combining the decentralized, bottom-up approach of hard-law bilateral treaties with top-down soft-law standardization through multilateral models.[1] Key concepts that now constrain countries' ability to tax multinational companies were also developed at this time, finally set in stone with the creation of the OECD model treaty in 1963. Throughout this century of negotiations, the tension between capital-importing lower-income countries and capital-exporting higher-income countries has been a consistent theme. Yet the center of gravity of the regime we have today, even taking into account the UN model treaty's greater emphasis on lower-income countries' taxing rights, is much closer to the position articulated by higher-income countries than by lower-income countries.

This chapter reviews the historical record, combining original archival research with existing accounts to give a political economy perspective on a story that is familiar to tax history scholars. It demonstrates that higher-income countries' domination of the international tax regime results from their stronger preference for cooperation among themselves, which drove repeated and insurmountable first-mover advantages. Today's international tax institutions were not primarily designed for lower-income countries but by and for higher-income ones. They resemble those countries' own tax systems and a consensus that formed among a transnational community of experts from the Global North.

Higher-income countries began to introduce the corporate income tax in its modern form in the early twentieth century.[2] Since business activities were already somewhat globalized at this time, this new tax was designed by states from the beginning bearing in mind the effects of its interaction with other states' tax systems. Most states wanted to be able to tax foreign companies' earnings within their borders, as well as the worldwide profits of their own multinationals, a situation that was not tenable if every state did it in an uncoordinated fashion. Consequently, soon after the First World War, states began to work together through the League of Nations to construct a set of international norms that shaped their domestic tax laws as well as the tools of cooperation.[3] While some lower-income countries were present in the League they joined its tax discussions late and were unable to influence them. In the 1960s, it was again a group of higher-income countries that consolidated the earlier work into the OECD's model bilateral tax convention. The growing pressures from globalization since then have transformed and intensified the original conflicts, forcing OECD states to elaborate an increasingly complex and detailed global tax regime. Their tax systems have converged on a common approach formulated over decades of collective experimentation and negotiation.

Although they did not design it, lower-income and transition countries began to be absorbed into this system from the 1970s, concluding more and more bilateral tax treaties and developing their tax codes on the basis of OECD tax concepts and standards, some of which they adopted wholesale.[4] Whereas the domestic tax laws of higher-income countries were mutually co-constituted with the international regime, for most lower-income countries the traffic has been one-way. Their very identities as fiscal states—from the purpose and definition of corporate tax to the fiscal state's responsibilities toward its taxpayers—have not formed in isolation but as participants on the outer edges of this regime. In most cases, elements of their tax systems that were inconsistent with OECD standards have been reformed to bring them in line with international norms, or at least overridden by bilateral tax treaties.

To tell this story, this chapter begins with the emergence of the "tax state" itself, exploring the connection among statehood, sovereignty, and taxation. It then considers how the tax state in lower-income countries developed differently, as much a product of exogenous influences as endogenous social forces. The rest of the chapter traces the development of the institutions of global tax governance from the League of Nations through to the OECD, illustrating how the different phases of cooperation established and consolidated higher-income countries' first-mover advantage as rule makers, in contrast to lower-income countries, which arrived later and became rule takers. In particular, the OECD's model bilateral tax convention became both the most widespread template for bilateral negotiations and the most powerful focal point around which the expectations of participants in the international tax regime have converged.

Prehistory

The history of taxation is intertwined with the history of the modern state itself. As Rudolf Goldscheid asserted, "The origin of the state lies in association for the purposes of defence and to meet common fiscal needs."[5] His fellow "fiscal sociologist" Joseph Schumpeter, in the first manifesto on the subject, *Crisis of the Tax State*, asserted that "the fiscal history of a people is above all an essential part of its general history," emphasizing that taxation not only was a useful lens through which to view political and social events but also played a causal role in those events.[6] While Schumpeter and Goldscheid may have been the first to explicitly emphasize the fiscal part of their story, others before them had recognized the importance of taxation for any understanding of the state. According to Edmund Burke, writing about postrevolutionary France, "The revenue of the state is the state. In effect all depends upon it, whether for support or for reformation."[7]

Schumpeter's argument ran as follows. As warfare between princedoms led more and more European princes to face financial difficulties in the fourteenth and fifteenth centuries, they turned to the estates they governed to finance the war effort, and in doing so a public financial realm came into being, separate from the prince's private finances: the tax state. Writing at the end of the First World War, Schumpeter traced the development of the Austrian tax state but argued that it faced a crisis, burdened by war debts and reaching the limit of its taxing capacity as it struggled to repay them.[8] Others, writing subsequently, have characterized the tax state's evolution into the "fiscal state," which is distinguished by its ability to borrow sustainably on the strength of its reliable revenue stream, and hence its greater financial capacity to react to wars and other emergencies.[9]

The "militarist" fiscal sociology account is found across many descriptions of state development. In Norbert Elias's history of state formation, the modern state is characterized by two mutually reinforcing monopolies: military force coerces the payment of taxation, which in turn funds military force.[10] Charles Tilly expanded on Elias's ideas as follows: "Where did the money [for warfare] come from? In the short run, typically from loans by capitalists and levies on local populations unlucky enough to have troops in their vicinity. In the long run, from one form of taxation or another."[11]

Income tax, the focus of this book, was first introduced in the UK in 1799 to fund the war with Napoleonic France, and continued to be tied explicitly to war efforts right through to the First World War.[12] In the United States, too, federal income tax was first levied by Congress in 1861 to fund its efforts in the civil war.[13] Wars also played a role in the introduction of income tax in France and Austria.[14]

The next stage of the account runs as follows. Extending the revenue base to more powerful, wealthy citizens who up to that point may have been insulated from the burden of coercive taxation created two imperatives: the establishment of administrative institutions to collect and manage the revenue separately from the prince's private household, and the formation of a social contract with these new taxpayers.[15] To collect taxes from these groups, the ruler relied on their consent, a shift characterized by Mick Moore as going from "coercive" to "contractual" taxation.[16] In sixteenth-century Austria, for example, Schumpeter describes how the estates' contributions to the defense of the princedoms came with an expectation of some capacity to influence both the distribution of the tax liability and the use to which the tax revenue was put.[17] Evidence shows that a higher tax burden on an elite leads to policies that favor it, and a higher tax burden in general leads to a more democratic or liberal polity: "In the long run, democratisation only occurs when rulers come to rely on citizen compliance for their means of rule," according to Tilly.[18]

The militarist account is only one lens through which to view the development of the fiscal state. Others have situated it within the deterministic sweep of economic and social modernization, the emphasis of institutionalist theory on path dependence, or have emphasized the role of elite and, later, popular consent.[19] The "new fiscal sociologists" argue that "taxation is central not only to the state's capacity in war, but in fact to all social life."[20] Because taxation is integral to the development of state-citizen relations, the fiscal component of sovereignty is an essential part of any story of the development of international relations, especially one that recognizes that both "war made the state, and the state made war."[21] The state needs tax revenue to safeguard the security of its citizens, but the act of taxation is also part of the social construction of the state itself, of its sovereignty within a given area.

Fiscal sovereignty is complicated, however, by the ability of economic factors to cross borders. If states attempt to exercise it in conditions of anarchy—without cooperation—it may be self-defeating. Without cooperation, overlapping claims to tax the same income will create onerous double taxation that deters trade and investment. Worse still, taxpayers may respond to a high tax burden in one country by moving to another or by placing their wealth in another jurisdiction, beyond the reach of their home state's administrative capacity. According to Peggy Musgrave, author of several seminal works in the tax literature interrogating this question, "It is likely that in the absence of cooperative agreements . . . countries will exercise their entitlements in a way to serve their national interests and that these interests may conflict with each other and with standards of inter-nation equity and allocative efficiency."[22]

Musgrave forms part of a long tradition of advocates for a formal international tax authority, whose proposals have failed to gain traction because of the strength of feeling about fiscal sovereignty.[23] Nonetheless, states have chosen to establish some degree of cooperation, because an anarchic "state of nature" would limit their ability to exercise their fiscal sovereignty in practice.

Indeed, it is hard to sustain a linear view in which national tax laws precede international cooperation, since the two have coevolved from the beginning. We are in a Waltzian world.[24] If economic factors can cross borders, it is hard to think that an absolute notion of fiscal sovereignty ever made sense.[25] As Allison Christians writes, "If tax sovereignty means anything, perhaps it is the idea that governments have a non-exclusive right to decide through political means whether and how to tax whatever activity occurs within their territories and whomever can be considered to be their 'people', and that they recognize a reciprocal right in all other states."[26]

When developing their own international tax systems (that is, their domestic laws as they pertain to multinational taxpayers) in the interwar years, states were already constrained by the way in which their laws might interact with those of other countries, and this was one of the main motivating factors behind their first steps at international tax cooperation.[27] Western states made explicit efforts to copy each other's laws at this time, while many lower-income countries emerged from colonialism with a facsimile of the colonizer's tax system.[28]

The Special Case of Lower-Income Countries

The development of the tax state in postindependence lower-income countries was somewhat different from the Eurocentric model. In part, this was a timing issue: when the contours of the international tax regime were put in place, lower-income countries were still under colonial rule, or had not yet been penetrated by significant amounts of foreign investment. On the one hand, the financing of a war effort against an external aggressor was not generally available as a pretext for asking citizens to make a greater tax contribution.[29] On the other hand, most lower-income states' fiscal situations were—and are—heavily influenced by external actors: tax systems were inherited from colonial governments and further influenced by donors, lenders, and technical assistance providers; overseas aid provided an additional source of revenue that changed leaders' incentives to raise and spend revenue in particular ways; tax levied on (and collected by) multinational investors, especially in those countries with extractive industries, made up a much larger share of tax revenue than in higher-income countries.[30]

Newly independent lower-income countries inherited tax systems from their colonial powers that shaped their legal codes, administrative structures, and even their ability to raise revenue. As Thandika Mkandawire demonstrates, "the end of colonialism left an institutional and infrastructural residue that still plays a major role in the determination of tax policies and the capacity to collect tax."[31] Victor Thuronyi identifies eight "families of income tax laws," traceable mostly to former empires.[32] Mick Keen notes that francophone African countries today still perform worse than their Anglophone continental neighbors at raising tax revenue.[33] Many countries also inherited tax treaties that had been put in place within the colonial system.

Since that initial starting point, probably an even greater influence on the design of lower-income countries' tax systems has come from thousands of technical assistance missions. In 1989, the economist Malcolm Gillis estimated in an edited volume written by many of those most experienced in technical assistance that "there have been perhaps one hundred identifiable attempts at major tax reform in developing nations since 1945."[34] Indeed, the history of such missions predates many lower-income countries' independence and can be traced to the "Shoup Mission" of 1949–50. A group of seven US academics led by the economist Carl Shoup are credited with the design of Japan's modern tax system, including the introduction of corporate income tax.[35] With the IMF and World Bank's emphasis on structural adjustment from the 1980s onward, tax reform advice and conditionality started to crystallize around a set of recommendations consistent with the "Washington Consensus" described by John Williamson. Tax reform was one of Williamson's original ten points, and his original essay noted "a very wide consensus" around the principle "that the tax base should be broad and marginal tax rates should be moderate."[36] Miranda Stewart describes the associated policies as follows: "The contemporary tax reform 'package' intended to achieve these goals includes a single-rate, broad-based VAT [value-added tax] to replace older-style sales taxes; a low-rate, broad-based corporate and personal income tax; the goal of tax 'neutrality' with respect to different investments and activities; and the gradual reduction and eventual elimination of import and export tariffs."[37]

Thus, while countries of the Global South no doubt looked to each other for inspiration and experience when building their tax systems, lower-income countries' tax systems have consistently been built with input from experts from the Global North. At times they have been imposed, whether through colonial measures or economic conditionality. Lower-income countries start from a position of learning from others. Chapter 4 considers how technical assistance in the area of international taxation contributed to the emergence of lower-income countries' tax treaty networks.

A second difference between higher-income and lower-income countries concerns the incentives their political leaders face. Higher-income countries introduced income taxation at a point where they urgently needed the public funds. For the governments of many lower-income countries, alternative sources of revenue can distort this incentive. There is some evidence, for example, that overseas development assistance (foreign aid) can crowd out tax revenue raising, since governments have a smaller incentive to impose tax costs on their citizens; when segmented, the effect appears to apply to grants but not loans, which must ultimately be repaid through tax revenue.[38] Similarly, in resource-rich lower-income countries, nontax revenue earned by the government from the extraction of oil, gas, or minerals can have a similar effect,[39] part of a broader "political resource curse" through which natural resource revenues are thought to have a detrimental effect on political institutions.[40]

Third, lower-income countries' dependence on foreign investment places them in a unique situation in comparison with higher-income countries. They are "dependent market economies," in which capital is primarily foreign owned,[41] and there is a lower capacity to raise revenue through the taxes used by higher-income countries: a much smaller proportion of their population is in formal employment and earning enough to pay personal income tax, the main source of revenue in higher-income countries.[42] Low-income countries collect taxes amounting to 18 percent of GDP, compared with 32 percent in high-income countries, yet both groups collect taxes from companies amounting to around 3 percent of GDP. The result is that one tax dollar in seven raised by lower-income countries comes from taxes on businesses, as compared with one in eleven for high-income countries.[43]

Lower-income countries often have higher tax rates than higher-income countries, but their tax systems are riddled with tax holidays and other incentives and are less well defended against tax avoidance by multinationals. The former problem comes about precisely because they are heavily dependent on foreign capital to enable them to exploit their abundant labor and land. The governments of lower-income countries are much more sensitive to the structural power of foreign capital, to the threat of discouraging inward investment through their tax systems. Indeed, a proliferation of tax incentives illustrates that they have been engaged in a race to the bottom since soon after independence, originally encouraged, but now discouraged in vain, by technical advisers.[44] The form of this competition, however, is influenced by the tax systems of *higher-income* countries.[45] In particular, as the latter have moved toward systems that exempt foreign income from further taxation at home, multinational investors have become more sensitive to changes in effective tax rates in their host countries.

In the story that follows, therefore, we must separate the rule makers and the rule takers. For the major players in the League of Nations, the Organisation for European Economic Cooperation (OEEC; the predecessor of the OECD) and now the OECD's fiscal committees, participation in the international tax regime has meant shaping a set of rules that regulate the interface between tax systems as they develop, adapting international rules to their domestic laws and vice versa. These countries learned from their own experiences and those of others, and shaped national and international tax rules accordingly. In contrast, for lower-income countries, those same rules came bundled in a consensus package of tax advice, broadcast to them through successive waves of colonization, technical assistance missions, conditionality, and development fads. Throughout the twentieth century, with a few exceptions, lower-income countries were purely in receiving mode when it came to international tax norms. Yet the rules governing the taxation of multinational companies are, if anything, more important to lower-income countries, because of their reliance on foreign capital and the disproportionate role of business taxation in their tax mixes. As we shall see, however, despite the differences in the interests of capital-importing and capital-exporting nations being fairly clear from early on, international tax standards represent the interests of the latter.

The League of Nations Era

As income tax systems became formalized in the Western world after the First World War, and rates rose to pay for the war effort, double taxation and tax evasion soon began to create problems for taxpayers and tax authorities. An International Chambers of Commerce (ICC) resolution in 1920, one of a series addressed to the League, called for "prompt agreement between the Governments of the Allied countries in order to prevent individuals or companies from being compelled to pay a tax on the same income in more than one country."[46] When the League's Provisional Economic and Financial Committee was created in October 1920, double taxation was included within its mandate, alongside matters such as postwar financial reconstruction. A Fiscal Committee in its own right was created in 1929.

During this period in which national and international tax regimes were simultaneously in flux, there were no existing rules to constrain the architects of the international tax regime. A handful of bilateral tax treaties had been signed, giving states some examples to work with, but there was no international consensus. To take a historical institutionalist approach, this was a critical juncture in which decisions with long-term implications were made and a few influential individuals were able to shape the design of a regime that has become notoriously sticky.[47] Accounts of the league's deliberations, contemporaneous ones by participants and observers as well as subsequent analysis by historians, emphasize the role of personalities and personal positions, both in creating conflict and in helping to overcome differences between national interests.[48] Edwin Seligman and Thomas Adams, for example, were both experts nominated by the United States at different times, and both were influential in the design of the US international tax system; they disagreed with each other on the source and residence matter.[49] Adams took a liberal view whereby more source taxation was in the interest of the United States because it would build a more inclusive international tax regime, which brought him into conflict with the staunchly residence-based views of his British counterpart, Percy Thompson.[50]

The central distributional dispute between higher-income and lower-income countries concerns the right to tax at "source," where a business makes its profits, versus at "residence," where it has its headquarters. Once the differences between tax systems and economic positions are taken into account, it is a thorny matter to resolve among any group of countries. As Thomas Rixen suggests, even OECD states cannot reach agreement on distributional questions in a multilateral setting, so they develop multilateral tools that will act as focal points for bilateral negotiations in which those distributional questions are resolved.[51] These tools, beginning with the first League of Nations models and running through to the present day OECD model and associated guidelines, are not neutral with respect to distributional questions, however. Source versus residence has been a constant theme in the development of the international tax regime since the 1920s.

The League proceeded through the drafting of a series of reports, beginning with the 1925 report of a Committee of Technical Experts to the Financial Committee, and concluding with the Fiscal Committee's tenth report in 1946, which also incorporated the influential London Draft. A brief examination of the countries participating in this drafting and the exchanges on the source-residence debate will illustrate the general orientation of the considerations. In 1923–25, during the drafting of the 1925 report, seven countries participated. Although these were all higher-income countries, source and residence was the main bone of contention between the combative British representative, Percy Thompson of the Board of Inland Revenue, and the others from continental Europe. The UK was still at this point an exporter of capital to mainland Europe, much of which was in heavy debt and reconstruction following the war, and thus Thompson preferred an emphasis on residence taxing rights, especially for the UK's general income tax. The other participants were keen to retain the UK's support, as a "great economy," and so the 1925 report, which included a number of resolutions establishing general principles on double taxation, had a stronger residence orientation than that preferred by the majority.[52]

When five new countries joined the committee to draft a model convention on the basis of the 1925 report, the new Argentinian and Venezuelan members quickly raised their concern that the resolutions of the 1925 report on income tax would disadvantage their countries, arguing for more source and less residence taxation.[53] But it was too late, and they were outnumbered. Sunita Jogarajan, in her exhaustive study of the records of these discussions, concludes that "the compulsion to follow the 1925 report significantly reduced the influence of . . . the representatives from 'developing countries.'"[54] The pattern occurred again when the franchise was opened to all countries in 1928: Bulgaria and Spain criticized what they regarded as an antisource bias in the 1927 draft convention, while Poland and South Africa took a more favorable view, citing investment promotion.[55] The momentum behind the existing draft prevented this discussion from influencing the outcome to any great extent, and the 1928 report, which incorporated three very similar model conventions, set the precedent from that time onward.

Numerous tax treaties were concluded during the 1930s and early 1940s, creating a desire on the part of the Fiscal Commission to revisit the 1928 models in the light of recent negotiating experience. While the European countries that had dominated the initial deliberations were embroiled in the Second World War, the Western Hemisphere continued to work. At a meeting held in Mexico in 1943, Latin American countries along with the United States and Canada agreed to the "Mexico Draft" convention, which drew on the 1928 report, but gave much stronger taxing rights to source countries. Following the end of the Second World War, and the conclusion of a treaty between the United States and the UK that effectively brokered a consensus between them, the Fiscal Commission held its final session at Somerset House in London. The meeting, which was dominated by European countries, agreed a new London Draft convention. The commission's report presents the Mexico and London Drafts side by side and states that, "virtually, the only clauses where there is an effective divergence between the views of the 1943 Mexico meeting and those of the 1946 London meeting are those relating to the taxation of interest, dividends, royalties, annuities and pensions."[56] These were no small disagreements, and the two models adopted diametrically opposed positions as to, for example, which country should be entitled to tax the interest payments on a cross-border loan. The commission suggested that "the work done both in Mexico and in London could be usefully reviewed and developed by a balanced group of tax administrators and experts from both capital-importing and capital-exporting countries and from economically-advanced and less-advanced countries, when the League work on international tax problems is taken over by the United Nations."[57]

While the United Nations did indeed take up work on double taxation within a "balanced group" of technical experts, this work did not progress very far. By the UN Fiscal Commission's second session in 1949, Cold War divisions had already begun to characterize its deliberations on double taxation treaties. According to the British delegate at the meeting, the Soviet, Ukrainian, and Czechoslovak members "took exception to international action in this field on the grounds that it represented pressure on the under-developed countries to the advantage of highly developed countries."[58] By its third session, a divide had also opened between higher-income and lower-income countries on the now-traditional source and residence lines. The International Civil Aviation Organisation (ICAO) had brought a proposal for reciprocal exemption of airlines, by which companies operating flights would be exempt from taxation in the countries to which they fly, paying it only in the country where they were based. India, Pakistan, Venezuela, and Cuba raised objections, pointing out that if only one country signing the treaty had an airline, "reciprocal exemption is quite unfair."[59] The ICAO proposal, which was consistent with the treaty policy of countries with their own airlines, fell after a vote in which the lower-income countries were joined by the Soviet group.[60] This compares to the reciprocal exemption of shipping companies, which had been comfortably agreed to by the higher-income-country-dominated League of Nations.

By the time the commission's work reached the Economic and Social Council (ECOSOC) in 1951, it appears to have run out of steam. Alexander Morosov, the Russian participant (also its representative on the Fiscal Commission itself), expressed his familiar objection that the commission's work on double taxation "was in reality intended to promote economic conditions favourable to the activities of British and American monopolies." He concluded that the commission "was engaged in futile operations, and that it was therefore useless to keep it in existence."[61] According to his Polish counterpart, "The majority of the Commission had, by certain of the recommendations adopted by that body, tried to exploit the authority of the Economic and Social Council to relieve investors from the highly-industrialised capitalist countries of the taxation which those less highly developed countries were entitled to enforce."[62] The British delegate, meanwhile, was "in agreement with the Soviet Union and Polish delegations as to the desirability of winding up the Commission's activities, although for other reasons than those advanced by them," taking the view that the commission was not a useful forum.[63]

Convergence on the OECD Model

With work at the United Nations grinding to a halt, the Executive Committee of the ICC passed another resolution in 1954, identifying double taxation as a "serious obstacle" to trade and investment in Europe and calling on members of the OEEC to take steps to relieve it.[64] The OEEC's secretary general was initially skeptical and noted that the ICC's proposal that the OEEC use the London Draft as the basis of its work was problematic because not all of its member and associate countries had endorsed it. "If an approach of this kind were to be adopted by the OEEC, therefore, it would be necessary for the Organisation to set up an expert body charged with the duty of attempting to produce a more acceptable draft."[65]

Soon after this, Switzerland and the Netherlands began to circulate proposals for a fiscal commission. A Dutch note in 1955 claimed that "the number and extent of problems relating to taxation has been steadily increasing, not only in the national field but also, and especially, in connection with the gradual intensification of international economic relations, in the international sphere."[66] It advocated work under the umbrella of the OEEC because it was consistent with the organization's mandate and because of the need to discuss in "a smaller circle than the United Nations."[67] In December 1955 the Netherlands and Switzerland were joined by Germany, publishing a joint memorandum proposing the creation of an expert committee of "specially qualified high-ranking Government representatives," and in January 1956 an ad hoc committee was created to conduct a study into the matter.[68] The ad hoc committee immediately recommended the creation of a full committee, citing "ample evidence that there are cases of double taxation which constitute obstacles to international trade and investment, and that action to remove these obstacles should be possible within a group of like-minded nations such as the members and associated countries of the OEEC."[69]

Within months, the new committee had begun to establish ways of working that are retained today, such as Working Parties delegated by the full committee to look in detail at each specific issue. It also began to elaborate the basis of the modern consensus on international tax. The result of these activities was the OECD Model Tax Convention on Income and Capital, the first complete draft of which was completed in 1963.[70]

The OECD model treaty is the basis of over three thousand bilateral tax treaties. It sets out the areas in which states will negotiate, and articulates an ideal type of negotiated outcome, although in areas such as the particular maximum tax rates specified, bilateral negotiations may vary from this outcome. The OECD model also incorporates various explicit and implicit principles of the international tax regime. Two sets of standards are incorporated into the model treaty but also have a life outside it: the OECD's Transfer Pricing Guidelines and its information exchange standard. It is through the constant updating of the model and its associated guidance that the foundations of the international tax system evolve.

Critically, the OECD model bears a closer resemblance to the London Draft than the Mexico Draft, which is hardly surprising given that it was drafted by officials from many of the countries that had been present in London in 1946 but not in Mexico in 1943. In the touchstone areas of dividends, interest, and royalty payments, it eschews the Mexico Draft's exclusive conferring of taxing rights on the source country in favor of a shared taxing right over dividends and interest, and exclusive residence taxing rights over royalties. In these critical areas, which will reemerge in the case studies that follow, the conflict between source and residence countries, in which the Mexico Draft had been a lone voice for the former, was finally settled in favor of the latter through the decisive role of the OECD model. That said, as the report of the London conference makes clear, in many other areas with distributional consequences, even the Mexico Draft did not represent a radical shift from the League-OEEC-OECD consensus.[71]

The OECD model was not the last word for lower-income countries. In 1971 the Community of Andean Nations (CAN) of Bolivia, Chile, Colombia, Ecuador, and Peru signed Decision 40, which created a multilateral tax treaty between the CAN members, binding them to be "guided" by a standard agreement in tax treaty negotiations with members outside the community, and to consult with other members before signing such treaties.[72] Decision 40 was a more radical departure than the Mexico model. Both the CAN multilateral treaty and the standard bilateral agreement gave exclusive taxing rights to the country of source for most types of income, creating a fundamental incompatibility with the OECD model treaty. The CAN model could not compete, however, with the preeminence of the OECD model. Natalia Quiñones observes that by the 2000s, "none of the . . . Members had applied it in their treaties and it was a known fact that most OECD Member countries would not even consider the CAN Model as a reference for negotiating a bilateral treaty."[73] Other regional groupings, such as the Common Market of Eastern and Southern Africa (COMESA) and the Association of Southeast Asian Nations (ASEAN), have formulated their own models, but these do not diverge radically from the OECD model.[74]

The United Nations also took up tax treaty work again, with the creation of the Ad Hoc Group of Experts on Tax Treaties between Developed and Developing Countries, which met for the first time in 1969. This committee eventually formulated its own model, first published in 1980, but this was now closely based on the OECD model, accepting the core concepts on which it was based, and the broad settlement from the London model. By 2017, a fourth iteration of the UN model had been published, with a growing number of divergences from the OECD model.[75] Some of these amendments explicitly reflect the committee's opinion regarding the appropriate balance between source and residence taxation.[76] Lower-income and higher-income countries have disagreed over the status of the UN committee and its model treaties, with lower-income countries seeking to upgrade it to an intergovernmental body and agreement, and OECD members consistently opposing this.[77] This disagreement reflects conflicting preferences about which body should play the main agenda-setting role.

Consolidation and Expansion

By any measure, the work of the OEEC/OECD Fiscal Committee has been a huge success. The committee's interim report in 1957 noted that its members had begun to "harmonise their views," which had "proved very useful during certain recent bilateral negotiations"; and by the time the OECD model was codified in 1963, around two hundred bilateral tax treaties had been signed.[78] Indeed, the OEEC committee had recognized that other countries would likely be incentivized to follow Europe's lead, because of its "position in the world economy."[79] Most pairs of OECD members had a tax treaty by 1980, and so the regime's expansion since then has been outward. There has been an exponential increase from the 1960s to the 1980s, driven by treaties between non-OECD members (figure 2.1). Consistently around 40 percent of tax treaties have been signed by lower-income countries, a number that far outstrips intra-OECD tax treaties. For the past three decades, growth has stabilized, with around one hundred new treaties concluded per year, on top of numerous renegotiations.

The success of the OECD's work is best indicated not by the number of treaties but by their content. Across the 39,600 relevant clauses in 2,200 treaties in my data set, all signed by at least one lower-income or emerging economy, OECD model provisions are used 61 percent of the time, while UN model provisions occur on the remaining 39 percent of occasions. Given that the UN model is explicitly designed for treaties signed between higher-income and lower-income countries, while the OECD model reflects purely the preferences of higher-income countries, this is a concerning outcome. Of course, because the OECD model reflects the preferences of OECD states, it partly reflects the power balance in negotiations: greater asymmetries in capabilities and investment positions lead to more OECD-type treaties.[80] But given that OECD model provisions also prevail in 46 percent of cases when neither signatory is an OECD member, the authoritative position of the OECD model is also a factor.

In addition to expanding in breadth, the OECD-centric international tax regime was also expanding in depth, becoming more legalized as countries attempted to

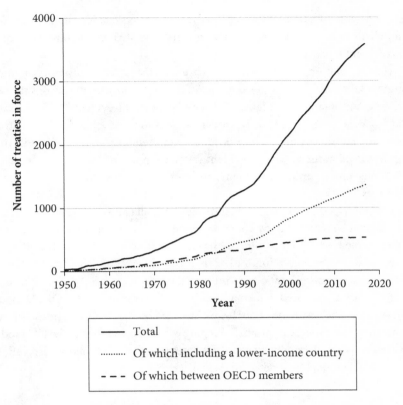

FIGURE 2.1.   Growth in the number of tax treaties

Source: IBFD, "IBFD Tax Research Platform," 2020, http://research.ibfd.org/.

spell out how the core principles would apply in new and more complex situations. The OECD model has been revised a dozen times, gradually increasing the specificity and complexity of the rules it entails, through the elaboration of a more detailed commentary. In 1979, the OECD published its report on transfer pricing, a document that spelled out how states should implement the approach to allocating profits to multinational companies that is found in article 9 of the model treaty. This was substantially revised in 1995, becoming the Transfer Pricing Guidelines, now almost as long as the model convention itself, but effectively an extension of the model treaty because they are referred to within its commentary. Multilateral tax instruments contain ten times as many words now as they did when countries first reached agreement on the OECD model.[81] A further deepening of the regime is found through the creation of the mutual agreement procedure (MAP). This is a dispute settlement mechanism that taxpayers can trigger in order to force states to negotiate with each other if they disagree over the interpretation of the treaty. Initially characterized by its "antilegalistic" nature,[82] the MAP has become more of an enforcement tool over time.

The OECD model bilateral treaty "represents the general consensus on international taxation."[83] It is a "focal point . . . defined as social conventions that are followed 'automatically' because they have become self-evident."[84] As Genschel and Rixen set out, "The OECD Model Convention was embedded in a broad epistemic consensus on 'how to do double tax relief properly', which in turn reinforced its status as the self-evident reference point in matters of double tax relief once cross-border investments and capital mobility started to increase in the 1970s."[85]

The model, commentary, and guidelines have all gained an authoritative status that can be referred to by courts in the respective countries when seeking to interpret the treaty.[86] That influence has extended, on occasion, to the interpretation of domestic legislation, rather than treaties.[87] With this in mind, OECD members can enter reservations on the model treaty, and since 1998 lower-income countries are also invited to formally set out their positions on the OECD model convention. The vast majority of lower-income countries' observations reflect a desire for greater source taxation, in keeping with the provisions of the UN model. Indeed, net-capital-importing countries enter more reservations or observations to the OECD model than net capital exporters.[88]

The Problems of Tax Avoidance and Evasion

Most literature on the politics of global tax governance focuses on the problems created when economic actors exploit weaknesses in the rules for international tax cooperation: tax avoidance, tax evasion, and the tax havens that help make them possible. While this book is focused on a different problem, it is worth considering the relationship between the source-residence tension and tax avoidance/evasion.

A state may claim the right to tax a person in principle, either because they are one of its residents or because they earn income within its borders. But there are practical constraints that may prevent it from exercising that right, and these constraints have helped shape the development of international tax norms to date. The two biggest are these: First, how can a state tax a person with sources of income in multiple countries if it cannot know whether the person has given an honest account of his or her global financial position? Second, how can a state force a foreign resident to pay tax on income earned within the state's borders if the foreign resident no longer has any income or assets in that state? The architects of the international tax regime in its earliest days were aware of this: the division of taxing rights between source and residence countries reflected practical realities as well as political settlements,[89] the problem of tax evasion was as much a part of the remit of the League of Nations Fiscal Committee as double taxation,[90] and tax treaties include instruments through which states share information with each other and cooperate to collect revenue from cross-border taxpayers.[91]

By the 1970s, however, tax avoidance and evasion had been intensified by a third problem, described by Ronen Palan as the "commercialisation of state sovereignty."[92] This refers to a jurisdiction offering residents of other countries the opportunity to adopt its nationality, attracting them with a preferential tax regime, without physically moving to that state. By becoming, on paper, a resident of this new jurisdiction, companies and wealthy individuals can exploit the international tax rules put in place by the states in which they operate, by which their taxing rights are curbed. In other instances, companies and individuals use the commercialized sovereignty of tax havens to conceal their wealth behind a veil of secrecy that cannot be penetrated by the tax authorities of the countries where they are actually present. Because this could not be resolved without either abandoning the key tenets of the international tax regime or introducing a coercive characteristic into its operation, the problem has proved particularly difficult to resolve.[93]

Tax treaties can include tools to help deal with such problems, but they are imperfect. Because they place constraints on signatories' ability to tax, they can also exacerbate it by creating opportunities for international tax avoidance. Here multinational taxpayers circumvent the intention of one country's tax laws by exploiting the differences between countries' tax systems and the constraints on their ability to tax international transactions as a result of tax treaties.[94] Treaty shopping, in particular, uses the terms of tax treaties that divide up the tax base, combined with the advantageous laws of low-tax conduit jurisdictions such as the Netherlands and Mauritius, to obtain advantages not intended by (at least one of) the treaty signatories.[95] Eduardo Baistrocchi has suggested that lower-income countries may deliberately avoid enforcing international tax rules as a form of tax competition, while Vincent Arel-Bundock argues that tax treaty shopping places pressure on countries to sign treaties.[96]

In the area of tax avoidance and evasion, higher-income and lower-income countries' interests are often aligned, since the winners from improved cooperation are states in which real economic activity takes place, while the "losers" from cooperation are tax havens and their users. Nonetheless, there are two differences. First, the asymmetrical nature of economic flows and enforcement capacities means that lower-income countries need a different form of cooperation than that of higher-income countries. For example, complex corporate tax structuring is a problem for higher-income countries, while lower-income countries often suffer from simpler structures that higher-income countries are better equipped to tackle.[97] In contrast, as capital importers, lower-income countries need access to information on multinational investors that may be more readily available to the higher-income countries in which they are headquartered.[98] The international tools of administrative cooperation formulated by higher-income countries may therefore not always meet the needs of lower-income countries. It is notable that the provision in tax treaties that obliges the capital-exporting state to collect tax on behalf of the capital importer, in cases where an investor from the former no longer has assets in the latter, is present in just 16 percent of treaties signed by lower-income and emerging economies, and much less than half of those signed since 2000, despite its presence in both the OECD and UN model treaties.

A second difference is that, while higher-income countries have the economic power to coerce tax havens into cooperating, lower-income countries that lack this coercive power must piggyback on initiatives designed by others or offer concessions during treaty negotiations. To obtain information from less cooperative tax havens, for example, some countries have found themselves obliged to sign a tax treaty that restricts their taxing rights and opens them up to treaty shopping. We can see, then, that the North-South axis colors this possibly existential challenge faced by the international tax regime.

Conclusion

In this chapter we traced the emergence of the multilateral institutions of tax cooperation, from the League of Nations in the 1920s–40s, via the United Nations, to the OEEC/OECD since the mid-1950s, supplemented since the 1970s by the UN again. The tension between capital-exporting and capital-importing nations, which is present within the OECD but much starker when lower-income countries are involved, has been present throughout. Hence, we see, broadly speaking, the same pattern in the interwar period as in the second half of the twentieth century. Higher-income countries reach an agreement among themselves that sets the parameters for future discussions in which lower-income countries can participate.

Higher-income countries have a greater shared interest in reaching agreement on a common set of international tax rules, and negotiations between them are less characterized by outright distributional conflict. This is because economic interactions among them are more intense and complex, and hence the potential for double taxation is more significant, while the economic relations are less one-sided. Negotiations between them in both eras took place primarily through technical experts, and it is notable that participants in the early work of both the League and the OEEC observed the importance of this epistemic consensus building. This shared understanding among participants, the foundation of their cooperation, was embodied in common language and principles that endure to this day, as well as in more transient formal agreements.

By the time that lower-income countries joined the discussions, the first-mover advantage of the higher-income countries was unassailable. At the League of Nations they entered into discussions after the contours of agreement had already been defined, while the UN committee that began work at the end of the 1960s was reduced to tweaking an OECD model treaty that had quickly attained hegemonic status. When lower-income countries asserted themselves more strongly, through the Mexico Draft in the 1940s and the UN Fiscal Commission in the 1950s, this merely provoked an unproductive stalemate that drove "like-minded" states to work through the OEEC. The CAN model also proved a nonstarter given its incompatibility with the OECD model. As chapter 8 will consider further, this historical record does not bode well for efforts by the OECD to open the institutions of multilateral cooperation to lower-income countries.

The chapters that follow will shift the focus from cooperation over multilateral soft law toward bilateral hard law. This is in keeping with the central puzzle of why lower-income countries have entered into bilateral agreements when the terms appear disadvantageous. It is also because multilateral tax institutions have been remarkably stable since the 1970s. Though the OECD and UN model treaties have been updated from time to time, these changes have been incremental adaptations and have hardly touched on the distributional questions at the heart of this book. The two main exceptions illustrate how stable the underlying settlement of the regime has been. A change to article 7 of the OECD model in 2007 that conferred greater taxing rights on the home countries of multinational firms has yet to gain widespread acceptance. At the UN, meanwhile, the inclusion of a new article 12A in the 2017 edition of the UN model permits the imposition of a withholding tax on technical service fee payments. This can be seen as a shift toward capital-importing countries, but it is hardly revolutionary: it was already under discussion at the UN in the 1970s and has become common, albeit in a minority of treaties signed by lower-income countries. Countries do have some autonomy to differ from the formal rules set out in the models, yet, as the subsequent chapters emphasize, it is the ideational consensus about tax treaties that exerts the most powerful conditioning effect.

THE COMPETITION DISCOURSE
AND NORTH-SOUTH RELATIONS

Nobody comes to invest because you have a tax treaty. When you see the rationale to attract investment, it sounds laudable. But when you look at the evidence, it's not the case.

—Tax treaty negotiator, African country

One reason that lower-income countries do not raise more tax revenue from multinational investors is tax competition. States can choose to exercise their sovereign right to tax as much as they like in principle, but in practice they are engaged in a strategic interaction that keeps effective tax rates down, enforced by mobile corporate capital and high-income labor.[1] As capital has become more mobile over time, states have come to take this much more into account, engaging in what some have described as a "race to the bottom."[2] Tax competition is a manifestation of what is often called the structural power of business: companies' ability to shape the options available to governments without explicitly lobbying for a given outcome, since governments anticipate their preferences and fear the negative consequences of contravening them.[3]

Competition for inward investment is the single most commonly cited reason for why lower-income countries have signed, or should sign, tax treaties. Yet, as we saw earlier, they are a poor choice of tool, given the uncertainty about their positive effects and the certainty about their costs. This is not a scenario limited to tax treaties but one that applies to other forms of tax competition: the effects of tax incentives and even headline corporate tax rates often seem to be overestimated by policymakers. The evidence that governments engage in strategic interactions over taxation is much stronger than the evidence that those strategic interactions influence investment flows. To understand tax competition, we therefore need to consider it through a cognitive lens, as a social rather than a brute fact. The *idea* of tax competition, potent in political debates as well as economic decision making, is sustained regardless of the shaky evidence that it brings welfare gains, especially to lower-income countries.[4]

This chapter combines the insights from work on boundedly rational learning—especially on BITs—with the classic conception of policy diffusion through competition, or "race to the bottom."[5] As the evidence presented in this chapter shows, lower-income countries have indeed signed tax treaties in order to compete for inward investment. The evidence to justify this competition is weak, and treaty negotiators themselves are often skeptical that tax treaties will attract investment. Others in lower-income countries do subscribe to the competition approach, but may be relying on ideas as well as, or instead of, purely rational analysis of the costs and benefits. Tax treaties are, however, a harder case than BITs for theories of bounded rationality, because the costs are more immediate and certain than any potential benefits, and hence information on the costs might be expected to be more "available" to policymakers. It is therefore important to consider how policymakers evaluate the costs and benefits, taking into account that the salience of information about costs may vary.

The chapter then turns the logic of competition on its head, demonstrating that the conclusion of tax treaties with lower-income countries has often been driven by higher-income countries in pursuit of outward investment opportunities. Tax treaties confer benefits in a lower-income country on only those multinationals based in the other signatory country, giving these companies an advantage over their competitors, who in turn ask their home governments to conclude tax treaties. Anecdotal evidence confirms that this mechanism has played an important role in the initiation of tax treaty negotiations between higher-income and lower-income countries. This apparently simple observation is largely absent from discussions in the literature on both BITs and bilateral tax treaties. Competition for outward investment cannot explain why lower-income countries, which incur most of the costs of tax treaties, would acquiesce to requests from higher-income countries. The final task of this chapter is therefore to consider the means through which higher-income countries have influenced lower-income countries' willingness to reciprocate.

Tax Competition

Higher taxation need not necessarily have a negative effect on investment and growth, but governments must take into account the behavioral effects resulting from the impact of taxation on taxpayers' economic incentives. They may reduce the incentive to work and invest, increase the incentive to avoid or evade taxes altogether, or encourage mobile economic actors to seek out less onerous tax regimes.

While some of these incentive effects occur within each state regardless of the conditions outside, the effect of levying taxation on mobile taxpayers is to create strategic interactions between states, tax competition. A large number of studies have attempted to model how corporate income taxation in the host state affects inflows of FDI. Meta-analyses of these studies find that a one-point increase in the corporate tax rate reduces FDI inflows by either 3 percent or 1.7 percent.[6] For lower-income countries, however, there is some econometric evidence that long-term investment may not be responsive to taxation, and especially to tax incentives.[7] In surveys, too, international investors in lower-income countries tend to cite other, more fundamental factors such as infrastructure and education above taxation.[8] Where FDI in lower-income countries is sensitive to tax competition, it may crowd out domestic investment and may be of a transitory, footloose kind that does not bring with it long-term benefits such as skills and technology transfer, or forward and backward linkages.[9]

Despite these limitations, tax competition is not merely a descriptive theory: it is a powerful idea that influences policy. There is an influential view in public choice economics, originating with Charles Tiebout, that competition between states for mobile factors of production is desirable because it will lead to the optimal balance between the provision of public services benefiting those factors of production and the levels of taxation levied on them.[10] Conversely, others argue that states should cooperate to limit tax competition, which if unmitigated leads to negative externalities such as mutual erosion of tax bases and increased regressivity.[11] There is, consequently, a broad consensus in the literature confirming strategic tax competition between governments.[12] Corporation tax rates, for example, have fallen consistently since the 1960s, while burgeoning tax incentive regimes can be seen in both lower-income and higher-income countries, in spite of consistent advice from international organizations that such competition is unlikely to bring investment gains.[13] There are caveats to this account: tax rates are not the only elements of tax policy that determine how much companies pay, and evidence also suggests that political factors such as governing party ideology and prevailing societal norms can limit the potency of tax competition.[14]

Tax competition as we discuss it here refers to "real" competition, which Peter Dietsch calls "luring," as opposed to virtual competition, or "poaching," when governments use tax rules to attract paper profits and portfolio income, detached from any real activity.[15] The two are connected, since a multinational company that can avoid tax by moving its paper profits may not be so sensitive to real tax competition, and hence virtual tax competition may reduce the so-called real tax competition pressure on governments.[16] While "poaching" by tax havens has dominated international relations scholarship on the international tax regime, this account is much more focused on the North-South politics of "luring."

Bounded Rationality and Tax Competition

As I noted earlier, the puzzle of widespread tax treaty adoption by lower-income countries resembles that for BITs in many respects: an apparent undervaluing of costs and overestimation of benefits, combined with the inconsistent evaluation of information drawn from other countries' experiences. The literature on the diffusion of BITs, in which Lauge Poulsen's *Bounded Rationality and Economic Diplomacy* is an influential contribution deploys a bounded rationality framework drawing from behavioral economics.[17] This, in turn, derives from Daniel Kahneman and Amos Tversky's prospect theory, which argues that people making decisions under uncertainty employ "heuristics" as shortcuts to evaluate information.[18] Rather than acting as Bayesian logic machines that evaluate all available information, people process information through a cognitive-psychological framework, privileging certain pieces of information and downplaying others.

In a study of public policymaking in Latin America, Kurt Weyland introduced the insights from prospect theory into studies of world politics. He began from three common heuristics that people use when evaluating information. First, the availability heuristic causes people to overvalue information that is more striking—for example, information that is simpler to understand or more dramatic. Weyland suggests that this explains why policymakers pay more attention to reforms adopted by countries close to home, rather than evaluating the full range of alternatives from around the globe. Alternatively, policymakers may look more favorably on the evidence about a policy that conforms to their ideological preferences, in comparison with a policy that contradicts them.[19] Second, through the representativeness heuristic, people tend to overestimate how generalizable the information gleaned from a small number of observations is. This would explain why certain policies seem to explode, spreading rapidly among countries. This "deviates from rational learning, which requires a careful cost-benefit analysis that considers a longer track record."[20] Instead, the "informational cascade" reaches a tipping point at which point countries stop accumulating new information and decide to adopt the policy.[21] Finally, the anchoring heuristic is the mechanism by which the stickiness of an initial piece of information biases further analyses. This can explain the adoption of near-identical policies by countries with diverse needs and contexts: policymakers have simply not studied their own problems and all potential solutions in detail.

Weyland describes an S-shaped curve when policies diffuse, and as Poulsen's account makes clear, this fits the BITs story very well: at first, countries were quick to copy each other without a detailed consideration of the costs and benefits of signing BITs, creating an exponential increase. This trend was reversed once policymakers realized the costs could indeed be significant.[22] Poulsen uses the availability heuristic to explain this pattern: lower-income countries entered into treaties without fully anticipating their consequences, because these consequences were remote and had lower salience, in comparison with the signal sent by their neighbors forging ahead with BIT signatures; they were slow to realize the implications for themselves when other countries experienced investor-state claims, especially when these claims were outside their own region, because the examples were, again, less salient.[23]

A bounded rationality approach differs from more sociological explanations because it is based on a change in policymakers' beliefs about cause and effect; to use March and Olsen's terms, a logic of consequences rather than appropriateness.[24] As Martha Finnemore and Kathryn Sikkink argue, norms can reach a "tipping point," beyond which they become "standards of appropriate behaviour," effectively the default behavior for states.[25] As the following chapter discusses, such a dynamic is clearly present within the technocratic expert community, but in this chapter our focus is on the causal ideas of tax competition held by actors with less specialist knowledge. The literature is not always clear about this distinction. For instance, when Frank Dobbin and colleagues laid out a typology of policy diffusion mechanisms, their "constructivism" category (now more commonly referred to as emulation) referred to the three means by which a policy might spread through its social acceptance as a policymaking norm: its adoption by countries that are seen as exemplars by others, its promulgation as a policy norm by expert groups even in the absence of an exemplar, and the adoption of a policy by countries sharing economic, social, political, or cultural similarities.[26] In practice, all three of these routes could constitute a heuristic, and thus be consistent with a bounded rationality framing. Similarly, while international organizations are sites for socialization, shared membership also provides a heuristic.[27] In several studies of different economic policy diffusion, Xun Cao finds that shared participation in intergovernmental organizations leads to diffusion through the "natural affinity" between members of the same intergovernmental organization, as well as through policy learning.[28]

Chang Lee and David Strang demonstrate a combination of bounded rationality and more intersubjective mechanisms in the example of changes in the size of the public sector in OECD countries.[29] Policymakers privileged information from certain examples more than others: countries with which they had a stronger trading relationship, and the United States, which served uniquely as a "Stackelberg leader."[30] They also gave more weight to information that was consistent with their "interpretive frame," a belief that downsizing will encourage economic growth.[31] Information consistent with this frame appeared more "available" than information that was not: changes to public sector size that were followed by changes in economic performance in the direction supported by the theory led to public sector downsizing in other countries, but changes with a null or opposite effect to that anticipated did not lead to increases in the size of the public sector. We might regard the logic of tax competition to be a similar interpretive frame.

We can apply these insights to relax the assumption of rationality inherent to most discussions of tax competition. Under economic competition, strategic interaction between countries causes them to adopt policies in order to make them relatively more attractive to foreign investment or to gain relatively more favorable access to export markets. This may lead to the diffusion of particular policies among countries competing with each other, or to the adoption of different policies in order to compete. Tax competition, in particular, is a convergence on lower effective tax rates in the hope of attracting investment. That hope need not, however, be rational, in at least three ways.

First, in the choice of policy: the government of one country may respond to the adoption of a particular investment-promotion policy in a competitor country by adopting it, perhaps ignoring doubts about its efficacy because of a fear of losing investment. This may be a rational choice to take a risk-averse approach in the absence of evidence, a mechanism that has been described as "rational emulation."[32] Nathan Jensen argues that at the US state level, tax incentives are used by governments, even when their effectiveness is questionable, as a credit-claiming device.[33] It may also, in the language of prospect theory, be based on cognitive heuristics. States compete with each other over corporation tax, but there is evidence to suggest that such competition is far from purely rational. Some attempts to study structural power in practice have found that the *perception* of business power matters more than the reality; indeed, different perceptions of the disinvestment threat among different actors in a country can lead to different preferences.[34]

Second, the choice of competitor country may be imperfectly rational. Quantitative models define competitor countries objectively, based on economic statistics (similarity in trade patterns, bond ratings, and infrastructure characteristics, for example), and hence implicitly assume that policymakers apply a similar evidence-based approach to determining the countries with which they compete.[35] Yet the *logic* of competition may also apply in a boundedly rational way, in which information about the actions of certain countries is more "available" than information on the actions of others, regardless of the extent to which they actually compete with each other.

Finally, policymakers may have an imperfect understanding of the relationship between a particular reform and flows of trade and investment. As the example of anti-money-laundering rules shows, countries may adopt reforms on paper in order to send a signal to other countries and to investors, without real commitment to enforcing them.[36] In corporation tax, policymakers' focus on the headline rate of tax may differ from businesses' interest in the effective rate, which is determined by other factors such as the generosity of capital allowances and the opportunities for profit-shifting.[37]

The possibility of bounded rationality in the operation of competition mechanisms is specifically excluded by many quantitative methodological designs, which identify competitive pressure by analyzing objective economic variables, assuming that policymakers with a competitive mentality have done the same. For example, Beth Simmons and Zachary Elkins examine the determinants of capital account, current account, and exchange rate liberalization, finding that economic competition drives the diffusion of such policies.[38] Elkins and colleagues also find that potential host governments seem more motivated to sign BITs when countries whose exports compete in similar third markets, and countries whose economic fundamentals make them comparably "attractive" to investors have done so.[39] It is possible that what is captured by emulation variables such as linguistic similarity and geographic proximity is not pure emulation but rather competition employing cognitive heuristics to identify competitors. Thus, the conceptual boundaries popularly used in the policy diffusion literature may obscure more complex mechanisms, which can be more readily uncovered using qualitative research.

Bounded Rationality in the Case of Tax Treaties

The technically complex, obscure, and low-salience nature of tax treaties makes them an ideal candidate for bounded rationality: the simplicity of the idea that tax treaties will attract investment by eliminating double taxation contrasts with their complex nature and uncertain effects. Specialized knowledge is required to assess the likely effects of tax treaties, yet evidence suggests that those calling the shots often fail to consult with revenue authority officials possessing such knowledge. Historically, many of these officials themselves lacked sufficient specialist knowledge to advise. According to a former technical adviser to Rwanda, which has renegotiated its treaty with Mauritius, the original agreement was "a classic case of somebody negotiating something they don't understand."[40] A technical adviser at an international organization observed that lower-income countries

often have contradictory policies within their tax codes, some of which are designed to maximize revenue, and others to give it away with the idea of attracting investment. "It's at that political, strategic level that more could be done" to
improve such coherence.[41]

Although in one case a negotiator described having been asked by her finance
ministry for an impact assessment, in many cases there is no detailed consideration of the costs and benefits by the lower-income country concerned, and no
policy on which to base decisions—a point emphasized by Catherine Ngina Mutava in her study of African countries' approaches to negotiation.[42] One negotiator
told me that "we are thinking that we should have a policy."[43] Another said that her
country had sought advice from international organizations on conducting impact assessments and was told it was impossible.[44] Furthermore, a high turnover of
staff means a lack of institutional memory, illustrated by the fact that negotiators
were rarely aware of the considerations around treaties that they themselves had
not worked on.[45] Most of the negotiators from lower-income countries interviewed, who would be most likely to understand the situations in which investors
would benefit from treaties, did not share the view that they would attract investment, even when they recognized that foreign investors in their country faced
some double taxation. The skeptical views are illustrated by the quotes reproduced
in table 3.1.

Other negotiators saw the matter differently, but they did not speak with any
great confidence or certainty. "We do have the idea that it will attract investment," said one.[46] Another negotiator, from a lower-income country, said, "You
must understand that we are afraid of losing investment. We are a poor country
and we're at the bottom of the pile."[47] A private sector interviewee explained
that a request to a company's home country government for a tax treaty with a
country in which it was considering an investment would rarely be the deciding factor in an investment decision, but that it would come into play when
evaluating the potential return on an investment, as a potential upside risk.[48]
While a few interviewees pointed to real examples of double taxation in lower-
income countries in the absence of tax treaties,[49] the consensus appeared to be

TABLE 3.1.   Quotes from lower-income country negotiators

A treaty is not a central factor to promote investment, it's more to eliminate double taxation.

I would agree that a DTA is not a major factor driving investment.

I know that there's a position that these treaties affect FDI, but I think it's not right.

Most of the time developing countries are disadvantaged by treaties. Treaties do not attract
investment. It is other factors.

Source: (In order, from top to bottom) Interview 37, Interview 23, Interview 4, Interview 20.

that in most cases these examples were unlikely to be material to FDI decisions or limited to a small subset of investors.

One way to verify whether the active pursuit of tax treaties by lower-income countries has been underpinned by an understanding of the treaties' actual tax effects is to look for evidence that requests received by higher-income countries from lower-income countries coincided with interest from investors. If they did not, this would indicate that the absence of a treaty was unlikely to have been an impediment to investment flows. Because higher-income countries' tax treaty policymaking is quite sensitive to multinational companies' needs, and since the sacrifice of taxing rights entailed by a treaty is largely by the lower-income country, a higher-income country's response to a request for a tax treaty is generally quite indicative of whether a treaty will really resolve problems that are preventing investment.

According to one former treaty negotiator in a higher-income country, "Requests come from developing countries and may wait for years before there's a response."[50] Another told me that this experience "is true to some extent, but our in-tray is not large."[51] As Allison Christians observes, when examining the legal consequences of the absence of a tax treaty between Ghana and the United States, "in today's global tax climate, a typical tax treaty would not provide significant tax benefits to current or potential investors. Consequently, there is little incentive for these investors to pressure the U.S. government to conclude tax treaties with many LDCs . . . even if concluded, these treaties would not have a significant impact on cross-border investment and trade."[52]

US diplomatic cables dated between 2004 and 2010 give numerous examples of lower-income countries seeking treaties with the United States. These include Vietnam, Hungary, Brunei, Croatia, Azerbaijan, Jordan, Malaysia, Libya, Honduras, and Turkmenistan.[53] In most of these cases, no treaty has since been signed, and correspondence in the cables suggests that US reluctance was because US multinationals did not consider these treaties necessary. For example, a "scenesetter" for an assistant secretary of state ahead of a March 2007 visit to Macedonia noted that while that government wanted to sign a tax treaty with the United States during official visits later in the year, US businesses did not see any need for it: "Regarding the double taxation issue, we are studying the Macedonian draft proposal and have advised the MFA [Ministry of Foreign Affairs] that action on such agreements would require strong lobbying from US companies doing business in Macedonia, which has not yet been the case."[54]

In December 2006, the US ambassador met with the Croatian foreign minister, noting "that the Barr Labs $2.5 billion takeover of Pliva Pharmaceuticals may spur interest in concluding a double taxation treaty between the US and Croatia, and said he would be urging Washington to take a fresh look."[55] Records of meetings with senior US Treasury officials illustrate this line consistently. In

2007, Croatia's finance minister was told that "investments, such as Barr, will help make Croatia a higher priority" for a tax treaty.[56] The following year, Qatar's finance and economy minister was informed that "the [US government] has limited resources to negotiate treaties and therefore has certain core requirements that would need to be addressed following consultation with U.S. companies to ensure that the proposed treaty would, in fact, address specific problems."[57]

In some instances, then, the governments of lower-income countries have sought tax treaties despite (or in the absence of) analysis by their own expert officials about the likely impact of the treaty, or against these officials' views about an appropriate negotiating position. The response from higher-income countries, where tax treaty policy may be supported by a greater awareness of the likely impacts, has sometimes been to delay or decline such requests.

Fiscal Costs versus Investment Benefits

Tax treaties are at first sight a harder case to explain through bounded rationality than BITs. The costs of the latter are incurred only if an investor makes a claim against a signatory state at some point in the future, and hence those costs may be less salient to the policymaker.[58] Many of the costs of tax treaties are immediate and significant: withholding tax revenue is reduced from the moment the tax treaty comes into force, and can be estimated in advance (although in interviews it became apparent that such forecasts are rarely made). Some other, larger costs emerge later and may be unanticipated—in particular, restrictions on capital gains charges, which have been the subject of legal disputes in countries such as Uganda years after a treaty was signed.[59] The costs of tax treaty shopping, too, follow later, as investors construct tax planning structures using the new treaty. Furthermore, the growth in tax treaty diffusion has yet to level off. Even countries for which significant negative consequences of treaty conclusion have clearly become apparent have generally not stopped signing tax treaties, choosing instead to cancel or renegotiate some problematic treaties and carry on negotiating new ones.[60]

This poses a question: Why have some governments acted in spite of information about the fiscal costs, while others have not? In the tax competition literature, the focus has been on the ideological and institutional constraints on governments.[61] Scott Basinger and Mark Hallerberg find that political costs faced by a government in the form of veto players and ideological opposition reduce the likelihood that it will cut corporate taxes in response to competitive pressure: the governments of competitor countries take into account the political costs of their competitors in setting their own corporate tax rates.[62] Duane Swank shows that the "neoliberal" tax policies diffuse from the United States to other countries through a process of competition for mobile capital, which is conditioned by national institutions: coordinated market institutions impede diffusion, and liberal market institutions assist it.[63] Thomas Plümper and colleagues consider how domestic constraints affect the balance between capital and labor taxes, demonstrating that fiscal constraints on a government as well as prevailing norms among voters constrain capital tax reductions.[64] The latter paper also demonstrates that competition over corporate tax rates is more intense between adjacent countries. Stakeholders beyond the policy elite may conversely intensify tax competition if ideas about structural business power diffuse to the domestic constituencies that shape politicians' incentives.[65]

Tax treaties, however, differ from corporate tax rates in that, while their costs are just as real, their visibility is lower, and the number of de facto veto points they must pass through is also fewer.[66] In the UK Parliament, tax treaties are ratified as statutory instruments through a delegated legislation committee, which rarely discusses them in any detail and has never declined to ratify a treaty.[67] In Canada, legislative scrutiny is similarly cursory.[68] In Uganda, tax treaties are laid before parliament, but only for information purposes, and in Denmark, parliamentary approval was only introduced in the last few years.[69] This lack of engagement by political actors illustrates that tax treaties are not clearly identified with any ideological positioning, most likely because they are regarded as serving a primarily administrative function. Furthermore, they reduce taxes on capital, which is generally considered a preference of the right, but they are also regarded as tools for investment promotion, which is a preference of the left because it may create jobs. There is no identifiable political constituency likely to oppose tax treaties, which may explain why they are rarely controversial.[70] A government's preference for concluding tax treaties is therefore unlikely in most cases to be impeded by vetoes imposed by its domestic constituencies or within the political system (chapter 4 will discuss how conflict between political and bureaucratic actors may occur at veto points).

More pertinent, perhaps, to lower-income countries is the importance of the fiscal costs of the tax treaties to political actors. The "availability" of this information may vary. While governments do not routinely collect information on the taxes foregone through their treaties, such information becomes apparent when NGOs or the media highlight tax avoidance structures that exploit tax treaties, or when a court case over eligibility to treaty benefits thrusts particular elements of a treaty into the limelight.[71] Fiscal cost information may also become more "available" if the underlying constraints on policy change. For example, political conditions may create incentives for a government to reexamine the tax revenue it raises from foreign investors, either because this is a vote-winning policy or because a government wants more tax revenue across the board to obtain autonomy from donors. Fiscal conditions may also influence how "available" the information about fiscal costs is: where tax revenue is scarce, or corporate tax makes up a larger share of total revenue, the revenue foregone through a treaty is likely to be a bigger concern. Finally, there is some evidence that individual policymakers differ in their predispositions to be concerned about fiscal costs. In one lower-income country, a finance ministry official who led treaty negotiations explained that "before we came, the leadership in Treasury felt that we were going to lose a lot of tax revenue. The perception then was that if we enter into these treaties we are going to lose tax."[72]

The significance that policymakers give the revenue sacrifice resulting from a tax treaty is therefore an important element of the revenue raising / investment promotion trade-off. The case studies later in this book will illustrate that where ministers and officials are very conscious of the fiscal costs, they are more likely to resist pressure to sign treaties, whereas if raising tax revenue is less of a priority, they are more likely to acquiesce.

Turning the Tables: Tax Treaties as Outward Investment Promotion Tools

So far, following the existing literature on tax and investment treaty diffusion, I have focused entirely on competition among capital-importing countries. I now turn to another possibility, that competitive pressure might act on capital-exporting countries, driving them to seek tax treaties with lower-income countries. Mark Manger has argued, with respect to preferential trade agreements, that "concentrated interests in FDI-exporting countries have a strong incentive to lobby for preferential agreements because they confer specific advantages over competitors. To be politically attractive, these agreements must have a discriminatory effect on trade and investment with non-members."[73]

Such a position is certainly logical for tax treaties, which provide a tax advantage to firms investing outward into the treaty partner over their competitors from countries where such a treaty does not exist. Indeed, there is ample evidence that business lobbying, exercised in the home country rather than the host, has been at the origin of many tax treaties between higher-income and lower-income countries. At a discussion in the Danish Parliament in June 2015, for example, business pressure on the Danish government was very evident. A private sector participant stated that "Danish industry sees DTTs [double taxation treaties] as an important competition parameter," while Denmark's tax minister stated that "we have several times heard expressions of interest regarding Nigeria, but we have been unable to get them to sign."[74]

In support of this proposition, a majority of negotiators interviewed from lower-income countries stated that their countries' patterns of treaty signatures were mainly the result of requests from other countries. "We're more or less on the waiting position. . . . They come to us," one stated.[75] According to another, "Normally we negotiate when we receive requests, and have always responded positively. It's always a request from the other party."[76] In this country's case, the treaty would be signed and ratified only after the treaty partner had pushed again, usually after further requests from the investor. Negotiators from two lower-income countries that had signed their first tax treaties indicated that, once it became known that they were open to concluding agreements, they had been inundated with requests from capital-exporting countries.[77]

Higher-income countries formulate their negotiating priorities through consultation with their multinational businesses. Many have an established procedure to solicit private sector input into their future plans for treaty making. European treaty negotiators interviewed were all happy to say that their countries actively solicit business input into their annual treaty priorities, and that this was the main factor determining those priorities, alongside other diplomatic and economic matters. Some typical quotes from these interviews are given in table 3.2. The same applied to middle-income countries whose negotiators were interviewed, in respect to their treaties with lower-income countries.

Indeed, many individual treaties are the result of lobbying by a single multinational around a particular investment in a lower-income country. Talking about a particular treaty that had been concluded on his company's behalf, a business interviewee in a higher-income country said, "We were the first [to invest in that country] but they knew there would be others. . . . If you went through any developing country and looked at big investments, you'd see a treaty just before or afterwards."[78] In Nairobi, Kenya's 2007 tax treaty with France is widely understood among tax professionals from the public and private sectors to have been specifically linked to France Telecom's investment in the country, although this was denied by a Treasury official. "The entry of France Telecom into Telkom Kenya has yielded a tax benefit across all sectors with the signing of a double taxation treaty between Kenya and France," a local newspaper report noted at the time.[79] Several interviewees from government and the private sector in different African and Asian countries hinted that certain tax treaties had been concluded in response to pressure from regional airlines.

Tax treaties are, therefore, frequently initiated at the behest of outward investors, via their home states, rather than by host country governments seeking to

TABLE 3.2. Quotes from lower-income country negotiators

When we agree our treaty negotiation program the main concern is how it is going to benefit [our] companies.

It's a matter of competition: we're a small country.

We do have a treaty with [an African country] because at that time we had a construction company [investing there].

[If a competitor is from a treaty country] this will make it impossible for [our company] to compete.

Source: (In order, from top to bottom) Interview 21, Interview 14, Interview 19, Interview 13.

attract inward investment. Lower-income countries usually accept these requests to negotiate for a variety of reasons: a positive but passive attitude to tax treaties, diplomatic necessity, lack of capacity to analyze the costs and benefits, or simply because they are following the path of least resistance. Almost all the negotiators that I spoke with indicated that they never decline requests for tax treaties from higher-income countries, except from tax havens. "We never reject a request for negotiation. This has something to do with diplomacy and international relations," said one African negotiator.[80] Several did indicate that responses to some requests might be deliberately stalled—for example, if it was politically necessary to conclude treaties in a certain order.[81]

Coercion

If the advantages of tax treaties accrue predominantly to the higher-income country signatory, and in many instances it is also the actions of that higher-income country that lead to the initiation of negotiations, this sheds a different light on why lower-income countries may have been willing—even enthusiastic—to sign tax treaties. The organizing concept in this case is coercion, a term with a much broader meaning here than its common usage. Following Fabrizio Gilardi, I use "coercion" as an umbrella concept referring to a hierarchical process through which a third party changes a state's incentives rather than its preferences.[82] Returning to Dobbin and colleagues' discussion of policy diffusion, three coercive mechanisms can be identified: changing material incentives through conditionality, changing material incentives through the formation of a policy consensus around a policy leader, and the influence of "hegemonic ideas." "What unites these studies," they say, "is their focus on the influence of an external source of pressure or ideas."[83]

There is some limited evidence of explicit conditionality associated with tax treaties. For example, several negotiators indicated, always about other countries rather than their own, that Spain had threatened to withdraw tax-related technical assistance, and even aid funds, as part of treaty negotiations.[84] British civil servants discussed using aid as leverage to obtain tax treaties in principle, but there is no evidence that they did so in practice.[85] Examining tax treaties signed between aid donor and recipient countries, Julia Braun and Martin Zagler found on average a 22 percent increase in development assistance in the year a treaty was signed.[86]

There are more examples of higher-income countries insisting on a tax treaty as a quid pro quo for some other form of agreement. A US embassy cable from 2009 outlines Colombia's pursuit of free trade agreements (FTAs): "According to the [government of Colombia], Japan has insisted on negotiating a BIT (fourth negotiation round is in late November), followed by a DTT, before it will begin FTA negotiations with Colombia."[87]

In 2007, Argentina requested a tax information exchange agreement (TIEA) with the United States. This is a kind of abridged tax treaty that would allow Argentina to obtain information about its citizens' US tax affairs, to help in investigations of potential tax evasion. The United States responded by stating that it was only willing to discuss a full tax treaty, which would give Argentina the same information but would also require Argentina to surrender some of its tax base to the United States.[88] This led to a stalemate, which has yet to be resolved. According to the commissioner general of the Kenya Revenue Authority, Kenya received a similar response when it requested a TIEA with Singapore.[89]

The second form of coercion, policy leadership, occurs when a country or bloc with market power takes an action that changes incentives for other market actors—whether deliberately or not. Thus, since OECD countries have all adopted a common approach to international taxation based on bilateral tax treaties, lower-income countries have an incentive to do the same. As mentioned in chapter 2, OEEC members were aware of this when they began to discuss tax cooperation, and they gained a substantial first-mover advantage from acting together. Eduardo Baistrocchi frames these advantages using the concept of a network market, which creates three types of network effects that incentivize adoption of a particular policy instrument: positive externalities, whereby the detailed elaboration of model tax treaties and case law on their implementation reduces the transaction costs for other countries choosing to adopt them, and for taxpayers operating in those countries; an expectation among market actors that countries will follow the lead of the OECD countries; and "lock-in" effects, a concept similar to path dependency, in which the existing regime has significant sunk costs that make it difficult for new, incompatible entrants to the market to gain ground, even if they have advantages over the existing technology.[90] In practical terms, this explains why lower-income countries might face a binary choice—sign OECD-type tax treaties or not at all—rather than supporting an alternative approach such as the CAN model.

Finally, coercion through hegemonic ideas refers to how "dominant ideas become rationalized, often with elegant theoretical justifications, and influence how policy makers conceptualize their problems and order potential solutions."[91] Norms emerge within a social hierarchy of states, and their association with this hierarchy is important: a norm may be more likely to spread in a universal way if it is associated with the behavior of an "advanced" state.[92] It may reach a tipping point "beyond which adoption provides legitimacy rather than improves performance."[93] Jason Sharman suggests that governments in lower-income countries may emulate others in adopting reforms associated with being "developed," regardless of the content of those reforms, "to show peers and reassure policymakers themselves that they are in line with shared values."[94] To quote Kurt Weyland, writing within the bounded rationality framework, "Governments dread the stigma of backwardness and therefore eagerly adopt policy innovations, regardless of functional needs."[95]

As I argued earlier, the tax treaties myth is itself a hegemonic idea that influences policy preferences in lower-income countries through bounded rationality. Beyond its simplistic logic of double taxation, however, the association of tax treaties with the OECD, and the widespread participation in the regime by a growing number of countries, creates additional pressure for lower-income countries to join that may be unrelated to the underlying tax reasons. David Rosenbloom, a former US tax treaty negotiator, famously stated that many lower-income countries regard tax treaties as a "badge of international economic respectability."[96] Arianne Pickering, a former Australian treaty negotiator, concurs that "a country may want to signal to the global economy and potential investors that it is a responsible member of the international tax community that is willing and able to conform with widely-accepted tax rules and norms."[97]

By concluding a tax treaty for broader reputational reasons, policymakers may therefore be acting in a purely rational incentive-driven way, making a conscious instrumental calculation based on a logic of consequences such as the tax treaties myth. Alternatively, they may be following a logic of appropriateness, taking for granted a norm that associates tax treaties with the way "advanced" countries behave.[98]

Conclusion

This chapter focused on the preferences of nonspecialist actors. It modified the standard model of tax competition, which is assumed to motivate lower-income countries to conclude tax treaties, in two ways. First, the tax treaties myth provided a "cognitive shortcut" for policymakers filtering information in a boundedly rational manner. This argument is similar to that used to explain the spread of BITs, but it is a harder case to explain because the costs of tax treaties are immediate and foreseeable, unlike those of BITs, which are uncertain and occur in the future. Thus, the "availability" of information about these costs is critical to the bounded rationality framework. In particular, when governments are focused on maximizing corporate tax revenue, those costs may be more salient, which means that such information may be more cognitively "available" than it is for governments with other sources of income.

The second change from the standard account of tax competition was to switch the focus onto competition among capital exporters. As a tool for attracting inward investment, a tax treaty is an odd choice, because it has the distorting effect of lowering tax costs for foreign investors from one country in comparison with those from other countries in the host country market. In contrast, for capital-exporting countries, the effect of that distortion is to give their outward investors a competitive advantage in the lower-income country over investors from other countries. For this reason, and as the evidence provided showed, it is commonly capital exporters that initiate tax treaty negotiations, not capital-importing lower-income countries.

Three mechanisms of coercion in the diffusion literature offer explanations for why a lower-income country would respond positively to a request from a higher-income country. First, capital-exporting countries have levers, such as aid budgets and sovereign wealth funds, that might change a lower-income country's incentives. Second, the first-mover advantage of OECD states creates incentives for other countries to sign treaties that are compatible with their approach to international tax. Third, the hegemonic idea of the tax treaties myth, or even that signing tax treaties is what advanced countries do, permeates analysis of tax treaties in lower-income countries. Having focused on ideas about tax treaties among policymakers who do not have a deep specialism in the subject, the book shifts its focus in the next chapter to look at international tax specialists, for whom tax treaties serve an altogether different purpose.

THE INTERNATIONAL TAX COMMUNITY AND THE POLITICS OF EXPERTISE

> **Double taxation is not Satan. But when you go to the OECD, and you say double taxation, everyone looks at you like you are the devil. You have one dollar of double taxation, that's the devil.**
>
> —Former international tax official, Latin American country

Since the origins of the international model treaties at the League of Nations, and the negotiation of some of the earliest bilateral agreements, tax treaties have primarily been the project of a community of international tax practitioners. Many have a common educational and professional background, they meet each other regularly, share in the performance of negotiations among states or between states and businesses, and have a vested interest in protecting the internal coherence of what they see as a technical project against political interference.[1] There is little pretense during the formal political scrutiny of tax treaties that they are understood by ministers and other politicians in any kind of detail. This chapter therefore turns the attention away from mechanisms that act on such policymakers and toward the experts who develop the multilateral models and negotiate the bilateral treaties themselves.

Whereas the tax treaties myth leads nonspecialists to seek treaties as a way of stimulating investment by lowering investors' tax costs, those with detailed technical knowledge take a different view. For them, tax treaties transmit a series of procedural and content rules concerning the taxation of investors, from the authors of model treaties—a community of specialists revolving around the OECD—to the signatory countries. They translate transnational soft-law standards into hard, enforceable law. To be sure, these negotiators have strong incentives deriving from the national sphere, which can produce intense disagreements in bilateral and multilateral negotiations. But they share the long-term project of creating a consistent global approach to taxation modeled on OECD standards, to enhance trade and investment flows, a public good to be diffused as widely as possible.[2] Political considerations are often regarded as exogenous constraints on this project.

To the extent that the dissemination of international standards via tax treaties lowers the risk-adjusted tax cost to investors, bilateral treaties could be conceptualized as a more nuanced version of the tax competition mechanisms discussed in the previous chapter: firms protected by tax treaties' reference to international standards incur an advantage over others that are not. Competition premised on the diffusion of international standards and competition premised on lower short-run tax rates do not always produce the same preferences, however, in terms of either treaty partners or the content of tax treaties. Furthermore, members of the international tax community do not necessarily support a form of competition that applies its standards as a private good, to benefit only investors between treaty signatory countries. They take a more skeptical view about the likely impact of any one tax treaty on investment flows.

This chapter describes the international tax community, the ideas that its members hold, and the means through which it influences policymakers. It considers two implications of the different perceptions of tax treaties in specialist and nonspecialist communities. First, in lower-income countries where there is little institutional memory and the national bureaucracy does not socialize people into the transnational community, civil servants acquire technical knowledge by learning from members of the international community. Expertise may make them more skeptical about the tax treaties myth, and more aware of the costs of tax treaties to their countries. They may also come to share in the international tax community's conceptualization of the merits of tax treaties that transcends this short-term cost/benefit calculation. A second implication is that the ideational difference between specialists and nonspecialists can lead to conflict between the preferences of the two groups within a country. This may prevent it from concluding tax treaties, even if both groups support this course of action in general terms. Specialists may seek to block the conclusion of tax treaties that have been motivated by short-term investment gains, or they may try to negotiate treaties in which political actors, whose consent is ultimately required for signature and ratification, have little interest. The politics of knowledge is a critical part of the political economy of the tax treaty regime.

The International Tax Community

The history of tax cooperation told in chapter 2 was a "quiet politics" scenario.[3] As Philipp Genschel and Thomas Rixen describe, the low political salience of international taxation from the 1930s to the 1960s had "allowed the experts to craft a compromise solution without major intervention from their political principals."[4] While state preferences no doubt influenced the shape of this consensus, tax historians commonly regard it as having formed among a transnational group of technical experts.[5] The preface to the report of the League of Nations Committee of Technical Experts on Double Taxation in 1927, one of the regime's foundational texts, stresses that "although the members of the Committee are nominated by their respective Governments, they only speak in their capacity as experts, i.e., in their own name."[6] One of the participants in the early League of Nations work, Edwin Seligman, observed that, while at first the technical experts' "concern was primarily to enter into some arrangement which would be politically agreeable to their respective countries . . . when they learned to know each other more intimately; and especially in proportion as they were subjected to the indefinable but friendly atmosphere of the League of Nations, their whole attitude changed. Suspicion was converted into confidence; doubt was resolved by the feeling of certainty of accomplishment; and aloofness gave way to warm personal friendship which contributed materially to smoothing out the difficulties."[7]

According to Sol Picciotto, "Perhaps the most important outcome of the interwar years was to begin to create a community of international tax specialists . . . a community within which ideas and perspectives as well as economic advantage could be traded."[8] An official history of the OECD model concurs that its "direct parents were . . . senior tax officials from European countries."[9]

It is very common to describe these international tax experts as an "epistemic community." In the tax law literature, for example, Allison Christians describes how OECD staff, civil servants representing national governments, and other professional stakeholders "form an intertwined epistemic community that holds an important and influential position in the law-making order."[10] These individuals "diagnose and prescribe tax policy reforms that are informed by, and that play out within, national legal regimes."[11] Diane Ring similarly suggests that international tax negotiations are best understood as "epistemically informed bargaining," in which an epistemic community "served as a driving force in the double taxation problem, both in terms of providing a forum for discussion and providing a base of expertise to structure the debate."[12] Jason Sharman argues that "tax administrators are enmeshed in a trans-national epistemic community."[13] Thomas Rixen, commenting on Stephen Webb, regards the community as being "comprised of tax bureaucrats and business association representatives," having "succeeded in excluding civil society from international tax matters by defining the issues as being 'purely technical' in nature."[14]

It is easy to see the attraction of this concept for scholars of the international tax regime. In its original formulation, an epistemic community is "a network of professionals with recognized expertise and competence in a particular domain and an authoritative claim to policy-relevant knowledge within that domain or issue."[15] Tax is a technically complex area in which a transnational community claims a monopoly on legitimate expert knowledge.[16] It advances a policy project through the process of international standard formation that takes place in arcane committees of the OECD, but that ultimately takes the form of national tax laws, mostly via bilateral treaties.

Establishing the causal links between national and international settings is, however, a challenge for the epistemic communities literature, which has tended to focus on demonstrating the existence of particular communities, rather than on understanding how and in what circumstances they are able to influence—or indeed may be influenced by—national policies.[17] Haas himself suggested their influence came mainly in times of uncertainty and crisis for policymakers, which is unhelpful for the century-long incremental development of the international tax regime. More useful is Haas's notion that policy influence comes in part through "infiltration" of government bureaucracies by community members, but this still characterizes the community as an exogenous influence on national bureaucracies. The concept of an epistemic community is thus ill suited for situations in which bureaucrats themselves form part of the community, where "the decision makers whom members of an epistemic community advise turn out to be themselves."[18]

Another theoretical concept with purchase in such situations is that of a transnational policy community, which "refers to a group of officials, whether public or private, that exhibits particular characteristics" including similarities in education and career development, a strong sense of affinity to each other, and a set of interests "defined and articulated in terms of widely accepted principles."[19] Such communities use club settings, in which "members place a limit to the range of actors involved in the making of policy and define what type of actor is relevant."[20] To characterize the international tax community, we would need to establish the "widely accepted principles" on which its interests rest, the mutual affinity and common characteristics of its members, and club membership rules. This is not so far from the characteristics of an epistemic community identified by Haas: shared normative and causal beliefs, evaluation of authoritative claims to knowledge, and policy project. Indeed, the transnational tax community exerts influence on national tax policy in the manner of both an epistemic community—through deference to its claim to authority and through infiltrating bureaucracies—and a transnational community, where policymakers' ideas form intersubjectively as part of the social group itself. Since the argument of this book is that specialist bureaucrats come to share the worldview of the transnational community, while others in government do not, both mechanisms are of interest.

Describing a transnational policy community, including its gatekeeping rules and underlying norms, does not necessarily tell us how material interests may have shaped it in the past or how they may continue to do so. Such an analysis is assumed by other frames, such as that of a transnational capitalist class.[21] The international tax community could easily be seen as a part of this group: a collection of bureaucrats and professionals whose shared agenda promotes the globalizing interests of transnational capital. Certainly, the free movement of goods and capital is an underlying normative concern of the transnational tax community, as one might expect given its convergence on the OECD. The choice of transnational policy community reflects an emphasis on two further characteristics, however: the diverse interests within a community that also includes those of governments determined to maximize revenue, and an autonomous logic that sustains the community's normative core and is derived from taxation principles, which cannot be reduced purely to these individual interests or to a capital-friendly logic of globalization.

Ideas within the Policy Community

The departure point for understanding the international tax community is its original aim of alleviating double taxation. Although this originates with a causal belief—that eliminating double taxation will enhance cross-border trade and investment—the abhorrence of double taxation has become a principled belief with its own normative weight, rather than merely a means to achieve an end. The strength of language used in one of the original League of Nations reports illustrates this: "Double taxation . . . imposes on such taxpayers burdens which, in many cases, seem truly excessive, if not intolerable. It tends to paralyse their activity and to discourage initiative, and thus constitutes a serious obstacle to the development of international relations and world production."[22]

The modern-day successor to that report, the OECD model tax treaty, adds that "it is scarcely necessary to stress the importance of removing the obstacles that double taxation presents to the development of economic relations between countries."[23] A report from consultancy firm PWC on international taxation in lower-income countries asserts, with no support, that "overall, double taxation is detrimental to economic development."[24]

The OECD model and its associated guidance today have come to embody a consensus view of how to tax cross-border income and capital that transcends the original double taxation problem. States now take care of the "heroic" double taxation that motivated the original League of Nations work through their national tax laws, and the words "double taxation" have been removed from the OECD model's title. Nonetheless, it is the alignment of national approaches to international taxation with the standards set out in the OECD model that keeps the instances of double taxation low, and this provides the international tax community with a compelling ongoing claim to authority. "Treaties are the means whereby sovereign states endeavour, usually on a bilateral basis, to harmonize the rules of their national laws," according to a former US negotiator.[25]

Within the community, certain foundational concepts are powerful social conditioning tools, underpinning instances that socialization scholars would recognize as "normative suasion," wherein actors are persuaded to change their positions through recourse to these shared norms.[26] Double taxation is anathema, and the taxation of multinational firms must comply with the "arm's length principle," which is designed to prevent both double taxation of and tax avoidance by multinational companies.[27] Policies are evaluated against compliance with these principles above all else, while criteria on which community members may differ, such as particular tax rates or the distribution of taxing rights between different countries, are subjugated below these overriding objectives. In one typical instance at a United Nations meeting, delegates from the US government and the accountancy firm PWC engaged in a lively debate with a speaker from Brazil over whether unconventional aspects of the latter's tax law were consistent with the arm's length principle.[28] In a fraught debate between members of the UN Tax Committee over a proposed new article to the UN model treaty conferring greater rights to tax on lower-income countries, opponents claimed that the new article would create double taxation, instantly shifting the burden of proof to proponents.[29]

When in 1986 the United States adopted transfer pricing laws that deviated from OECD guidance, its tax policy was roundly criticized by businesses and tax officials from other countries, provoking a decade-long international debate. A short statement by UNICE (Union des Industries de la Communauté Européenne), which represents European businesses, referenced the arm's length principle in nearly every paragraph: various different parts of the US regulation were "a dangerous departure from the arm's length principle," "a threat to the arm's length principle," "at odds with the arm's length principle," and "alien to the concept of arm's length."[30] The OECD formed a task force to review the US proposals and effectively negotiate with the United States. It concluded that the US rules "could risk undermining the consensus that has been built up over a number of years on the application of the arm's length principle and thereby increase the risk of economic double taxation."[31]

Club Membership and Hierarchy

If this is the ideational foundation of the community, what about the spaces in which shared understandings develop? The boundaries of club membership are most clearly illustrated in accounts of the contemporary politicization of tax politics, many of which focus on how actors such as activist organizations that are not part of this community attempt to influence it, and the community's resistance to such influence.[32] NGOs, for example, have most successfully influenced deliberations by adopting the mantle of tax expertise themselves.[33]

The burden of participating in numerous international meetings is a common complaint that I have overheard among government officials and business representatives during coffee breaks at such meetings, but it is clear that close social relationships develop as a result. One staff member of an organization that frequently hosts international tax meetings observed during one such coffee break, "These people are friends, they stay at each other's houses."[34] According to a former treaty negotiator from an OECD country, participation in OECD meetings "was very much a club, people didn't want to lose that gig, a really clubby arrangement."[35] Elements of this "clubbiness" observed at international meetings include delegates' habitual reference to each other in formal discussions by first name, and the clearly warm nature of informal discussions between long-standing members—regardless of their professional affiliation—during breaks and over dinner. It is also clear that such comradeship exists principally among long-standing members of the group from OECD countries, the private sector, and international organizations. Lower-income country delegates—who are newer, attend fewer meetings per year, and generally change over positions more quickly—appeared at the meetings observed to interact primarily among themselves, and with less familiarity. In this sense, the community can be thought of as having a core-periphery structure, with long-standing members from OECD countries forming a close social group, and lower-income country participants occupying a satellite role. It is a common observation that discussions at the UN Committee of Experts are dominated by OECD members who have coordinated their positions in advance, unlike lower-income country members who act in isolation.

Some country delegates, as well as some external commentators such as prominent lawyers and academics, are particularly influential.[36] Competition for authority within a community is a key theme of the "linked ecologies" approach, which defines the unit of study in terms of relationships and interactions rather than professions and institutional affiliations.[37] As Sending and Neumann argue, there is no reason researchers should a priori assume and reproduce the traditionally understood boundaries between realms, such as institutional affiliation or professional qualification; rather, communities should be identified empirically.[38] Individuals with diverse backgrounds and patterns of interaction in multiple ecologies employ "epistemic arbitrage," gaining a more authoritative position through their familiarity with (and in) multiple different ecologies.[39] This is an especially appropriate concept for international taxation, a field that combines law, accounting, and—to a lesser extent—economics, as well as spanning public and private boundaries and organizing at national and supranational levels. The international tax community's most authoritative participants are able to leverage knowledge from these multiple ecologies, as well as to "be heard" in multiple professional spaces.[40]

Consider first the links between different professional ecologies at a national level. "The concept of a single 'tax profession' or tax practitioner is difficult to comprehend," write Rex Marshall and colleagues; they go on to say, "In practice, the term 'tax practitioner' covers a diverse group of individuals, business structures and professional groups."[41] Yet these people with different professional trainings, representing organizations on different sides of various distributional conflicts, do identify as part of a common "tax profession." For example, the Chartered Institute of Taxation in the UK was founded in 1930 by a mixed group of accountants and lawyers drawn from private practice and the Inland Revenue, to "promote the study of taxation, hold examinations, facilitate the exchange of information, make representations and establish and maintain a high standard of conduct."[42] Tax is a hybrid discipline combining law and accountancy, requiring familiarity with both, and individuals with more diverse careers are more often found in positions of authority within formal institutions.[43] Inside law and accountancy firms, businesses, and revenue authorities, international tax is a niche field within the already specialist field of tax, and those who practice it are small in number, often building closer professional links with fellow specialists outside their own institutions.[44]

Next, consider the public and private sectoral ecologies. While one may naturally assume that governments and businesses may be in conflict over how much of a firm's profits should be paid as tax or retained by the company, in practice international tax policymaking has always been a collective endeavor between the two groups. In their history of the League of Nations years, Graetz and O'Hear describe how the ICC "exercised primary leadership in the movement against international double taxation," developing terminology and concepts that were adopted as the basis of subsequent work by the league's technical experts.[45] In many respects, it was negotiations between the ICC's national chapters that established the contours of an international agreement, ahead of discussions among the league's committee. Resolutions passed by the ICC, according to an observer, were "used as the firm basis on which draft conventions have been built or actual treaties adopted."[46] Furthermore, the ICC's Double Taxation Committee (representing businesses) and the league's Technical Expert committee (representing governments) had overlapping memberships. Thomas Adams, the US government-appointed member of the League committee, chaired a committee for the US Chambers of Commerce as well as participating in the ICC's work; his successor, Mitchell Carroll, was a lawyer advising multinational firms on their tax affairs, as well as working on behalf of the United States at the League.[47]

Today, as noted above, representatives of multinational companies and tax advisers regularly mix at international tax meetings. In addition to private sector representatives' attendance at meetings of the OECD and United Nations, governmental and international organization representatives are commonly in attendance at events organized by tax professionals, such as an annual conference organized jointly by the US Council for International Business and the OECD.[48] At the national level, in the UK, for example, interactions between governments and private sector lobbyists are frequent, and "the corporate tax reform policy community has a tightly integrated and fairly constant membership," according to John Snape, leading to "an almost astonishing assimilation of professional expertise to the legislative function, born no doubt of many a congenial meeting over coffee and biscuits in Whitehall."[49] The UK government used secondees from Deloitte to help develop reforms to its laws surrounding taxation of multinational companies, who subsequently returned to the firm to advise private clients.[50] Although the relationship between government and businesses can be more antagonistic in lower-income countries, there are many similar examples to the UK: Thailand, for example, formed an advisory committee with representation from the "big four" accounting firms to develop more competitive international tax laws;[51] in Zambia, the Revenue Authority contracted tax adviser Grant Thornton to perform some of its tax assessments.[52] Advice to the European Commission on international tax law and administrative reforms in lower-income countries was contracted out to accountancy firm PWC.[53]

Added to this is the "revolving door" phenomenon, as individuals move between tax roles in government, the private sector, and international organizations.[54] A majority of the tax advisers interviewed for this research had worked in the past for governments or tax authorities. The creation of semiautonomous revenue authorities at arm's length from the civil service has led to the appointment of tax commissioners and others in senior roles from the private sector, in countries as far apart as Uganda and Colombia, while the British tax authority has a governing board drawn primarily from the private sector.[55] The community within which international tax norms are formed and propagated thus permeates the public/private border, and furthermore, those whose authority is recognized within both ecologies have greater influence as a result.

A final overlap between ecologies concerns national and international settings. As well as interaction between the different groups mentioned above at the national level, many of the most influential people within national-linked ecologies also operate at the international level. The international ecology is distinct from each of the national ecologies from which its members also hail, and, as Leonard Seabrooke suggests, they are "in a different social space and reconfiguring how they work rather than replicating their national institutions or changing their own to reflect other national institutions."[56] Seabrooke argues elsewhere that international professional networks "provide a common language to those generating economic policy knowledge and they also stretch and test allegiances to national interests when these conflict with the professions' ideologies and beliefs."[57]

The community of international tax professionals is thus heterogeneous, with a ragged boundary, incorporating people from different countries, professions, and sectors. These individuals are united by a common set of ideas that are embodied in norms such as the arm's length principle, departing from an abhorrence of double taxation. To participate, one must be fluent with the ideas and language of the community, which is complex and technical. Authority within the community is a function of the ability to deploy this language and to leverage experience from within different professional ecologies.

The International Tax Community and the Global South

Up to now, my discussion of community and ecologies has centered on OECD countries, but almost every country has at least a handful of international tax professionals in government and the private sector who come into contact with the broader international environment. I consider this to be a *socializing* environment, in which "a process of inducting actors into the norms and rules of a given community" is at work.[58] When an individual is socialized, they move from a "logic of consequences," based on material incentives and outcomes, to one of "appropriateness," in which actors determine the appropriate course of action by reference to social rules.[59] Mechanisms of socialization have been divided into three categories: those based on instrumental calculations in response to social incentives; role playing, in which actors emulate those around them in order to fit in; and normative suasion, in which actors are persuaded by others to change their opinions through recourse to intersubjectively derived shared values.[60] Alastair Iain Johnston distinguishes between a first stage of socialization, in which an actor makes a "conscious instrumental calculation" to follow the logic of appropriateness (changed constraints), and a second stage that leads to the "taken for grantedness" of institutional norms (changed preferences).[61] Michael Zürn and Jeffrey Checkel suggest that compliance with norms based on a purely instrumental motivation may lead to the internalization of norms over time, as a result of the cognitive dissonance created.[62]

Identifying whether preferences and identities have truly changed over time—whether norms have really been internalized—is empirically very challenging.[63] For example, Kerrie Sadiq describes Australia's integration into the international tax regime as a four-stage process, the first stage of which, she argues, required a conscious decision to recognize the concept of an externally derived, preexisting legal regime. But she maintains that Australian policymakers' actions were based on instrumental calculations about the constraints created by this regime, rather than any change in preferences, "assessing the gains in tax revenue as well as other economic benefits from attracting capital imports as well as international perception against the forfeiture of a certain amount of autonomy and sovereignty."[64] In this book, I treat statements made by actors in nonattributable interviews as an accurate reflection of the ideas they hold, and I identify logics of both consequence and appropriateness in those statements.

We can consider two ideal-type mechanisms through which influential positions within a bureaucracy come to be occupied by individuals who have been socialized. They differ in terms of sequencing. In the first type, individuals who have already been socialized into a community through professional training or a scientific career subsequently move into policy jobs. For example, Jeffrey Chwieroth finds that countries are more likely to adopt neoliberal economic policies if they appoint to senior posts economists who have trained in an academic environment likely to have socialized them into neoliberal orthodoxy.[65] The relevant appointments for tax treaties would be senior roles in tax policy within the finance ministry, and tax commissioners, but these roles tend to be occupied by career civil servants who may not have a formal tax training at all. Lower down the bureaucracy, international tax is a niche field that generally develops as a specialism once people are employed within relevant roles in industry or the public sector. If civil servants from lower-income countries take academic training in international tax, they generally do so after they have been appointed.[66] Such individuals are therefore unlikely to have been socialized into the international tax community before when they began their roles.

A second mechanism, which is more likely to be relevant to international tax, occurs when individuals become socialized in the course of doing their jobs, as they interact with members of a community. For tax treaty officials from lower-income countries, this is most likely to occur when existing community members "teach" newer members about community norms.[67] Former treaty negotiators, tax lawyers, and international organization staff—all members of the epistemic community—played an influential role in shaping the approach to tax treaty negotiation in Cambodia and Zambia. Teaching and learning may occur through the numerous tax treaty negotiation trainings that are organized for lower-income countries, usually delivered by the OECD and UN Tax Committee, but sometimes under the auspices of lower-income country organizations such as the ATAF. A United Nations treaty negotiation manual for use at such trainings, for example, contains only a very brief section on the arguments against signing treaties, focusing almost entirely on the arguments in favor.[68] The international meetings of the policy community, at which lower-income countries are increasingly represented, include a growing number at the OECD and the annual sessions of the UN Tax Committee. Treaty negotiation rounds themselves, which can take one or two weeks, are often described by their participants as teaching and learning environments too. Several interviewees indicated that they had used negotiations with lower-income countries to teach them about the technical detail of tax treaties.[69] As the tax manager of Maersk, the Danish multinational shipping company, put it: "By negotiating these agreements, they are led into a train of thought about how various forms of tax are administered."[70]

As André Broome and Leonard Seabrooke argue, learning in such a socializing, specialist context means that "policy space is reduced as actors converge on a shared policy language and learn to solve problems through common diagnostic practices embedded within 'best practice' policy norms."[71] Thus, the "learning curve" leads to an equal and opposite "policy curve," as the logic of appropriateness circumscribes possible policy responses (figure 4.1a).

In the case of tax treaties, however, policy autonomy requires a degree of technical knowledge, without which policymakers will either be unable to analyze policies correctly or will be reliant on external sources of expertise. Learning may lead to socialization, as Broome and Seabrooke suggest, but in these circumstances it can also create policy space as the technical knowledge gained by bureaucrats allows them to question their own prior assumptions and those implicit in the knowledge imparted by the international community. I suggest that the "policy curve" is therefore shaped like a normal distribution (figure 4.1b). With a small amount of capacity, individuals resort to nonspecialist norms, which close down policy space. Fully absorbing specialist norms through socialization restricts policy space in a different way. Yet considerable learning is nonetheless necessary to maximize policy space.

This dynamic can be observed in the cases discussed in chapters 6 and 7. Zambia and Vietnam negotiated large numbers of treaties without first establishing a baseline of technical knowledge. They were unable to critically analyze the

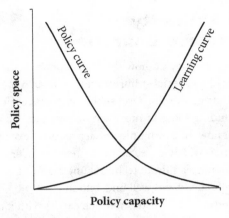

FIGURE 4.1A. Policy space and capacity-building curves

Source: Based on André Broome and Leonard Seabrooke, "Shaping Policy Curves: Cognitive Authority in Transnational Capacity Building," Public Administration, *May 2015, https://doi.org/10.1111/padm.12179.*

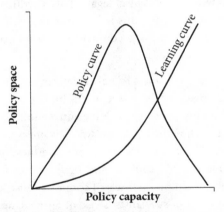

FIGURE 4.1B. Policy space and capacity-building curves for tax treaties

Source: Author.

circumstances in which tax treaties were likely to have significant benefit and costs to them, or when or how to counter the negotiating preferences of higher-income countries. There are signs that, by the 2000s, technical officials from both countries had internalized international norms, although these officials' autonomy over treatymaking differed significantly. Yet the beneficial impact of strong technical capacity on policy space is visible in Zambia's renegotiations to fix past mistakes and Cambodia's careful early negotiations.

Epistemic Authority
in Lower-Income Countries

The previous section considered how the international tax community may influence the ideas held by specialist bureaucrats. But such mechanisms can only influence bureaucrats at a junior level such that their remit is specialized. For nonspecialists, including those in more senior bureaucratic and political roles, we need to consider how the community influences people outside its own boundaries. Such influence is widely expected to be greatest under conditions in which policymakers experience significant technical uncertainty, but the means through which they exert influence is not well understood.[72]

Taxation is entirely a legal construct, which carries with it a certain inevitable deference to tax professionals, who are seen to monopolize expert knowledge not just on its interpretation but on its very nature.[73] So it is not surprising that concerns about the domination of international tax policy by a technical community are also highlighted by critical legal scholars writing in the Bourdiesian tradition. The starting point for this is Pierre Bourdieu's article describing a juridical social field as "the site of a competition for monopoly of the right to determine the law." As he argues:

> It divides those qualified to participate in the game and those who, though they may find themselves in the middle of it, are in fact excluded by their inability to accomplish the conversion of mental space—and particularly of linguistic stance—which is presumed by entry into this social space. The establishment of properly professional competence, the technical mastery of a sophisticated body of knowledge that often runs contrary to the simple counsels of common sense, entails the disqualification of the non-specialists' sense of fairness, and the revocation of their naïve understanding of the facts, of their "view of the case."[74]

This view describes with prescient accuracy the tax community's interactions with the broader political and public space. John Snape regards international corporate taxation as an example of how "private regulation is transformed into public law with the complex reasonings of specialized professional disciplines as its chief characteristic."[75] Sol Picciotto sees a resonance for international tax in the way that "law operates to defuse social conflicts and depoliticize them, shifting political and economic conflicts on to the terrain of debates over the symbolic power of texts."[76] He argues that the cohesiveness of the international tax "interpretive community" of stakeholders from organizations with apparently conflicting interests is maintained by elaborating new rules that maintain a broad ongoing consensus, and by "limiting the membership of the interpretative community and trying to ensure that they are like-minded."[77] Secretive meetings in the 1960s and 1970s have given way to public discussions to which access is instead restricted by the technical complexity of legal rules and the language used to debate them. This leads to a self-reinforcing in-group of people "able to invest in learning the arcane terminology and linguistic techniques familiar to that group."[78] This linguistic gatekeeping, he argues, is bolstered by a social and financial pressure not to question the community's foundational principles.

Certainly, where there is political involvement in the specifics of multinational corporate taxation, this is an exception rather than a rule.[79] As Pepper Culpepper emphasizes, civil servants and business representatives may exercise a de facto veto over political actors because of the disparity in knowledge. Business power in "quiet politics," he argues, "is not primarily because of the structural power to disinvest, which Lindblom emphasized. It is instead because they [businesses] know the facts on the ground, and that expertise is extremely valuable in negotiating with other members of the policy subsystem. On the rare occasions when politicians turn their attention to typically low salience areas, they enter with an asymmetry of expertise vis-a-vis the representatives of business."[80]

Charles Lindblom refers to the complicity between civil servants and their private sector interlocutors in his classic analysis of business power, in which he argues that one strategy employed by businesses is to attempt to keep policy issues below the political radar. He suggests that civil servants will often support such efforts because "they are caught in a potential crossfire between privileged controls and polyarchal controls."[81] Ash Amin and Ronen Palan also emphasize that there is no reason to assume a priori that actors within government bureaucracies and multinational firms are in an antagonistic relationship.[82]

Beyond international tax rules, tax policy in lower-income countries has historically been shaped by an outside professional community. There is a critical strand of literature on tax reform that describes how a "tax consensus" developed among development policy advisers in the 1980s and was transmitted to lower-income countries through conditionality and technical assistance. According to Odd-Helge Fjeldstad and Mick Moore, this consensus focused on the elimination of trade taxes and their replacement with the VAT, as well as a bureaucratic reform: the creation of semiautonomous revenue authorities that were not under the direct control of finance ministries.[83] This view, they argue, formed among "an epistemic community of taxation professionals, employed in national tax administrations, in consultancy companies and in international financial institutions, and organised in regional and global professional associations" during "a period of unusually radical tax reform in the developing world since the 1980s."[84] "The key factor," writes Miranda Stewart, "is the development of an international consensus, or 'norm', of tax reform and policy driven largely by the international institutions, and propounded by non-government tax experts."[85]

Three main concerns are highlighted by authors discussing this tax consensus: its close association with the neoliberal Washington consensus, its "one size fits all" approach, and, crucially, the depoliticization of decisions with important distributional impacts, which critics argue should fundamentally be part of the democratic process.[86] Lisa Philipps describes how "tax and budgetary issues are frequently constructed as technical matters that can be resolved rationally according to economic, mathematical or other ostensibly neutral principle," with policy-making processes dominated by technical experts despite the political nature of outcomes.[87] Stewart concurs that "tax reform projects have been mass-produced and have spread rapidly across the globe through broad, superficial, and generalized tax policy recommendations grounded in the consensus. . . . The contemporary mass production of tax reform militates against any real domestic political participation in the determination of tax policies and laws in the countries undergoing reform."[88]

This literature has focused on domestic tax reforms, in particular the elimination of trade tariffs and the introduction of VAT, during the past three decades. Yet international institutions and experts play a similar driving role in the international tax reforms adopted by lower-income countries, in particular with respect to transfer pricing and tax treaties.[89] A review of lower-income country tax systems commissioned by the European Commission from PWC, for example, urges that "donor support initiatives should eventually aim at lifting the TP [transfer pricing] legislation and its application in developing countries to a common international standard. In our opinion, this is vital to reduce economic uncertainty and foster investment and growth."[90] In Vietnam, the business lobby group the Vietnam Business Forum (VBF) regularly urges the government to "align . . . Vietnam tax policy with international practice," calling in 2014 for it to "study and provide guidance base on the description and regulation about permanent establishment under international practice and standard as the UN and the OECD."[91]

The international tax community can thus be characterized as a transnational policy community whose ideas are formed intersubjectively in the social context it creates. Through formal professional competence, high technical and linguistic barriers to participation, and its own pivotal role in standard setting, the community claims a monopoly on the "correct" way to do international tax. Because tax is a legal construct, this claim extends to defining its every aspect. The community itself is dynamic and fluid, the nexus of several overlapping ecologies: accountancy and law, private and public, national and international. Many of the leading roles in international tax are played by individuals who have authoritative positions within these multiple ecologies. The community influences policy in part by socializing bureaucrats who occupy relevant specialist positions into its norms, and in part through nonspecialist policymakers' deference to its expertise. Policymakers' technical uncertainty, the emphasis in the epistemic communities literature, certainly leads them to defer to the community, yet the community itself actively creates such uncertainty, through the proliferation of ever-greater complexity.

The OECD as a Site of Authority

It is impossible to discuss international tax without discussing the OECD. Its hegemonic status is widely recognized by tax law scholars, and so a theoretical understanding of the organization is essential for this book.[92] Yet in comparison with other international organizations, international relations scholarship on the OECD is relatively limited.[93] Work on the OECD's role in international tax relations has generally been focused on its initiatives to target harmful tax practices and tax havens, which are largely distinct from its work on tax treaties.[94]

International organizations are of particular importance in the field of socialization, both as providers of advice and, along with their associated communities, as settings for socialization.[95] According to Martha Finnemore, international organizations should be considered as autonomous actors, "shapers of actors or interests," above and beyond the sum total of their member states.[96] She points to the "teacher" role fulfilled by international organizations, "according them more autonomous and causal status, particularly as shapers of actors and interests."[97] Friedrich Kratochwil and John Ruggie argue that "in the international arena, neither the processes whereby knowledge becomes more extensive nor the means whereby reflection on knowledge deepens are passive or automatic. They are intensely political. And for better or for worse, international organizations have manoeuvred themselves into the position of being the vehicle through which both types of knowledge enter onto the international agenda."[98]

The OECD's model tax treaty and associated guidance have a hegemonic status, forming the basis of all bilateral tax treaties. Variations, such as the UN model tax treaty, still take the OECD model as their point of departure, although they adapt it independently. Yet the OECD has achieved this outcome not as a purveyor of hard law but rather as a site in which soft-law instruments are created and promulgated. For this reason, much scholarship on the OECD focuses on its ideational leadership. As Charles Nelson wrote as early as 1970: "The OECD is important not for the decisions it makes but for the decisions it prepares. . . . There are very few

important international economic problems which the OECD can legitimately resolve. . . . This is the most important single characteristic of the OECD. The major
decisions prepared within it are inevitably formalized and carried out elsewhere:
in the IMF, in the GATT [general agreement on tariffs and trade], in the UNCTAF
[*sic*; United Nations Conference on Trade and Development], in the World Bank,
or through traditional diplomatic channels."[99]

Bengt Jacobsson suggests that the OECD has a meditative function, through
which standards are developed, and an inquisitive one, its distinctive peer review
process through which states' compliance with those standards is assessed.[100]
While the peer review process is a part of the OECD's taxation work, until recently
this was in areas other than tax treaties, and so it is on the meditative role that
this discussion will dwell. It is worth noting, however, that the OECD's authoritative
position as the grouping of the world's most "advanced" democracies occupies a
mutually reinforcing role with respect to its peer review process. Peer reviews simultaneously rely on and bolster the OECD's position as a source of authoritative
knowledge about how an advanced economy should behave, because it can
"modify the reference groups of national bureaucrats, their aspirations, and their
behaviour."[101]

An influential paper by Martin Marcussen segments the OECD's ideational role
into five categories: an artist, which formulates, tests, and diffuses policies; an
agent, which transfers ideas from more prosperous to less prosperous states; an
agency, which takes emerging ideas from states, develops them, and then sells
them back in a more refined form; an arbitrator, through which civil servants are
socialized; and finally, an authority, used by states to back up their positions.[102]
Each of these roles helps explain the OECD's central role in the world of tax
treaties.

Consider first the artist role. The OECD is the place in which international tax
standards are formulated and reformulated, since it inherited the responsibility
for the model tax treaty from its predecessor the OEEC. Whenever tax specialists
within its member states identify a need for new or changed standards, it is to
the OECD that they turn. This was the case in the late 1990s, when states began
to be concerned about tax havens, and it applied again in 2012, when corporate
tax avoidance rose up the political agenda.[103] Arthur Cockfield suggests that this
is part of a trend toward doing the technical work on new standards at the OECD
first, rather than first developing standards at the national level and then using
the OECD as a forum to reconcile different approaches. "Because of the history
of cooperation along with more recent efforts, it may be the case that the OECD
member states have learned to trust the OECD process to the point where they
are increasingly prepared to accept the OECD's leadership in resolving other areas

of international tax policy concern, including binding multilateral mechanisms in limited areas such as transfer pricing arbitration."[104]

Studies of the OECD have emphasized the informal interaction between specialist bureaucrats as a forum for socialization since its early days as an organization. Henry Aubrey emphasized that the formal part of meetings and the "informal contacts in the corridors and over meals" led to "mutual appreciation and trust" between civil servants.[105] Marcussen, citing Gunnar Sjöstedt, describes how officials in OECD deliberations "develop a common language . . . start using the same kind of causal reasoning," and "develop a common selective perception of the world and they start to employ a common frame of reference and a common worldview. The latter helps them to define what can be considered as a relevant problem in the first place and which instruments can legitimately be employed to solve this problem."[106]

Scott Sullivan, in an authorized account that presumably reflects the OECD's self-perception, describes how OECD committees "serve as a crucible for its members' future actions. . . . In the corridors and coffee bars between sessions, officials with similar interests but very different backgrounds meet, argue, forge friendships."[107]

A focus on the OECD's members and their interactions through the OECD, however, risks underspecifying the entrepreneurial role of the OECD secretariat. For Rianne Mahon and Stephen McBride, the organizational culture within the OECD is an important contributor to its meditative function. "OECD staff conducts research and produces a range of background studies and reports. In this, they draw on their disciplinary knowledge, supplemented by what Dostal refers to as an 'organizational discourse'—'claims encapsulating long-term political projects as defined by the organization in question'. The latter reflects the effects of organizational learning."[108]

A survey of career histories of staff from the OECD's Centre for Tax Policy and Administration (CTPA), forty-five of whom had a profile on LinkedIn, illustrates that the OECD tax bureaucracy reflects the public-private policy community. Some 42 percent of its staff came to the OECD from multinational businesses, accountancy firms, and law practices, while 58 percent worked in finance ministries and revenue authorities; when full career histories were taken into account, 75 percent of CTPA staff had worked in tax specialist roles in both the public and private sectors at some point.[109] The OECD secretariat is therefore the embodiment of an expert community whose reach transcends the public and private boundaries. As Jason Sharman argues, the normative weight of the OECD's output rests on its "technocratic identity . . . as an international organisation composed of 'apolitical' experts."[110]

Secretariat staff and civil servants interact frequently through the OECD's various tax committees, working parties, and forums. For Allison Christians, it is this tripartite interaction among national government representatives, experts from academia and business, and secretariat staff (largely drawn from the first two groups) that defines the OECD's way of working. "These tax policy groups form an intertwined epistemic community that holds an important and influential position in the law-making order. Together, the CTPA (OECD employees) and the CFA [Committee on Fiscal Affairs] (public servants or national representatives) diagnose and prescribe tax policy reforms that are informed by, and that play out within, national legal regimes."[111]

If the internal milieu of the OECD is a potential socializing context for the tax profession, the external-facing aspects of Marcussen's typology also seem highly apposite. He describes the OECD's "agent" role as the manner in which it transfers policy from more prosperous to less prosperous nations.[112] As a socializing forum and a promulgator of standards, it is not just that the OECD is a focal point for other states, as Thomas Rixen argues, but also that its standards are associated with the "advanced" reputation of its member states.[113] As Tony Porter and Michael Webb write, the OECD's technical work "is reinforced by the diffuse sense that the OECD's knowledge is an expression of the best states' best practices."[114]

This authoritative role toward nonmembers is established not merely passively by the OECD but also through active outreach. This takes two forms: civil servants from lower-income countries are invited to participate in various forums in Paris, and the OECD also engages in sensitization and capacity-building work. Since the mid-1990s, the CTPA has maintained an active program of outreach to lower-income countries, based on training workshops and seminars with civil servants, many of whom went on to lead their country's tax treaty negotiations.[115] Such outreach is premised on the technical superiority of the OECD's international tax instruments, as demonstrated by their adoption across its members and more widely. A prominent policy paper from the OECD states: "There is already a significant amount of work being done by the OECD and other international organisations to support developing countries to address these [international tax] challenges. This work aims at disseminating effective international standards, improving access to data and information, building capacity and assisting in tax audits."[116]

Another part of the OECD's meditative function, as described by Marcussen, is the manner in which it is cited as an authority by its members (and, we might say, by other actors in the international tax milieu). For example, a consultancy report on transfer pricing written for the European Commission by PWC states: "The OECD Guidelines could serve as common global standards for TP and we would advocate that developing countries orient themselves to these standards when adopting and implementing TP legislation. . . . The selected countries should particularly draw attention to the development of a network of DTAs. This can foster the local investment climate by providing a legal mechanism to address potential cases of double taxation."[117]

The OECD is *the* guardian of concepts that are foundational to the international tax community, but it is not the only organization in which the tax expert community operates. Some regional organizations of lower-income countries have developed their own model treaties, but in every case these organizations use the OECD's model treaty as their jumping-off point.[118] The UN Tax Committee, a group of twenty-five tax treaty negotiators (acting, like the League of Nations group, in their personal capacity) produces its own model treaty that is supposed to be explicitly designed to take into account the special needs of lower-income countries. The UN model treaty differs from the OECD model in the wording of a number of clauses, some of which can be found in a majority of tax treaties signed by lower-income countries.[119] In practice, however, the committee's debates exist within a framework of legitimate dissent, whereby differences in interests between higher-income and lower-income countries are tightly contained within the overall framework of the standards formulated by the OECD, such as the arm's length principle, which are not questioned. Many of the senior roles within the UN committee are occupied by individuals who also play leading roles within the various OECD working parties.[120]

More importantly, the UN committee serves as a forum for socialization of lower-income country officials. This objective is set out clearly in an internal UK civil service document from the 1970s: "Our view, which is shared by the Americans and the Dutch, has been that it is of little use to try to 'educate' developing countries—at the United Nations Expert Group on tax treaties and elsewhere—about acceptable international fiscal standards if, when it comes to the crunch, we are prepared to sacrifice principle in order to secure an agreement."[121]

We can see, therefore, that the OECD is at the heart of a tax ecosystem that incorporates other international organizations, business groups, and countries, held together by the glue of a community of tax professionals who are simultaneously participants in these different organizations' work. The OECD's central position is a function of two mutually reinforcing perceptions: the technical superiority of its standards, and their endorsement by the world's most advanced economies, the members of the OECD. The international tax community's emphasis on tax treaties as the correct way of establishing the tax treatment of multinational companies gains authority from the organization's wider economic policy authority.

The Tax Policy Community and the Making of Tax Treaties

This section takes the prior analysis and situates it in the national-level tax policymaking procedures, in particular the process of treaty making. That process, from the initial policy considerations through to ratification, is guided in almost every country by a small team of technical professionals. The formation of a strong specialist international tax unit within a finance ministry or revenue authority, with institutionalized links to the OECD, UN Tax Committee, or other socializing environment, is likely to determine the extent to which officials learn. But these professionals' autonomy is circumscribed by a number of veto points, at which political or other bureaucratic actors may have some formal or informal ability to block the progression of the treaty.[122] While the process varies across countries, these veto points are generally ex ante negotiating authority, opening negotiations, agreement at official level ("initialing the draft"), signature, and ratification. If the preferences of specialists and nonspecialists do not align, the ability to negotiate a treaty is likely to depend on control of those veto points.

Such tensions have been inherent since the very first tax treaty to be negotiated between two countries—Prussia and the Netherlands in the 1910s. First, the treaty was not ratified by the Dutch side because of objections from the business community to its information-sharing clauses, which only emerged at the last minute when the outcome of negotiations was made public.[123] The treaty was described as a "personal project" of lead negotiator Jan Sinninghe Damsté. An attempt at renegotiation stumbled because, according to a communication from the Dutch ambassador to Germany, "this matter was previously dealt with by the Minister of Finance, and . . . the current official did not understand these matters."[124]

Let us begin at the policymaking level. In her study of business power in corporate tax policymaking in Latin America, Tasha Fairfield argues that "administrative constraints" and "technical principles" limit the businesses' structural and instrumental power over tax policy at the national level.[125] In international tax, even at the national level, it is the transnational policy community that provides the technical language, norms, standards, and guidelines that frame debate, embodied in the OECD model. The model certainly delimits the set of acceptable options in the minds of policymakers, to the extent that it is argued to have a "soft law" status.[126] Kerry Sadiq characterizes the process of international tax policymaking in Australia as follows: "The Australian Federal Government inherently accepts the existence of an international tax regime and adopts both the international tax policy and practice aspects embodied in that regime through its domestic rules and double tax treaties."[127] This is also the case outside the OECD, where policymakers may feel constrained to follow international best practice.[128]

Few countries have an explicit policy regarding whom they will negotiate with.[129] As a result, decisions about whom to negotiate with are made by civil servants, often with little ministerial oversight. In one country, a treaty had been negotiated by a previous tax commissioner, understood by current officials as a "personal project" based on his personal connections to the treaty partner, and quietly shelved when the commissioner was replaced. Seven years later, when its existence was uncovered by a senator, it was ratified, to the consternation of the revenue authority.[130] In another, ministerial approval to open negotiations was fully understood to be a box-checking exercise and had never been declined.[131] Uganda even initiated a review of its treaty network with the aim of soliciting some political guidance where previously decisions had been made entirely by tax officials.[132]

As discussed in the previous chapter, tax treaty negotiators from most capital-exporting countries consult at the prioritization stage, with businesses and with other government departments. In some countries, the decision to enter negotiations requires direct ministerial approval, while in others ministerial involvement comes later, once the text is ready for signature or even further down the line. The UK case study in chapter 5 records how the minister responsible sought to have approval of treaty texts before signature, rather than simply being shown them before he proposed their ratification to Parliament.

Negotiators' autonomy is in part circumscribed by the law that gives them force. For example, in the UK, the Taxation (International and Other Provisions) Act of 2010 defines the double taxation that is to be relieved by tax treaties, and specifies the taxes to which the mechanism can apply. To give effect to an agreement that exceeds this mandate, the law would have to be changed, as it was in the case of the UK-Brazil negotiations (discussed in chapter 5). Within the legal parameters, only new precedent generally requires ministerial approval.[133] In contrast, section 88 of Uganda's income tax act merely states that an international tax agreement "shall have effect as if the agreement was contained in this Act." Uganda's chief negotiator indicated that the country's review of its tax treaties was in part designed to give a political steer where previously negotiators had only their own opinions to guide them in negotiations.[134]

An important addition to this discussion is the role played by model treaties in setting the parameters of negotiations. OECD member states have their own national model treaties, which are largely used in private to set out their opening negotiating position,[135] and which are published by a small number of countries.[136] They also adhere to the articles of the OECD model convention, which they have negotiated among themselves in advance, except where they have specified reservations to its text.[137] Itai Grinberg argues that "at least within the OECD, tax treaty negotiators feel substantially constrained to accept OECD Model Treaty provisions in their future negotiations with other sovereigns."[138] Other countries may also refer to regional models, such as the COMESA, SADC (Southern African Development Community), and EAC (East African Community) models in Africa or the ASEAN model in Southeast Asia. These models are generally formulated by the treaty negotiators themselves, in particular at the OECD, where a dedicated working party of civil servants updates the model convention, which is then approved by the CFA, made up of "high-level officials in national treasuries and tax administrations."[139] The process of modifying the OECD model has become more consultative, with business groups submitting comments on published drafts or participating in working groups.[140] Political oversight, however, remains minimal for the most part.[141] The UN committee's members are formally acting in a personal capacity rather than on behalf of their countries, and the model they draft has no intergovernmental status. Notably, the COMESA model treaty was drafted by European private sector consultants, while the accountancy firm KPMG drafted an ASEAN position on tax treaties.[142]

Tax treaty negotiations are generally led by a country's finance ministry or its tax authority, with the exact division of labor depending on the institutional structure. In countries such as the UK and Cambodia, it is the tax authority that leads, while in others such as Zambia and the United States, responsibility lies with the finance ministry, although the revenue authority may also participate in negotiations.[143] Foreign affairs and investment promotion ministries also often participate but contribute little, if at all. In the UK, for example, the Foreign and Commonwealth Office (FCO) approves treaty texts before they are signed, but in general its only input is on the definition of the contracting states.[144] In all the case studies in this book, negotiations were led by officials from finance ministries or revenue authorities, with varying degrees of specialism in international tax; in wider interviews, a handful of examples were given of negotiations led by other government ministries, such as in one case an investment promotion authority.[145]

Tax treaties are intergovernmental agreements that, once signed, become a part of their signatories' tax laws. Ratification follows different procedures in different countries. Typically, in lower-income countries, tax treaties are ratified by the cabinet, with no parliamentary approval. This is the case, for example, in Uganda, where treaties are merely laid before parliament, and Zambia, where they never pass through parliament.[146] TJNA's lawsuit in Kenya concerned in part the lack of parliamentary ratification of the treaty with Mauritius: Kenya's new constitution requires parliamentary ratification of treaties, but the government argued that the tax treaty was merely an administrative agreement, a position supported by the High Court.[147]

In higher-income countries, it is more common—but not universal—for parliaments to approve new tax treaties. A survey of the parliamentary ratification of Canada's last thirty-three treaties revealed "expeditious implementation through Parliament with little or no scrutiny," with deliberations not coming to a single vote in one of the two chambers.[148] In the UK, tax treaties are made law as statutory instruments, a mechanism that is designed for noncontroversial laws that are passed through a delegated legislation committee. Ratification rarely entails more than a token debate in this committee, and no treaty has ever been rejected or sent back for renegotiation.[149] In Denmark, parliamentary ratification was introduced during the 1990s but is equally uncontroversial.[150] At the other end of the spectrum, the US Senate is famously thorough in its scrutiny of tax treaties. It forced a change to the US-UK treaty before ratification in the 1990s, and in some cases has held up ratification altogether.[151]

There is certainly considerable heterogeneity across countries in the number of veto points and players. A combination of formal rules and their authoritative position could give a coherent team of tax treaty experts near-total control over the treaty-making process. Some treaty negotiators interviewed did indeed claim that ministerial and parliamentary scrutiny, where it existed, was largely a rubber-stamping exercise.[152] In contrast, others had been unable to realize their preferences because other stakeholders, who did not share their ideas about tax treaties, exercised a veto at various stages of the process. Even where there was no parliamentary ratification, some negotiators explained that the approval process could get held up because finance ministers did not approve signature.[153]

Finally, there is specific evidence that tax treaties are sometimes pushed through by nonspecialists in spite of the reticence of tax treaty specialists themselves. A study of tax treaty negotiations in Colombia, for example, suggests that tax officials received a political instruction to negotiate treaties swiftly in pursuit of "investment at any price."[154] One negotiator from a lower-income country interviewed for this book explained that his country had signed a treaty with Mauritius, a tax haven, on very disadvantageous terms because the negotiation had been initiated by the country's newly created investment promotion authority and conducted without any revenue authority involvement. The tax implications were not considered, and the country did not even formulate an opening position before beginning negotiations.[155] There are numerous examples of heads of state signing agreements over the heads of their negotiating teams or instructing them to negotiate in a hurry.[156]

Conclusion

This chapter focused on tax treaty specialists: those who formulate international models and national policies and negotiate treaties themselves, as well as the other actors within their community, such as from businesses and academia. This transnational policy community has a distinct conceptualization of the role of tax treaties grounded in a set of norms concerning the appropriate way to tax multinational firms. The community wields the threat of double taxation as a tool through which to strengthen its influence over tax policymaking. The effect is to depoliticize negotiations between states that have distributional consequences, with political involvement treated as an exogenous constraint rather than an endogenous part of the policymaking process. Much of this is achieved using increasingly obscure language and elaboration of ever more detailed terms, as well as by the community's claim to authority derived from professional expertise. The community is predominantly composed of professionals from OECD countries, and this is one reason why, despite being in the majority, lower-income countries are still "norm takers" in the international tax regime.

The ability of the international tax community to exercise power within national bureaucracies varies over time and between countries. In lower-income countries, the number and experience of international tax bureaucrats varies, which is one reason for the variation in approaches to international tax: as individuals become socialized into the international tax community, their attitude toward tax treaties may changes: as they first learn about their costs and benefits framed in terms of their preexisting ideas, which may create a skeptical outlook; if they internalize the community's ideas about the desirability of convergence around OECD standards using tax treaties, it may create an enthusiastic outlook.

The influence of specialist tax bureaucrats over treaty making in a country depends further on their autonomy within the government structure. The number and nature of veto players varies between countries, and veto points may cause treaties to fail because of differing preferences over treaty partners, treaty content, or the whole project of tax treaties itself. These differences do not necessarily emerge because different actors have different material incentives, but because they hold different ideas about what tax treaties are for and, indeed, about the function of international tax rules.

THE UNITED KINGDOM

Above all, [tax treaties] impose acceptable standards . . . where such standards would otherwise be absent.

—Deputy chairman of the Board of Inland Revenue

The United Kingdom has the widest tax treaty network of any country in the world. It played a very involved role in the development of the League of Nations and OECD model conventions, and the UK-US treaty of 1945 is regarded as having set the precedent for modern tax treaties.[1] This chapter focuses on the 1970s, a period when the tax treaty network expanded rapidly into recently independent lower-income countries that were certainly keen to attract inward investment. Britain entered into negotiations with about forty lower-income countries during the period 1970–79, successfully concluding agreements with just over half. Most of these agreements are still in force today.

A conventional tax competition logic would suggest that the UK concluded a large number of tax treaties with lower-income countries because they were competing for British investment. In keeping with the arguments of previous chapters, this chapter develops that tax competition logic in two directions. First, it demonstrates that the main driver of the UK's treaty negotiations with lower-income countries was competition between the UK and other home countries of multinational investors for outward investment opportunities. Second, it shows that two different logics of competition existed: one within the tax expert community, and another among nonspecialist stakeholders. For the tax specialists, including treaty negotiators in the Board of Inland Revenue, the goal of tax treaties was to export "acceptable" OECD tax standards wherever British firms operated. Nonspecialist stakeholders were motivated by a combination of the tax treaty myth and the perceived effects of tax treaties on the short-term effective tax rate of UK multinationals. This led to clashes of preferences, which the Inland Revenue generally dismissed as misunderstandings or parochialism. The role played by expert technical knowledge in shaping the preferences of tax specialists is illustrated by the private sector actors, who did not align with each other but with the two civil service camps, based on their level of expertise.

Evidence presented in this chapter is drawn from civil service documentation released under the United Kingdom's thirty-year rule. It covers the decade from 1970, the most recent full decade for which these records were available, and one in which many treaties still in force today were negotiated with lower-income countries in Africa and Asia. The documents reviewed include internal civil service correspondence, minutes of negotiation meetings, and correspondence between the UK and other countries' negotiating teams. The focus is therefore on the variables driving the UK's actions, rather than those internal to the lower-income country. We cannot tell conclusively from this evidence what motivated the lower-income country, but by mapping the process of each negotiation, it is possible to determine the extent to which the lower-income country was driving forward negotiations, or acquiescing to the UK's enthusiasm. Where the latter is the case, this illustrates how competition among capital-exporting countries is responsible for the emergence of new tax treaties, rather than purely among capital-importing countries as much of the literature assumes.

The rest of the chapter proceeds as follows. The next section briefly discusses the archival documents used. The chapter then establishes some general findings about roles and attitudes of different stakeholder groups in the treaty-making process, drawing from some specific examples as well as overriding policy considerations. I then move on to consider three cases in particular: the UK's negotiations with Egypt, Nigeria, and Brazil. Egypt shows the conclusion of a new agreement, Nigeria the renegotiation of a colonial agreement, and Brazil an unsuccessful negotiation in spite of strong demand from British businesses. In each of these cases, we see evidence that lobbying by tax specialists from British firms was crucial to determining the UK's position, as well as evidence of conflicting preferences between treaty negotiators and nonspecialist stakeholders.

Context

The evidence used in this chapter is from the UK National Archives, which releases civil service files thirty years after they have been closed (seventy years for files that include information on identified people's tax affairs). Each file is recorded in an online database that includes its name and a short description. To find the relevant files, I searched this database for the terms "double tax," "double taxation," and "tax treaty," which yielded 2,301 results when I first conducted the search in 2014. The majority of these were country-specific files originated from the Inland Revenue or the FCO and its predecessors. They include internal civil service correspondence, correspondence between countries, and minutes of negotiation meetings. This means that they include both the internal thinking of the UK and the positioning of the negotiating partner, supplemented on occasion by intelligence about its motivations from other British sources.

Most of the country files indicate that sporadic contact between the two sides was the norm before any serious negotiations were initiated. The UK may have made tentative inquiries, as in the case of Latin American countries, or an ambassador from a lower-income country may have expressed an interest that the UK judged not to reflect a serious intent on behalf of that country's tax treaty decision makers. The UK entered into serious discussions with around forty lower-income countries during the 1970s, shown in table 5.1. The median length of time from the UK's first successful contact with a country with a view to negotiating a tax treaty to signature was just over three years, but a significant number of negotiations took over six years. The median time from first contact to ratification by both parties was as much as five years.

Negotiations were undertaken by a small team of officials within the Board of Inland Revenue. Most of the information used in this chapter is drawn from that team's files, although most treaties also have a corresponding Foreign Office file, which may include communication between the embassy and the desk officer in London, but is often purely procedural. In general, for each treaty the file begins with correspondence with the report of a conversation with a lower-income country, or correspondence either between the Inland Revenue and its counterpart or between the Inland Revenue and the British embassy. Preliminary discussions then give way to a formal request to start negotiations, and the Inland Revenue circulates a written request for comment to the Treasury, FCO, and the Department (or Departments, depending on the date) of Trade and Industry (DTI).

A typical negotiation consisted of an exchange of drafts (or simply the UK sending its draft and the lower-income country responding with comments), then a first round of negotiations in person. Finding a mutually convenient time to meet was a lengthy process when correspondence was principally by air mail, and a year's delay at this point for purely practical reasons was not atypical. After the first round of negotiations, the file usually includes formal minutes and a more informal memo circulated to accompany them, giving the negotiators' impressions of their opposite numbers. Further correspondence on outstanding issues usually led to a second round of negotiations, at which the agreement was initialed, signaling acceptance at an official level. The treaty was then subject to final checks, including translation and finalizing the definition of countries with the FCO, before it was signed. Sometimes errors, legislative changes, or a change of heart by one side could lead to

TABLE 5.1. UK negotiations with lower-income countries, 1970–79

	INITIATOR OF NEGOTIATIONS	DISCUSSIONS OPENED	FIRST ROUND OF NEGOTIATIONS	TREATY SIGNED	TREATY IN FORCE
Argentina	UK	1979	1980		
Bangladesh	UK	1976	1977	1979	1980
Botswana	[Renegotiation]	1974	1974	1977	1978
Brazil	UK	1972	1973		
Colombia	UK	Informal discussions only			
Czechoslovakia	UK	1975	1977	1990	1991
Egypt	UK	1976	1976	1977	1980
Fiji	—	1973	1974	1975	1976
Gambia	—	1974	1974	1980	1982
Ghana	[Renegotiation]	1974	1974	1977	1978
Greece	UK	Informal discussions only			
Hungary	UK	1976	1977	1977	1978
India	UK	1976	1976	1981	1981
Indonesia	—			1974	1976
Iran	UK	1973	1975		
Ivory Coast	—	1978	1979	1985	1987
Jamaica	[Renegotiation]	1969	1969	1973	1973
Kenya*	[Renegotiation]	1971	1971	1973	1977
Korea	—	1974	1975	1977	1978
Lesotho	—	Informal discussions only			
Malaysia	[Renegotiation]	1971	1975		
Mauritius	—	1974	1975	1981	1981
Mexico	UK	1978			
Morocco	Counterpart	1970	1976	1981	1990
Nigeria	UK	1978	1979	1976	1978
Philippines	Counterpart	1974	1975	1976	1978
Poland	UK	1975	1975	1975	1978
Romania	Counterpart	1975	1975	1975	1977
Saudi Arabia	UK	1977			
Spain	UK	1973	1975	1975	1976
Sri Lanka	Counterpart	1972	1974	1979	1980
Sudan	[Renegotiation]	1973	1974	1975	1977
Swaziland	—	Informal discussions only			
Tanzania*	Counterpart	1976	1977		
Thailand	UK	1974	1976	1981	1981
Tunisia	Counterpart	1975	1976	1982	1984
Turkey	UK	1978			
Uganda*	—	1971			
Yugoslavia	—	1975	1976	1981	1982

Source: National Archives, various files. Where no information was available in the archives, this is indicated by a dash. Blank spaces indicate that this stage of negotiation did not take place.

*Kenya's, Tanzania's, and Uganda's negotiations with the UK began as part of a joint negotiation on behalf of the East African Community.

amendments being made at this stage, either to the text itself or via a protocol, signed at the same time. Ratification followed, which in the UK involved the minister of state presenting the agreement to a parliamentary committee: the file usually includes a copy of the briefing given to the minister, explaining any salient or unusual features of the treaty, and giving suggested answers to anticipated questions; while these briefings are usually formulaic, they sometimes include information explaining the UK's reasoning. It was not unusual for signature or ratification to be delayed in the lower-income country, and the files sometimes show the UK negotiators seeking to expedite ratification by the other side.

There are also some files relating to the UK's general negotiating position, such as correspondence within and between departments relating to a cross-departmental review of DTTs. Another set of files records meetings and correspondence with business organizations, including quarterly "state of play" reports on all the UK's negotiations, which were compiled as briefing documents for civil servants attending these meetings. These are discussed in more detail in the sections that follow.

The UK's Active Pursuit of Tax Treaties

Since the earliest files discussing potential treaties, correspondence inside the UK civil service indicates that the UK was not merely a passive respondent to requests from lower-income countries, "stand[ing] ready with model treaties in hand," but rather it was actively shaping its own treaty network.[2] Already in 1957, discussion of a potential agreement with Colombia states, "For years we have been unsuccessfully trying to conclude an agreement with a South American country without any success. . . . This is, therefore, the only area of the world, apart from the countries behind the Iron Curtain in which we have made no progress."[3]

With Turkey, the UK proposed talks in 1978 and again in 1979, but a note in 1981 indicates that the Turks "have expressed no enthusiasm" for a treaty.[4] Similarly, the UK sent a draft treaty to Czechoslovakia in 1975, but in 1976 a civil servant wrote that "despite reminders, the Czechs have not responded."[5] In the latter case, negotiations did take place in 1977 and 1978 but ended in a stalemate because "the Czechs [were] refusing to reduce their tax on royalties."[6] Iran's previous "apparent lack of response" to the UK gave way to a "willing[ness] to have talks" in 1974, but later the same year the civil service files record that "our embassy is pressing the Iranians as much as we can."[7] Another example is Mexico, with which the UK requested negotiations in 1978 after an approach to the Inland Revenue from business groups.[8] The next mention in the "state of play" reports is in 1981, which record that the UK had been "told they are not yet ready."[9]

While business lobbying often underpinned the decision to pursue a treaty with another country, the Inland Revenue frequently made a first approach once it saw that a country had begun to negotiate with competitor states. In 1961, for example, the UK sent a draft treaty to Thailand after the latter began to negotiate tax treaties with other countries, even though there was no interest from British businesses.[10] In the early 1970s, it tried again, noting a handful of requests from businesses as well as that Thailand had by that point concluded tax treaties with many competitor countries. After a meeting in 1972 with "the only one who is able to talk about Double Taxation Agreements" in Thailand's revenue department, a British Foreign Office official concluded that, "in principle they would be interested but it was not likely that Thailand would take the initiative."[11] A memo from October 1973 notes that "Thailand does not seem to be very interested in a DTA with the United Kingdom."[12]

Similarly, when the UK approached Bangladesh about a treaty in 1976, a background note in the file states that "there is not much pressure in the United Kingdom for a treaty with Bangladesh,"[13] and that the UK's initiation of the treaty was "partly because other countries had opened negotiations with Bangladesh."[14] Bangladesh's revenue officials were apparently not interested at first, and the UK "made the running," including by applying diplomatic pressure.[15] By the second round of negotiations in Dhaka, the head of state, Ziaur Rahman, was being given daily updates on progress.[16] Nonetheless, the reluctance of Bangladesh's negotiators to surrender their taxing rights is visible in the meeting minutes. A Bangladeshi negotiator argued that the UK should break precedent and allow Bangladesh to retain higher withholding tax rates because it was "practically the poorest of the world's underdeveloped countries," to which his UK counterpart responded that "the United Kingdom did not regard a double taxation convention as a vehicle for giving financial aid, no matter how deserving the partner country."[17]

If the UK was keen to sign treaties with all lower-income countries, but many of them rejected its overtures, this would be consistent with the view that it is policy in the lower-income country that is the primary determinant of the timing of treaty negotiations. The picture painted by the files, however, goes beyond that. The UK actively reached out to certain lower-income countries to urge them to open negotiations, exerting diplomatic pressure where necessary. For many, the decision to respond positively to British overtures was characterized more by acquiescence than by enthusiasm. Excluding renegotiations, three-quarters (seventeen of twenty-three) of the negotiations listed in table 5.1 for which information is available were initiated by the UK. Where lower-income countries made the first move, this was often because they wanted to renegotiate the terms of an existing agreement put in place when that country was a British colony.

Actors and Actions in UK Treaty Making

In this section, I outline the roles of different groups of stakeholders in the decision-making processes surrounding the UK's tax treaties. Specifically, I examine the preferences of tax treaty specialists in the Inland Revenue, who led negotiations, and those of nonspecialists, in particular those in the rest of government. I also consider what happened when these different preferences created conflict between the two groups.

Tax Experts: Dissemination of Technical Standards

For specialists inside the Inland Revenue, the major causal effect of tax treaties was not, despite their formal title of "for the avoidance of double taxation and the prevention of fiscal evasion," the elimination of double taxation (fiscal evasion rarely seems to get a mention either). The reason for this was that the UK, like many other countries, had taken unilateral steps to prevent double taxation of its firms operating overseas by giving them a credit against their UK tax bill for any taxes paid overseas.

Recognition of this dates back to at least 1957, when an Inland Revenue civil servant wrote that, with regard to one treaty, "the United Kingdom taxpayer gets very little benefit out of it: he will get credit for the tax paid in Colombia against the tax due on the same income in this country whether we have an agreement or not."[18] Two decades later, in 1976, a cross-department review of the UK's approach to international double taxation, led by the Inland Revenue, made the case even more boldly: "In the absence of an agreement there is no question of United Kingdom investors being doubly taxed."[19]

What, then, was the purpose of a tax treaty for the Inland Revenue? That same note from 1957 records that, for a board of directors in the UK, "the advantages of a double taxation [agreement] need no stressing."[20] It goes on to argue that a tax treaty "at once assures the directors that they will be taxed according to internationally accepted rules and they will not be subject to discrimination."[21] These are often referred to as "intangible benefits," and they are mentioned by government officials throughout the period under consideration. According to the 1976 review, "These include protection against fiscal discrimination, the establishment of a framework within which the two tax administrations can operate, and the expectation that an overseas authority which has negotiated a treaty will at least try to apply it reasonably." The deputy chairman of the Board of Inland Revenue in 1976 was Alan Lord, who twenty years earlier had represented the UK on the new OEEC committee that would eventually become the OECD's CFA. According to him: "Above all, treaties impose acceptable standards for allocating profits to branches and subsidiaries and for dealing with transfer pricing in countries (some of them within the EEC [European Economic Community]) where such standards would otherwise be absent."[22]

For the specialists, tax treaties were therefore tools through which the UK, which had always taken a prominent role in the development of the international tax system, ensured other countries' participation in it. This would be especially beneficial for British businesses in the case of lower-income countries, including those newly independent, where, as one official wrote, "protection against fiscal discrimination is generally worth more . . . because they are more likely to include deliberately discriminatory fiscal practices in their general law than are developed countries."[23] A memo from as early as 1949 expresses the view that "the United Kingdom particularly has much to gain from the increasing adoption, particularly by under-developed countries, of sound principles of income taxation and from the conclusion on sound lines of conventions for the relief of double taxation."[24] Treaties were largely understood as means to ensure that British firms could be competitive *when they decided to invest*, rather than to make investment in the treaty partner more attractive in the first place. Thus, treaties would increase investment from the UK to the treaty partner, but not by influencing business decisions; rather, they gave British investors a helping hand.

The effect of treaties on outward investment from the UK was not a trivial matter during the 1970s but an important policy question. Treasury policy was to limit the impact of outward FDI on the balance of payments by encouraging it to be done out of retained earnings, investment currency, or foreign currency borrowing. In 1973, at a meeting of the cross-Whitehall Tax Reform Committee handling changes to corporation tax, a Treasury official argued against measures that would prioritize overseas investment, because of the effect on the balance of payments. The concern was about foreign exchange reserves, which could be protected more through income from exports than from direct investment; furthermore, the likely shift in manufacturing abroad as a result of outward investment would increase imports.[25] Discussing this point, the 1976 review concluded that the treaty network at that point "neither encourages nor discourages overseas investment in fiscal terms compared with domestic investment, except where matching credit [i.e., tax sparing clauses] is provided."[26] Around this time, the Inland Revenue was arguing against conceding Brazil's demands for more comprehensive concessions in a tax treaty on the grounds that they "would mean that we were according outward investment a higher priority than hitherto with all that that implied for the balance of payments and the domestic economy."[27]

The community of tax specialists who shared this analysis and these objectives was not limited to the Revenue itself: it extended into the private sector. In December 1971, Alan Davies of Rio Tinto Zinc (RTZ), chair of the tax committee of the Confederation of British Industry (CBI), wrote to Alan Lord. The letter outlined the limitations of the Revenue's current approach to consultation, which was to solicit comments from industry by letter once negotiations were initiated. Davies cited "a peeved feeling on our side that some more confidence would be justified," and argued for more informal discussion about the progress of negotiations.[28] The informal tone of Davies's letter perhaps reflects a personal familiarity with the Inland Revenue officials concerned. For example, he attended meetings of the United Nations Ad Hoc Group of Experts on Tax Treaties between Developed and Developing Countries, representing the ICC, as did Inland Revenue negotiators.[29]

The result was a system of regular quarterly meetings between tax specialists from industry groups (the CBI, British Insurance Association, and Chamber of British Shipping) at which detailed information on the "state of play" in negotiations was divulged, and comments sought on specific topics.[30] The first such meeting took place in March 1972, and they continued for at least the next decade. At each meeting, the Inland Revenue participants were supplied with a status report on current and planned negotiations, which they shared verbally with the business representatives on the condition that the information was not shared outside of the small, expert group. When negotiations reached a difficult point, the matters of contention would often be discussed in this forum. The question of withholding tax clauses in the treaty with Kenya, discussed in the prologue to this book, came up at the very first meeting. The discussions are summarized in the minutes with a statement that "an agreement on some basis preferably with as low a rate as possible was preferable to no agreement at all."[31]

Before finalizing a treaty with Thailand, the Inland Revenue consulted with its tax contacts in the shipping industry, who were concerned about the precedent the agreement would set. A subsequent briefing note for the second round of negotiations stated that "the question is one of principle, and as the amount of money involved is small, we have decided, after consultation with the General Council of British Shipping, to have no Shipping Article in the Convention to avoid providing a precedent with other, and more important, countries."[32]

In contrast, a parallel negotiation with Tanzania broke down over the shipping question after discussions among the same group of experts.[33] The context to this firm line was the creation of a precedent ahead of anticipated negotiations with India, where the sums at stake were much larger.

Thus, British negotiators saw tax treaties primarily as instruments that ensured British overseas investment would be taxed in a manner consistent with the standards set out in the OECD model convention, which they had helped draft. When negotiating with lower-income countries, they commonly encountered situations in which their opposite numbers wanted a greater share of the tax base than the OECD model treaty permitted them, and where the successful conclusion of a tax treaty might depend on some deviation from the OECD approach. Decisions about how to respond to such dilemmas were made by Inland Revenue civil servants in consultation with their fellow tax experts from the business world.

Other Actors: Competition for Outward Investment Opportunities

Here I consider the preferences of nonspecialists, for whom tax treaties were also tools to increase the competitiveness of British firms abroad. A lack of detailed taxation knowledge, frequently lamented both by them and by the specialists, left them to rely on their own ideas, which were not necessarily grounded in facts. This would lead to conflicts, during which the Revenue would sometimes try to convince them that their faith in the effect of tax treaties was misplaced. "There can be little doubt that tax treaties are a means of stimulating trade and investment between the treaty partner countries," wrote the private secretary to the Treasury minister responsible for tax policy in 1976. "On the other hand their importance is sometimes exaggerated."[34] The UK's lead negotiator noted in 1974, referring to Brazil, that "we should not over emphasise the importance of a DTA. It generally only affects income *flowing* from one country to another whereas in the short term a company will not remit much in the way of profits and will not be too bothered in the absence of an agreement."[35]

Most civil service nonspecialists who engaged with tax treaty matters during the 1970s wanted British firms that were eligible for investment-promoting tax relief in lower-income countries to receive a corresponding credit (often referred to as tax-sparing credit) against UK tax, to ensure that they could retain the benefit of the tax relief when they repatriated their profits. As the 1976 review notes, in outlining the priorities of different departments, "the main cash benefit for the investor [from a tax treaty] is matching credit for pioneer reliefs."[36] The difficulty was that this was not the Inland Revenue's priority from tax treaties, and at times (as in the case of Brazil, below) the two priorities even came into conflict.

A good example can be seen in the negotiations with Zambia, one of the few cases in which negotiations were initiated by the lower-income country. When the Revenue consulted businesses ahead of these negotiations, tax-sparing provisions emerged as a priority for UK firms.[37] British negotiators did not disclose this to Zambia, which had already indicated an interest in a tax-sparing clause when requesting negotiations.[38] Instead, they tried to use Zambia's desire for a tax-sparing clause as a bargaining chip, offering it if Zambia would accept an agreement that prevented it from charging any withholding tax on royalty payments.[39] Zambia chose instead to keep its 10 percent withholding tax and forgo the tax-sparing clause, and so the British negotiators had to write to their Zambian counterparts soon after the conclusion of negotiations to unilaterally offer the tax-sparing credit that they had previously withheld, claiming that they had subsequently been pushed by another country to offer similar terms.[40]

The Inland Revenue sought to keep input from other departments limited and compartmentalized, and did not welcome their attempts to influence its priorities. The Treasury, DTI, and Foreign Office would each be consulted on treaties once negotiations were opened, and on specific questions concerning their content, but the Revenue would often reject their requests to be able to influence its priorities.

During late 1972 and 1973, an extraordinary correspondence opened up between the FCO and Board of Trade, on the one hand, and the Inland Revenue, on the other. The former were frustrated by their inability to influence the latter's negotiating priorities. At a cross-Whitehall meeting in April 1972, the Revenue had merely invited them to submit "shopping lists" for treaties they would like it to negotiate.[41] "We have already forfeited opportunities for investment in Brazil, notably to the Germans and Japan and, as a matter of commercial policy, it is important that we should not place our traders at a disadvantage when seeking out investment opportunities in the future," argued one official from the Board of Trade in February 1973. "As you know, we have been concerned that the corporation tax system should not so limit the scope for tax sparing as to damage the UK's ability to export to and invest in developing (and highly competitive) overseas markets. For this reason, we place great importance on the conclusion, as quickly as possible, of double tax agreements with our developing trading partners which allow for tax sparing."[42]

The Revenue rebuffed this pressure, even refusing to share a list of current negotiating priorities or negotiations that were under way, because "a high degree of confidentiality attaches to our negotiations with particular countries."[43] The reference to confidentiality is ironic, because this correspondence took place at the same time as the Revenue had begun quarterly meetings with tax specialists from businesses, at which exactly this information was disclosed.

"I find the Inland Revenue's attitude and behaviour quite extraordinary," wrote an official in the FCO's financial relations department, as part of correspondence that passed between these other departments. "I cannot imagine that any other department in Whitehall would behave in this way. Nor would we have allowed any other Department to get away with behaviour like this for quite so long. I am quite clear we must call a halt now."[44] Another lamented "a dispiriting and unfruitful confrontation with the Inland Revenue."[45] The problem for the FCO, in particular, was that it lacked a coherent position within itself, and the technical expertise to develop one. "The subject is difficult and mastering it is undoubtedly time-consuming" mused one FCO official.[46]

It was not only officials from other departments who had trouble influencing Inland Revenue officials: their own ministers faced the same problem. In general, politicians had little involvement in tax treaties at all. At the start of the 1970s, negotiators worked within enabling powers set by Parliament and would seek ministerial guidance only when making a concession that had not previously been given in negotiations. There seems to have been no political involvement in the decision with whom to negotiate, and the minister in charge, the financial secretary to the Treasury, usually did not see a treaty until bringing it before Parliament for ratification.

The technical complexity of tax treaties was inevitably a barrier to effective political scrutiny, but this must surely have been combined with the short tenure of financial secretaries: eleven people occupied the position during the 1960s and 1970s, with an average tenure of two years.[47] As a civil service memo from 1975 notes: "It is however a long time since the agreements took their present form and the Treasury Ministers of today have had no experience in this field outside government."[48]

The longest-serving financial secretary, Robert Sheldon, in post from February 1975 to April 1979, was also the only one for whom the Treasury archives record any attempt to scrutinize the activities of his civil servants on their treaty-making activities. In December 1975, Sheldon was being briefed ahead of a parliamentary debate at which he was to propose the ratification of several tax treaties. He expressed concern that he was expected to propose an agreement in Parliament that he had not seen beforehand. He suggested that parliamentary approval be dropped and replaced with greater ministerial oversight.[49] At a subsequent meeting in May 1976, Sheldon wanted "to reassure himself in the absence of quantifiable data that when he is asked to recommend a double taxation agreement to the House as a reasonably balanced deal he can happily do this."[50]

During the December 1975 debate, Sheldon undertook to look into the costs and benefits of tax treaties. This commitment provoked lengthy exchanges within the civil service, both to examine costing methodologies and to explain what officials saw as the problem with this approach. "What might be a reasonably balanced agreement as a whole," Sheldon's private secretary wrote to him, "might appear otherwise if the disadvantages were more easily quantifiable than the advantages." Furthermore, such costing information might undermine negotiations. Demonstrating that the UK had obtained a good deal might provoke the other country to seek to change it, while a bad deal would set a precedent.[51]

These notes indicate the difficulty faced by a minister trying to exert some influence over a policy area with which he was unfamiliar. During the mid-1970s, the UK had been seeking to amend the articles of its tax treaties covering the taxation of dividends, to reflect changes to its corporation tax system. The civil servant who first briefed Sheldon commented, "I got the impression that he does not realise—or did not until I pointed it out to him—that double taxation agreements also deal with other matters than dividends. . . . He seemed surprised when I told him we had sixty plus agreements in operation."[52]

This lack of understanding is also apparent in the minutes of the May 1976 meeting. Sheldon questioned "what the OECD Model was and what we would do if it turned out not to provide an advantageous pattern for the UK."[53] This question illustrates a lack of basic familiarity with the area, and is all the more surprising because Sheldon's brief would also have included ministerial responsibility for the UK's input into the OECD model. To make matters worse, Sheldon cut the meeting short before officials could give a full explanation.

A third category of nonspecialist stakeholder was those within business, who were evidently very keen to influence UK policy. At the nonspecialist level, businesses were able to influence the positions of other parts of government, including the FCO and DTI, but this rarely translated into treaties. Geographic departments in the FCO, in particular, were often persuaded by businesses, which lobbied British embassies, to advocate new British tax treaties. For example, "UK finance houses and business interests are adamant that we are losing a significant amount of business in Spain because there is no double taxation agreement," wrote an official in the FCO's southern Europe department.[54] These positions fed into the central FCO departments, in particular the economists' department and financial relations department, which as we have seen were furious that the Inland Revenue would not heed their concerns about the competitiveness of British businesses. Meanwhile, the Inland Revenue seemed content to divide and rule the geographical departments.

Business lobbying via these departments met with limited success, partly because those other parts of government had limited influence on the Revenue but also because one part of the private sector undermined the other, a fault line that sometimes ran within, rather than between, businesses. As the Brazil case study, below, will illustrate, private sector tax specialists sometimes directly contradicted their nonspecialist colleagues when in discussion with the Inland Revenue. While some of these specialists evidently felt it necessary to sacrifice the intellectual purity and consensus of the epistemic project for the sectional interests of their own firm, in many cases the business-Revenue consultations were more a strategic discussion of how to manage their respective nonspecialist constituencies.[55]

A memo from the CBI to the DTI, covering a wide range of policy and not written by tax specialists, states that tax treaty "negotiations should not be left exclusively to the Inland Revenue (whose main concern is naturally the minimisation of losses to the Exchequer)."[56] A year later, an Inland Revenue official was "subjected to a two-hour intense grilling" by CBI representatives who were not tax specialists at a cross-Whitehall consultative meeting. They had apparently "suggested that future negotiations for double taxation agreements would better be dealt with by a department other than the Inland Revenue since the negotiations were currently carried out for the United Kingdom by narrow specialists who were so blinkered by the technicalities of taxation that they failed to see the full view of the picture."[57] The CBI delegation also expressed the view that the Inland Revenue's consultation with tax experts from industry "was not really satisfactory since it was restricted to 'taxmen.'"[58]

The "taxmen" from industry felt obliged to apologize for their colleagues' actions in subsequent discussions with the Inland Revenue.[59] Later that year, a covering note from the chair of the CBI's tax committee to the Inland Revenue accompanying a copy of the CBI's submission to the UK-Egypt joint economic commission made another apology for the author's nonspecialist colleagues. "We were intending to discuss this question with you before we let the Department of Trade have any comments," it said, but short notice had prevented it. "Our overseas Department receives such requests from the Department of Trade from time to time and we are now trying to ensure that any answer is given by the tax experts who attend the joint CBI/ICC Working Group meetings at Somerset House [the Inland Revenue office] rather than by those who are not too familiar with the technical implications. This should avoid any future complications over such representations."[60]

We can see, therefore, that nonspecialist actors had different priorities than those of the Inland Revenue and the tax committees from business with which the Revenue consulted. Civil servants outside the Inland Revenue, as well as the business lobbyists with whom they interacted, were frustrated by their inability to influence the Inland Revenue.

Sample Negotiations

The previous section demonstrated two different motivations among different stakeholders for the UK pursuit of tax treaties. The tax treaty specialists sought to surround British businesses with the protective shield of OECD standards, while others focused on the specific tax advantages that British businesses would gain and the competitive edge this might give them. Tax competition driven by nonspecialists faced a potential "firewall" if it met opposition from specialists.[61] In this section I extend the analysis with greater specificity, by focusing on individual treaty negotiations. Egypt is an example of a successful negotiation, Nigeria of a renegotiation, and Brazil of an unsuccessful stalemate. In all three cases, we see evidence that the preferences of British businesses were the primary motivating factor behind individual negotiations. We also see, however, that these priorities had to coincide with the range of options deemed acceptable by Inland Revenue negotiators. In both the Nigerian and Brazilian examples, the lower-income country sought to negotiate on its own terms, not those dictated by the OECD model. While British businesses were desperate, the Inland Revenue held firm to its view of the "acceptable standards" a treaty should contain, and the only difference in outcomes between the two cases was that Nigeria backed down while Brazil held firm.

Egypt

The UK's 1976 treaty with Egypt is a typical example among those examined for this chapter. It resulted from pressure exerted on the UK government by British businesses operating in Egypt. Influential businesses sought a treaty either to limit Egypt's ability to tax their operations in accordance with rules set out in the OECD model or to pursue a tax-sparing clause. They explicitly pointed to the competitive disadvantage they faced in Egypt in the absence of a functioning treaty. Negotiations took some time to get off the ground, because Egyptian revenue officials were concerned about the revenue losses; yet when negotiations took place, Egypt did not have the technical capacity to defend its tax base. British officials, meanwhile, did not engage enthusiastically until the CBI informed them that British businesses were keen to see an agreement.

Egypt and the UK exchanged correspondence about tax treaties sporadically during the 1950s and 1960s, without ever concluding an agreement. Each side took the initiative at different times, while changes in civil service staff or government, reforms to tax policy, and at one point the Suez crisis caused changes in priorities.[62] By the late 1960s a strong preference for a treaty had emerged from the two national airlines, both of which were state owned.[63] In March 1969, the Egyptian embassy in London formally requested a limited DTA, which would exempt each country's national airlines from taxation in the other.[64] But later that year, when an embassy official spoke with Egyptian tax authority officials, they denied all knowledge of or interest in this proposal, and talks never went ahead.[65] The only party to seem aggrieved by this was the British Overseas Airways Company (BOAC), which declared itself "bitterly disappointed" that talks had failed, because Egyptian demands for taxation on it were "unreasonable" and "impossible."[66]

In February 1971, the UK formally requested negotiations on a comprehensive tax treaty, noting that "interest has been expressed by a number of British companies."[67] This followed a letter from the British embassy stating, "I have twice heard suggestions that a general double taxation agreement would be both welcome and useful" because some UK firms had faced "harsh tax assessments."[68] However, the request does not seem to have had the support of the Inland Revenue, whose officials observed in an internal memo: "The importance of a comprehensive agreement with Egypt is not clear. We have not called for representations [from industry] as such and neither have any requests been made to us from outside concerns apart from BOAC to take the initiative."[69] The request appears to have met with a similar fate in Egypt. According to a report from the British embassy in Cairo, "A tax official, on discovering that such an agreement would benefit Britain rather than Egypt because EgyptAir succeeds in never declaring a profit in London for tax purposes, whereas BOAC usually faces a stiff tax bill in Cairo, had decided to sit on the notes and do nothing."[70]

The logjam was finally broken four years later, when a joint UK-Egypt economic commission was under way, managed by the Department of Trade, covering a variety of areas of economic cooperation. The CBI's position document on the economic commission recorded "a wide expression of interest in a double taxation treaty with Egypt and there would seem to be little doubt that if a satisfactory agreement can be reached there would be substantial interest among those members we have consulted, in investment in Egypt."[71] The tax treaty was negotiated in one two-week meeting in May 1976. An Inland Revenue note indicates that the Egyptians "were willing to be led by us most of the time in the drafting" and "for the most part the Egyptians were content" with the British positions.[72]

Egypt's interest in the treaty, however, appears to have been quite weak. The ratification process in Egypt dragged on for years after 1976, during which time it became apparent that the treaty's real immediate impact was in increasing British firms' competitive position. A meeting with a construction firm in 1976 records its frustration that competitor firms from treaty countries benefited from tax-sparing provisions. "They were worried that the absence of a treaty would mean them losing an order and not getting a foothold in Egypt."[73] A letter from BOAC, now British Airways (BA), in 1978 complains that "BA are now the only major airline in Cairo not exempted from Egyptian tax."[74] In early 1979, an Inland Revenue document notes that, in the light of delays at the Egyptian end, "we are under some pressure from United Kingdom companies with interests in Egypt to push the convention through Parliament and into force as quickly as possible."[75] The agreement was ratified by Egypt the same year, and by the UK in early 1980.

Brazil

The UK devoted far more time and effort to negotiations with Brazil during the 1970s than almost any other lower-income country. It is a negative outlier, an unusual case in which strong pressure from business lobby groups did not translate into an agreement, even though there was no organized opposition. When talks were suspended in 1976, the Inland Revenue acknowledged that "it is British investors who will be the sufferers."[76] The transnational expertise perspective outlined in chapter 4 offers an explanation for this outcome. The British position was that it could only conclude an agreement with Brazil, "providing for significant amelioration of aspects of their tax code that run clearly counter to OECD principles; and if they are not interested, so be it."[77] This nonetheless poses the question why nonexpert interest group pressure was ineffective in the UK, when several other OECD countries had accepted Brazil's non-OECD terms.

Tax treaties with Brazil were in strong demand. Foreign businesses wanted to be part of the country's "economic miracle," and this allowed Brazil to adopt a "take it or leave it" approach to certain unconventional demands. Talks between the UK and Brazil had failed in 1967 but were taken up again beginning in 1972. A particularly difficult issue for the UK was Brazil's insistence that the UK grant extensive tax-sparing concessions. In common with many UK treaties, this would mean crediting the value of a Brazilian tax exemption against the UK company's tax bill as if it had paid full Brazilian tax, but unusually it would also mean doing the same for the reductions in withholding taxes on cross-border payments that Brazil would be able to levy on British investors as a consequence of a treaty. In the reported words of a Brazilian negotiator, "Whilst Brazil does not want the United Kingdom to lose tax, she cannot allow the United Kingdom to collect more tax as a result of the convention."[78] Such a concession required an amendment to section 497(3) of the Income and Corporate Taxes Act of 1970 in the UK, the provision that gave effect to tax treaties, and this was passed in 1976.

The second Brazilian demand was more difficult.[79] Under Brazilian domestic law, firms had to pay a withholding tax on the gross value of any royalty paid to a foreign recipient. Unusually, however, they were not permitted to deduct the value of the royalty payments when calculating their net profits. They also paid tax on the payments through corporate income tax, leading to a high effective tax rate. While the UK's unilateral double tax relief system gave investors a credit for taxes paid abroad, the effective rate in Brazil exceeded this credit, and so the company bore the cost, reducing its competitiveness. Brazil insisted that any tax treaty leave this state of affairs intact, though it was in direct contravention of the OECD model's provisions. Several OECD countries had reached agreements with Brazil that permitted this practice to continue, because other concessions obtained in treaty negotiations, such as lower withholding tax rates, gave their firms a competitive advantage.[80] This both increased the pressure on the Inland Revenue from British businesses and reduced its leverage in negotiations with Brazil. British companies "are undoubtedly at a competitive disadvantage as compared with companies from other countries," noted a background brief in August 1974.[81]

Businesses did not directly lobby the Inland Revenue; rather, they went via other ministries. "Pressure for an agreement with Brazil comes from the DTI, ODA, our Embassy in Brazil and, although perhaps to a lesser extent, from the CBI, in particular RTZ," wrote an Inland Revenue official in November 1973.[82] In October 1974, a memo from the Department of Industry to the Inland Revenue pressed the case for a treaty, citing "specific evidence of orders being lost by British companies apparently because of their relatively lower post-tax returns forcing them to quote higher prices in compensation."[83] With no movement by December, the Department of Trade weighed in, beginning a correspondence between its secretary of state, Peter Shore, and Chancellor of the Exchequer Denis Healey.[84]

As the pressure from business lobbyists on other government departments ratcheted up, tax specialists within British businesses reassured the Revenue that they were broadly in agreement with its view that the Brazilian terms were unacceptable.[85] In 1974 the Inland Revenue called a special meeting with its regular interlocutors, tax specialists within British multinationals. The latter group agreed with the Revenue that Brazil's terms on royalties would be detrimental in the long term, in view of the precedent that would be set:

> The CBI Secretariat (but not the Overseas Tax Panel) are well aware of the powerful trade and political pressures in favour of having an agreement (apparently *any* agreement) with Brazil which he [Paul Moran of the CBI] thought could lead to an explosion in the autumn. His personal view was that the Revenue and Treasury Ministers could be under pressures from other Ministers which might lead to an agreement, in spite of the unsatisfactory features that had been discussed. Much of the pressure is based on ignorance of the effects of unilateral relief and of the likely terms of a treaty, and it appears that much of it is generated in Brazil and by companies whose only overseas operations are, or are likely to be, in Brazil and which operate on the basis of official handouts.[86]

Minutes of the meeting and a follow-up letter from the CBI record the industry tax experts' frustration at being unable to correct their colleagues' "ignorance" because of the confidential nature of their meetings with the Inland Revenue.[87] Inland Revenue memos contrast the "non-fiscal voices" within the CBI with those of "the CBI's Tax Committee, as a Committee of tax experts" and observe that "the CBI will no doubt have to consider how to deal with the situation in which it is speaking with two voices."[88]

In 1976, British negotiators were able to travel to Brasilia with their new legislative mandate on tax sparing, but with instructions "to refrain from agreeing to the unacceptable features of Brazilian law which they wish to enshrine in the treaty, but to avoid a breakdown in the talks."[89] While the negotiations did not create any further progress, the visit was illuminating for revenue officials. In negotiations, the head Brazilian negotiator (as reported by British negotiators) "frankly admitted that the treatment of royalties was unsound tax practice but made it clear his hands were tied," because of what the minutes describe as "a political decision."[90]

The Brazilian officials' frustration at political constraints preventing an agreement is revealed more sharply still by a note relating comments made by another negotiator: "Dornelles' No2 (Noqueira) at a dinner given for us last night by the Ministry of Finance told me that they are extremely anxious to get a treaty with the U.K. because their chances of getting one with the U.S.A, Switzerland or the Netherlands are ranked as nil. Switzerland is now second largest investor and will not even discuss a treaty on 'German package' lines. The U.S.A. have an annual meeting with the Brazilians for window dressing purposes only. The Netherlands merely write once a year to enquire whether there has been any change in Brazil's policy."[91]

After the negotiations, British officials held several meetings with business representatives in Rio de Janeiro. They reached the conclusion that, with one small exception that could probably be resolved unilaterally, there was no genuine problem with double taxation for most firms, despite the idiosyncrasies of the Brazilian tax system. "The impression all three of us got," wrote the chief negotiator, "was that the business community in Brazil were doing very well indeed and that a tax treaty would be a bonus rather than a matter of life or death to them. . . . They would not be at all impressed with [a treaty] which served only to confirm the undesirable features of Brazilian law."[92] He concluded that the FCO's picture of British businesses' views may have been distorted by the Consul General in Rio de Janeiro, who had become "positively paranoiac about the whole question of a tax treaty with Brazil and has got past the stage, if he was ever there, of being able to consider objectively the arguments against accepting the Brazilians' terms."[93]

The Brazil files stop at the beginning of the 1980s, but the same debate continues. In 1992, in a separate file, an Inland Revenue official wrote that "Brazil continues to be the big prize: but it is not ripe for an immediate approach and what indications there are suggest that it will be a difficult nut to crack."[94] The absence of a treaty with Brazil is still raised by British business lobby groups today, and was mentioned in Parliament in 2014, when the UK-Zambia treaty was ratified: according to the minister responsible, the UK and Brazil still cannot agree on terms.[95] The Inland Revenue's position is, in effect, that the benefits of maintaining an influential OECD model outweigh the costs to particular UK firms operating in Brazil, and that those costs may in any event be exaggerated.

The debate over the UK-Brazil tax treaty illustrates that the preferences and instrumental power of corporate capital in the UK were not monolithic but varied depending on technical knowledge. Had the aim of the UK's tax treaty negotiations been simply to give British firms a competitive edge by lowering their effective tax rate in Brazil, as British firms in Brazil were lobbying for via the British embassy and the DTI, an agreement would have been possible. But it would have come at the cost of implicitly endorsing Brazil's approach to taxing royalty payments. This would have undermined the longer-term project of exporting norms embodied in the focal point of the OECD model, which motivated members of the international tax community both in the Inland Revenue and in businesses.

Nigeria

Unlike Egypt and Brazil, Nigeria already had a tax treaty with the UK when it first requested negotiations in 1963. This may explain why it took twenty-four years to conclude a new one. The existing treaty was a colonial-era agreement that was, naturally, strongly biased in favor of the (now former) colonial power. While Nigeria's request for a new agreement related primarily to its desire that inward investors from the UK be eligible for tax-sparing credits in the UK,[96] the Inland Revenue had by 1969 decided not to push forward with renegotiations "since the UK would only stand to lose by a new agreement which was bound to be less favourable than the old."[97] As in the case of Brazil, this cool attitude came against opposition from the High Commission and Foreign Office, which, like the Nigerians, favored a renegotiation to introduce tax-sparing credits.[98]

When negotiations began in earnest a decade later, it was because Nigeria had announced the abrogation of all its colonial-era tax treaties, and the concurrent imposition of new taxes on air and shipping companies.[99] A telegram from the Inland Revenue to the British embassy in Lagos noted that the government "is very concerned at serious implications of termination of Double Taxation Agreement for British airline and shipping companies," and asked the embassy to request immediate renegotiations "in view of the strength of representation already being made here at senior official level and the probability of escalation to Ministerial level in the near future."[100]

The Nigerian government was willing to sign a new treaty, but according to an Inland Revenue official, its proposed draft "would require us to make concessions which are far in advance of the terms which other developing countries have accepted in treaties with us."[101] Progress was made in the first round of talks, including an agreement limited to air and shipping that relieved some of the immediate pressure on negotiators, but at the second round soon after February 1979 it became apparent to British negotiators that "an agreement on the terms offered would have been unattractive in itself and would have served as an unfortunate precedent for future agreements."[102]

The main concern was the rate of tax that could be imposed on fees for technical consultancy and management services, on which Nigeria had declared what one negotiator explained was a "total war."[103] The British economic arguments about the distortionary effect of taxes on management fees carried little weight because Nigeria's position was to use tax to discourage their payment at all. The Revenue discussed the situation in confidence with tax experts within the CBI, who "share our reluctance to reach an agreement until the Nigerians make concessions."[104]

The UK view did not change after 1980, but Nigeria moderated its position, and a new treaty was initialed in 1982. However, the treaty was not actually signed until 1987. The problem seems to have been with the Nigerian treaty approval process, which, unusually, required parliamentary ratification before signature. Although the negotiators on both sides were happy with the treaty, Nigerian officials in other ministries did not take any action to progress it, according to correspondence in the files.[105] Thus, the signature and ratification were blocked by actors outside the specialist treaty negotiating community.

In both the Nigerian and Brazilian cases, the UK dug in its heels and refused to deviate from the position set out in the OECD model. Why did Nigeria capitulate, while Brazil continued to resist? Drawing conclusions about the negotiating partner's preferences from the UK files is difficult, but we can at least speculate. The Brazilian officials claimed they wanted to accept the UK's terms, and accepted the rationale behind the British position, but they were constrained by political factors preventing them from accommodating the UK. Nigeria's cancellation of a treaty and five-year delay between initialing and signature indicate that—like Egypt—it was more concerned with maximizing tax revenues than with any urgent need to sign a tax treaty. So why did it make the concessions? The files do not contain an answer, other than that the climbdown came after Nigeria had negotiated with a clutch of OECD countries, opening up the possibility that its negotiators had learned what higher-income countries considered "acceptable" tax practices during earlier negotiations. An internal British note describes the original draft proposed by Nigeria as "an opening bid from a country which has had little recent experience in negotiating double tax conventions."[106]

Conclusion

The UK in the 1970s was a quintessential example of a capital-exporting country negotiating a wide tax treaty network. This is usually assumed in policy discourse and in the academic literature to have been a result of competition among lower-income countries to attract British investment. By examining civil service documents, I have demonstrated that this interpretation is incomplete. British firms were at a competitive advantage in any given host market with respect to firms from other countries if those other countries had a tax treaty with the host and the UK did not. As a result, it was usually the UK, not the lower-income country, that made the first move, and indeed the UK was frequently turned down by lower-income countries.

A further disaggregation into different stakeholders allows us to see the two potentially competing ways in which this competition effect worked. For the Inland Revenue negotiators and other tax specialists in the UK (and, the files suggest, their colleagues in other OECD countries), UK firms would benefit if the host country had to follow the "acceptable fiscal standards" set out in the OECD model. In contrast, pressure from businesses was often driven by the pursuit of short-term or parochial gains, especially tax-sparing clauses. Notably, since the UK began to exempt the foreign profits of British multinationals in the mid-2000s, the tax-sparing clauses that motivated both business lobbyists and lower-income countries are now largely redundant.

Importantly, the in-group for decision making within the UK was not defined by occupation but by specialism. Business lobbying was only effective insofar as the Revenue could be convinced that the terms of an agreement were consistent with its overall aim, because the UK treaty-making apparatus gave it a veto, and was further insulated by the technical obscurity of tax treaties that prevented other stakeholders from influencing its activities. Private sector officials who had a tax specialism were brought inside this tent, and their views were influential in decisions made by the Inland Revenue in the Brazil and Nigeria cases, as well as numerous others. Information readily supplied to the business tax experts was at the same time withheld from government officials from other departments on the grounds of confidentiality, and their views dismissed as "ignorant." Even the government ministers supervising tax officials were unable to exert influence because they lacked the technical understanding.

Having focused on the capital-exporting side of the negotiation, the book switches to a focus on capital importers in the next two chapters. These cases support the contention that tax competition is a strategic interaction between capital exporters and capital importers, but they also demonstrate how the latter operates. Just as in the UK, technical knowledge influences preferences concerning tax treaties. In the lower-income country case studies, we see how this can vary over time within the same country, as well as between different stakeholder groups at a given moment in time.

ZAMBIA

They ask for an arm and a leg and you give them both legs.

—Finance Ministry official, Zambia

This chapter complements the previous one by considering the other end of negotiations, in a lower-income country. One of the few negotiations between the UK and a lower-income country during the 1970s that was initiated by the lower-income country itself was the 1972 treaty with Zambia. In comparison with other agreements signed by the UK at the time, this was an easy negotiation for the UK, in which Zambia did not gain an outcome that protected many of its source taxing rights. Zambia permits us a within-case comparison, by looking at two different time periods: the 1970s, when Zambia was an enthusiastic negotiator, and the 2000s and 2010s, when it was not.

This first UK agreement was part of a flurry of negotiations at the beginning of the 1970s, and during that decade Zambia signed ten tax treaties, with countries of Western Europe and Japan. No other sub-Saharan country signed as many: Kenya and Tanzania, the next closest by number of signatures, signed six each.[1] Yet as figure 6.1 shows, on average, Zambia's early 1970's treaties imposed far greater restrictions on its source taxing rights than those signed by other African countries, and also Zambia's later treaties. In Zambia in the 1970s, a context where nobody in the bureaucracy had a detailed knowledge of international tax, the tax treaties myth took hold, but without the commensurate negotiating capability. The large tax revenue from Zambia's mining industry during the early 1970s meant that the tax costs of the treaties Zambia was negotiating were less important to those driving the negotiations.

In contrast, from democratization in 1991 until the Movement for Multi-party Democracy (MMD) finally lost power in 2011, a period when sub-Saharan

FIGURE 6.1. Negotiated content of tax treaties signed by sub-Saharan countries, 1970–85

Source: Martin Hearson, "Tax Treaties Explorer," 2020, http://treaties.tax.

countries signed 313 treaties among them, Zambia signed just three, with China, Mauritius, and the Seychelles. Ministers and senior officials, who were veto players in the ratification process, were concerned about the fiscal costs of tax treaties, because Zambia's tax-to-GDP ratio had declined since the 1970s and multinational corporate tax was becoming increasingly politicized. Tax treaty officials, exposed to external advice and socializing environments, formed an agenda for treaty negotiation and renegotiation. But they were blocked by nonspecialists, whose concern about protecting tax revenues made them skeptical. From 2011 onward, there was an alignment between technical officials and their leadership, resulting in a program of renegotiations and only three further treaties, all with African countries.

The discussion of the earlier time period primarily uses historical documentary sources. These include negotiation correspondence and meeting minutes from Zambia's negotiation with the UK, obtained from the British National Archives, and informal intelligence on Zambia's broader treaty negotiation program, from the same files and from US diplomatic cables.[2] I also use written accounts from individuals involved in economic policymaking in Zambia at the time, and official documents published by the Zambian government—in particular, the annual reports of its commissioner of taxes, which include sections on tax treaty negotiations. I was also able to speak by telephone and email with two former advisers to the Zambian government during the 1970s who have published work about their experiences, Charles Irish and Andrew Sardanis.[3]

The data for the later time period are drawn from fifteen semi-structured interviews. Fieldwork in Lusaka followed a snowball sampling approach, beginning from contacts made through NGOs and at international meetings. Interviews were conducted with a total of three current and two former officials drawn from the finance ministry and tax authority, including those with responsibility for treaty negotiations in these two institutions during the later waves of negotiations. These were triangulated through interviews with three tax advisers in the private sector, two British officials familiar with the Zambia-UK renegotiation, two expatriate technical assistance providers, and several other stakeholders from NGOs and academia in Zambia. These interviews have all been anonymized, at the request of some government interviewees.

The Early Years: 1970–84

Zambia's first tax treaty after independence was with regional neighbors in the EAC, in 1968. After this, it sought to obtain new treaties with higher-income countries, focusing first on countries with which it had not inherited an agreement from colonial times. This first wave of negotiations included Japan, Ireland, Italy, Germany, Denmark, and (unsuccessfully) India and Pakistan (table 6.1). These negotiating priorities follow quite closely the pattern of Zambia's main sources of foreign investment at the time (table 6.2). While the signatures came in the early 1970s, many of the negotiations appear, technically, to have taken place before this date, as the detailed timeline of treaty negotiations in table 6.1 shows.

In his 1968 report, the commissioner of taxes announced a plan to review and renegotiate the country's colonial-era agreements.[4] At independence in 1964, Zambia, like other former British colonies, had inherited a set of tax treaties signed on its behalf by Britain. There were six treaties with European countries, one with the United States, and a collective one with Kenya, Tanzania, and Uganda—the EAC countries. Colonial-era agreements between higher-income and lower-income countries tended to restrict the latter's right to tax quite considerably, in a manner that was inconsistent with the newly founded countries' desire to finance themselves, a state of affairs that provoked many lower-income countries to cancel or renegotiate those treaties.[5]

TABLE 6.1. Zambian negotiations, 1970–81

PARTNER	COLONIAL AGREEMENT INHERITED?	NEGOTIATIONS OPENED	AGREEMENT REACHED	SIGNED	IN FORCE
Japan	No	1967	1968	1970	1971
Ireland	No	1967	1968	1971	1972
Italy	No	1968	1971	1973	*
Germany	No	1968	1971	1974	1976
Denmark	No	1971	1972	1974	1975
Norway	Yes	1971	1971	1971	1973
United Kingdom	Yes	1971	1972	1972	1973
France	Yes	1971	*	*	*
Sweden	Yes	1971	1971	1974	1976
United States	Yes	1972	*	*	*
Netherlands	Yes	1978	1978	1978	1982
Switzerland	Yes	*	*	*	*
Finland	No	1979	1979	1979	1986
India	No	1968	?	1981	1981

Source: Reports of Zambia Commissioner of Taxes, 1967–74; IBFD, "IBFD Tax Research Platform," 2020, http://research.ibfd.org/.
* = Treaty not concluded
? = Date not known

TABLE 6.2. Foreign investors in Zambia's state-owned enterprises, 1974

COUNTRY	COLONIAL AGREEMENT INHERITED?	INDUSTRY
Canada	No	Mining, brewing
Germany	No	Chemicals
Italy	No	Road transport, oil & gas, manufacturing, engineering
Japan	No	Chemicals
Liechtenstein	No	Manufacturing
Romania	No	Mining
South Africa	Yes	Mining
Sweden	Yes	Manufacturing
Tanzania (government)	Yes	Road transport, oil & gas
UK	Yes	Mining, import/export houses, oil & gas, brewing, sugar, chemicals, manufacturing, building supplies, milling
United States	Yes	Mining, manufacturing

Source: Timothy M. Shaw, "The Foreign Policy System of Zambia," *African Studies Review* 19, no. 1 (1976): 44–46.

The Zambian review seems to have taken several years to get off the ground, and most of the renegotiations took place in around 1971–72.[6] Not every one of Zambia's treaty partners agreed to reopen its existing treaty with Zambia: an attempt to renegotiate with France in particular was unsuccessful. Some recently independent countries, such as Kenya, Uganda, and later Nigeria, chose to abrogate their treaties in such circumstances, to force countries to the table and secure a better deal; others, such as Malawi, concluded that renegotiation was not a priority at all.[7] Zambia, on the other hand, opted for a piecemeal approach, renegotiating individual treaties to replace old agreements where it could. As a result, its colonial-era agreements with France and Switzerland have remained in force.

Competition for Inward Investment

What were Zambian negotiators trying to achieve? It is clear that investment promotion was a priority. One of the first acts passed by the new government of Zambia was the 1965 Pioneer Industries (Relief from Income Tax) Act, which granted tax incentives to encourage investment in sectors outside the dominant mining sector, and in the nonmining areas of the country.[8] Many foreign investors were unable to secure the full benefits of these tax incentives, however, because their lower tax bills in Zambia simply led to higher tax bills in their home countries.

Zambia thought that the inclusion of a tax-sparing provision in a tax treaty would resolve this issue, giving full effect to the incentives outlined in the 1965 Pioneer Industries Act. All eleven treaties concluded between Zambia and OECD member countries during the 1970s and 1980s either provided explicitly for tax-sparing credits or contained provisions that had the same effect.[9] The priority accorded to the tax-sparing clause is illustrated in the formal letter from Zambia to the UK requesting that negotiations be opened. "In recently negotiated Agreements, Zambia has followed substantially the O.E.C.D. Draft Convention and it is suggested that any new Agreement should substantially follow this Draft Convention. Zambia would, in particular, wish to discuss matters arising from the operation of the Zambian Pioneer Industries (Relief from Income Tax) Act."[10]

While the treaties may have improved the effectiveness of Zambia's investment promotion measures, by the time that they were concluded they also undermined some of its newer policies toward foreign investors. From 1968 onward, Zambia attempted to balance investment promotion with other concerns: preventing the repatriation of capital by investors, increasing the participation of Zambian entrepreneurs in the country's economic development, and rebalancing the government's tax base away from large but volatile mining revenues. The reform agenda began with President Kenneth Kaunda's 1968 "Mulungushi" and "'Matero" declarations, which announced the partial nationalization of the nonmining and mining industries, respectively.[11]

According to Andrew Sardanis, an expatriate civil servant who helped design them, the goal of the Mulungushi reforms was "to give space to African business-men to develop away from competition from better financed and more experi-enced foreign-owned enterprises."[12] A *Financial Times* journalist, Antony Martin, argued at the time that the reforms were inspired in part by "a growing awareness that it would be futile for Zambia to rely primarily on foreign investment for its development."[13]

As the price of copper began to fall in 1971–72, the government tightened exchange controls and imposed import licensing restrictions to tackle its declining balance-of-payments deficit.[14] There was growing concern that, as Ann Seidman explained in 1974, "an increasing portion of the after-tax surpluses in the private sector was removed from the country—even after the economic reforms of 1968 and 1969—largely in the way of profits, interest, dividends, compensation for government acquisition of shares in industries, and salaries for expatriates. Together these totaled almost K200 million in 1971 . . . about a third of Zambia's investible surpluses."[15]

Kaunda delivered a speech in 1973 criticizing the mining companies, complain-ing among other things that "in the last three and a half years . . . they have taken out of Zambia every ngwee [penny] that was due to them."[16] As well as dividend repatriation, Kaunda complained that agreements with the mining companies per-mitted them to "provide sales and marketing services for a large fee. Although most of this work is performed in Zambia the minority shareholders have entered into separate arrangements with non-resident companies for reasons best known to themselves."[17]

Fluctuating Importance of the Fiscal Cost

At the beginning of the 1970s, Zambia's tax-to-GDP ratio was a phenomenal 34 percent.[18] This is comparable with the rate in OECD countries today, and more than double the average for sub-Saharan countries.[19] It is no surprise, therefore, that Zambia's treaty negotiations at the beginning of the 1970s were not driven by a technical analysis of the actual effects of these treaties' negotiated content, and that negotiators had made no attempt to cost them. The report of Zambia's inspector of taxes in 1972–73 quotes the cost of the reduced withholding tax rates in treaties in force at that time, expressed as refunds to taxpayers from the domestic law rate. "An increase in claims for refunds is expected," it notes, "but no estimate of the total refunds can be made."[20]

The withholding taxes on interest, royalty, technical fee, and dividend pay-ments made to overseas recipients had been introduced in 1971 and 1972, after agreement was reached on the new tax treaties but before they were signed. The taxes were primarily imposed as part of efforts to limit the repatriation of capi-tal, but the government also recognized that "only with a significant increase of the fiscal revenues from sources outside the mining sector will it be possible to maintain the share of fiscal revenue in the GDP at a level of about 34 percent."[21]

Despite difficulties in administrating them effectively, the new withholding taxes were also significant in revenue terms. By 1974, they were already raising 17 million kwacha, out of total government revenue of 628 million.[22] They could have raised more, but the newly implemented agreements with Ireland, Japan, Norway, and the UK were already costing Zambia 10 percent of its potential reve-nue from the dividend withholding tax.[23] All the treaties prevented Zambia from imposing withholding taxes on technical and management fees, and capped the taxes it could levy on the other types of payments. But the first two agreements to be reached, with Japan and Ireland, also ruled out any withholding taxes on dividends—and in Ireland's case, interest and royalties altogether. Because most of Zambia's foreign investment came from treaty partner countries, these agreements significantly blunted the effectiveness of withholding taxes, as both revenue-raising and exchange control policies. It appears that, with such a high tax-to-GDP ratio, nobody was looking closely at the impact of tax treaties, especially in the earliest negotiations.

Low Technical Knowledge among Negotiators

In late 1972, Charles Irish, a three-years-qualified American lawyer, arrived as a lecturer at Zambia University and an adviser to Zambia's finance ministry. Irish was aghast at what he regarded as the unfair nature of the tax agreements signed by Zambia with higher-income countries (he referred to it as a "bias for residence" taxation). He described the agreement with Germany as "horribly inequitable," while negotiators from the United States "were putting forward a treaty that was so one-sided it should have made them blush."[24]

For example, both Zambia and Kenya signed treaties with the UK, but the terms of Zambia's treaty, signed in 1972, were much less favorable than those of Kenya's treaty, signed in 1973. British negotiating records make clear that Kenya was much more focused on renegotiating an agreement with a wider scope for it to impose withholding taxes than the colonial agreement it inherited. Negotia-tions broke down over this point, until Kenya canceled the colonial-era agree-ment; and even after the two sides had reached an agreement, Kenya sought and obtained further concessions from the UK before ratifying. Tellingly, Kenya's negotiating team included an expatriate civil servant from the UK as well as the Kenyan lead negotiator; Kenya also attended meetings of the United Nations ad hoc committee on tax treaties, and negotiators frequently bolstered their positions with reference to what they had learned in discussions there.

In 1974, Irish published a paper castigating the system, singling out the withholding tax revenue lost by Zambia through its treaties with the UK, United States, Germany, and Japan. He wrote: "The practical effect of the present network of double taxation agreements between developed and developing countries is to shift substantial amounts of income tax revenues to which developing countries have a strong legitimate and equitable claim from their treasuries to those of developed countries. Concomitantly, these double taxation agreements result in a very considerable and unnecessary loss of badly needed foreign exchange reserves for developing countries. In other words, the present system of tax agreements creates the anomaly of aid in reverse—from poor to rich countries."[25]

According to Irish, negotiations at this time were pushed by a finance minister and his permanent secretary seeking to send a signal to investors, with little regard to the content. Interviewed in 2014, Irish stated that Zambia's negotiating strategy was not based on an analysis of the technical detail of treaties. "My impression of that time was that the revenue concerns were of less importance than the prestige concerns, and if you were able to conclude a tax treaty with the UK or the US then that was seen at the time in the minds of policymakers as opening the door to the possibility of foreign investment from those countries. There wasn't a very good awareness of the revenue consequences of the treaties, not very much at all."[26] In his paper, he concluded that lower-income countries "feel compelled to accept any double taxation agreement in order to remove impediments to foreign investment contained in the internal tax systems of developed countries and to provide assurances of stability to foreign investors" and displayed "unawareness of the adverse nature of tax agreements with a bias for residence."[27]

Andrew Sardanis, an expatriate who was permanent secretary to the finance ministry in 1970–71, concurs. Zambia's treaty with Ireland remains a standout example of a one-sided treaty, leaving Zambia with very few taxing rights at all. According to Sardanis, "The fact is that most of the times, we let the other side write the agreements. . . . We were all very raw in those days and we also had our likes and dislikes. We liked Ireland because of its history of conflict with the UK and because many Irish in Northern Rhodesia were sympathetic to us during the period of apartheid.[28]

Three organizational factors are likely to have exacerbated the failure to fully appreciate the consequences of treaty negotiations. First, in Irish's words the civil service was "dominated by people who didn't have very much formal education," lacking experienced bureaucrats who might have scrutinized the content of treaties.[29] This difficulty is corroborated by annual tax commissioners' reports, which outline the department's ongoing struggle to recruit, train, and maintain skilled staff. Successive commissioners complained of poor facilities, the lack of a sufficient budget, and the failure to fill more senior posts with competent staff.[30] Little wonder that, in Charles Irish's words, "the income tax departments of developing countries are woefully undertrained and understaffed and are barely able to cope with the administration of domestic tax laws, much less give serious consideration to complex international tax matters."[31] For the Ministry of Finance it was the same, according to a study of mineral taxation reforms, which notes that "Zambia did not have the needed cadre of technically-trained public officials and professional economists to contest the companies' claims."[32]

This was compounded by a second factor: President Kaunda's predilection for moving ministers and senior officials between posts on an almost annual basis. Dennis Dresang and Ralph Young describe a "merry-go-round" in ministerial posts, the product of political and later economic instability within the government.[33] From 1965 to 1975, ministerial reshuffles or organizational changes that shifted ministerial responsibilities took place every ten months,[34] while the average period of a permanent secretary in post was eighteen to twenty-four months.[35] The post of tax commissioner, with responsibility for tax treaty negotiation, was occupied by a different person each year from 1970 to 1974. The Ministry of Finance changed permanent secretaries at least four times in six years between 1967 and 1974.[36]

The minutes and correspondence from Zambia's negotiations with the UK bear out Irish's assertion that this state of affairs led to tax treaties that were "too often the product of unquestioned acceptance of the developed country's position after little or no substantive negotiation."[37] Zambia's negotiations with the UK in 1971 were carried out personally by the newly appointed E. C. Chibwe, on a whistle-stop tour of European capitals, flanked by two officials from other departments who did not appear to speak in the negotiations.[38] The Zambia-UK treaty was initialed in less than four days, an unusually easy negotiation. Having emphasized the tax-sparing clause in their letter requesting an agreement (written under a previous tax commissioner), Zambia's negotiators dropped this demand when forced to choose between it and retaining the right to levy a 10 percent withholding tax on royalty fees.[39] Zambian officials made clear that the royalty rate was of crucial importance, despite the fact that royalty flows were, according to British data, "negligible."[40] That Zambia caved in when faced with this ultimatum, rather than holding on for British concessions in a second round of talks, may be indicative of pressure on negotiators to reach agreement quickly, but it is inconsistent with the motivation behind the original request for negotiations. Furthermore, British investors did not consider the treaty to be valuable. It seems hard to sustain the view that Zambian negotiators had a clear consensus as to why they wanted a treaty with the UK, what they needed to concede to get one, or that they understood the aspects of the treaty most likely to bring the most costs or benefits.

A third factor was the role that appointments to senior positions played in political patronage, especially during the period when treaty negotiations were under way. Until the institution of the one-party state in 1972, senior posts in the Zambian government were used to balance the representation of different factions in the ruling coalition.[41] The finance brief came with substantial prestige and was allocated accordingly: it changed hands in 1967 as part of the balancing act, then twice in 1969, when it was first added to the portfolio of Vice President Emmanuel Kapepwe, and then moved to a new post of minister of development and finance.[42] Zambia's lead tax treaty negotiators, its tax commissioners, were thus operating without any specialist technical support below them, and without any focused scrutiny above them.

During the late 1970s and 1980s, Zambia's position toward inward investors became, if anything, more favorable, with a relaxation of exchange controls in 1976 and a new package of tax incentives in 1977.[43] Yet Zambia became a more cautious, better tax treaty negotiator. The agreements signed between 1978 and 1985, with Finland, India, and Canada were reached at a much slower pace, and figure 6.1 shows much improved negotiating outcomes.

By his own account, the presence of an expatriate international tax specialist— Charles Irish—had made a difference.[44] This is corroborated in US diplomatic cables that record Zambia's negotiations with the United States. In October 1973, the US embassy in Lusaka informed the US Treasury that Zambia's Ministry of Finance "had decided [to] seek [an] agreement more favorable to GRZ [Government of Zambia] in revenue terms than past agreements."[45] Instead of just one round of negotiations, the cables indicate that at least three rounds took place. Zambia's delegation was led by a less senior official, its deputy commissioner of tax, and also included Irish.[46] The agreement was never signed.

In summary, the late 1960s and early 1970s saw Zambia rush into negotiating a number of tax treaties with the aim of attracting inward investment through "prestige" and tax-sparing clauses. The decision to negotiate, with whom and on what basis, was made in the first half of the 1970s without any detailed knowledge of the specifics of tax treaty content, with a focus that oscillated between tax-sparing clauses and defending withholding tax rates. As a result, Zambia displayed an almost reckless disregard for the treaties' implications, making concessions that undermined policies it was simultaneously trying to implement to raise more revenue and keep capital in the country. Zambia also lacked a clear sense of the concessions that it might have been able to extract from treaty partners, as illustrated by the better results obtained by other African countries in negotiations with the same countries, and the better results Zambia itself obtained once it had the support of an external specialist adviser.

The Skeptical Years: 1991–2011

The reintroduction of multiparty democracy in 1991 saw the election of only Zambia's second government since independence. From 1997 onward, Zambian bureaucrats began participating extensively in international training and conferences on tax treaties. In the early 2000s, Zambia was even among twenty-five countries represented on the UN Committee of Experts dealing with tax treaties. Interview evidence indicates that a number of negotiations and renegotiations took place during this time. Despite all this activity, no treaties came to signature until 2010, when agreements with China, Mauritius, and the Seychelles were signed. This period in which few treaties were signed stands in contrast to both the 1970s and the position from 2011 onward, when a Patriotic Front (PF) government replaced the MMD (table 6.3). Mauritius and the Seychelles, of course, are tax havens, and these treaties open Zambia up to the risk of tax avoidance; the agreement with China is also quite one-sided, which provoked the United Kingdom to ask for a renegotiation to match its terms. This section discusses the reasons for the lack of new treaties, as well as these three rather surprising signatures.

TABLE 6.3. Zambia's negotiations since 2010

COUNTRY	YEAR	ADMINISTRATION
China	2010	Banda (MMD)
Seychelles	2010	
Mauritius	2011	
Botswana	2013	Sata (PF)
United Kingdom*	2014	
Netherlands*	2015	
Norway*	2015	
Ireland*	2015	
Switzerland*	2017	Lungu (PF)
Malawi	2017	
Morocco	2017	
India*	2018	

*Renegotiation

Growth of a Cohort of Technical Experts

As part of a classic structural adjustment program, the new MMD government immediately began to implement an aggressive suite of Washington Consensus policies, eliminating tariffs and exchange rate controls, privatizing much of the state-owned industry, and introducing a VAT.[47] Within two years, it had passed an act creating a new semiautonomous Zambia Revenue Authority (ZRA), a reform that swept through Anglophone Africa during the 1990s as a means of increasing the efficacy of revenue collection.[48] Semiautonomous revenue authorities are governed at arm's length from the government; they are free to set their own employment practices to reduce the extent of patronage in their staffing and to improve staff retention.[49]

The creation of a specialist organization dealing with tax administration, combined with an influx of technical assistance on tax issues from donors such as the UK, Germany, and Japan, quickly brought senior Zambian officials into contact with an international network of tax treaty negotiators. A review document prepared by the OECD secretariat and the government of Zambia in 2011 describes the extent of this interaction:

> Officials from the Ministry of Finance and National Planning together with the ZRA are working closely with their counterparts in other jurisdictions through double taxation agreements and organisations such as: the African Union; OECD; African Tax Forum; World Customs Organisation; SADC; COMESA Technical Committees on Customs; etc. Zambian Officials are often invited to attend discussions on issues pertaining to tax administration and customs border control organised by international organisations. An example of the outcomes of networking on tax treaties are the double taxation agreements that Zambia has signed with a number of countries.[50]

As one negotiator, who was senior within the ZRA at this time, explained, "From about 1997, the ZRA having been formed in 1994, there was a lot of interest from the OECD to get non-OECD countries to appreciate the issue of [tax treaties]."[51] Zambia went "religiously" to OECD tax treaty meetings in Paris and participated in numerous OECD trainings.[52] Throughout the 2000s, it was represented almost every year at either the OECD's Global Forum on Tax Treaties in Paris or the annual session of the United Nations Committee of Experts on International Cooperation in Tax Matters in Geneva. Its representatives were generally top-ranking officials from within the revenue authority.[53] At these meetings, according to an analysis of OECD documents by Lynne Latulippe, "the

OECD's activities created and maintained non-members' perception that tax treaties were necessary to attract FDI, although it did not produce any direct evidence of the consequences or the influence of tax treaties."[54]

Several examples illustrate the prevailing direction of discussions in these forums. In 2002, members of the SADC signed a memorandum on tax cooperation that committed them to "strive to ensure the speedy negotiation, conclusion, ratification and effective implementation of tax treaties" and "establish amongst themselves a comprehensive treaty network."[55] COMESA entered into a similar project in 2009.[56] Zambia's decision to accede to requests from Mauritius and the Seychelles for tax treaties, despite the risks originating from their positions as tax havens, was linked by many interviewees to the SADC protocol. As one government interviewee explained, "First of all there's the issue of expanding the network. Being part of SADC, SADC protocol says you're going to have treaties with each other. There's this thing that says you're in this together. If you just look at tax on its own you're never going to sign any treaties."[57]

In 2006, UNCTAD, in a project funded by the Japan Bank of International Cooperation, produced the *Blue Book* for Zambia, which included the following among its ten recommendations for capacity-building assistance: "Carry out a [tax treaty] negotiation round with China, the Republic of Korea and three other South-East Asian countries with strong investment interests in Zambia. This can be facilitated by UNCTAD. The participants will consist of teams of DTT negotiators mandated by their country to negotiate and conclude such agreements. The round will last five days. UNCTAD's secretariat will provide assistance for the facilitation and the organization of the round (preparatory work, invitations, exchange of drafts and comments, preparation of the negotiating matrix, secretarial backstopping during the round)."[58]

Zambia's specialist international tax officials at the time saw tax treaties as intimately linked with investment, but not as drivers of new inward investment. As they saw it, investors from countries without tax treaties might face double taxation, and this was a problem that should be resolved. According to a senior ZRA official at the time, "We wanted to expand the network. It was about the time we had opened up, and there was a lot of interest in terms of FDI coming into the country. It was about the time investors were coming in, and we wanted to have treaties there to avoid double taxation."[59]

His counterpart from the Ministry of Finance also explained that treaties "come from the [existing] investors' influence. It's when they need to repatriate income."[60] One of the former negotiators even expressed a quite cynical view about the political reality of his position. "I know there's empirical evidence that it has no effect on investment, but the reality country-to-country is that there's a bluff goes on, and countries don't want to take the risk of losing big investments. . . . China you know is a powerhouse. They come and say, 'for us to further this investment, we need a treaty.' That's what it's about: bluffing."[61]

Conflict within Government

Despite devoting so much energy to tax treaty negotiations throughout the 1990s and 2000s, Zambia had concluded only three tax treaties by 2011, with China (as recommended in the *Blue Book*) and the Seychelles and Mauritius (SADC members). Negotiators at the time indicated that many renegotiations, including with South Africa, Tanzania, and the UK, were stalled once officials had reached agreement, while others failed to get off the ground because of slow ministerial approval.[62] No treaties were actually signed until 2010, and it is common knowledge among negotiators and advisers in the private sector that these—as well as several that have not been signed—had been negotiated some years before.[63]

Treaty negotiators and private sector tax advisers all explained in interviews how officials were unable to secure ministerial approval for signature and ratification. "Government was not sure what were the benefits," said one former negotiator. "Some people had read that DTAs give away revenue. Somehow it never got past cabinet. The revenue authority was finding it a bit frustrating."[64] Another concurred: "You send it to the minister for permission, and it just sits there."[65] One factor appears to have been changes in government, with new presidents coming into office in 2002 and 2008. "When you have a change in government, you have to go back to the drawing board," explained a negotiator.[66]

The growing concern about Zambia's tax performance, and especially about taxes paid by mining multinationals, clearly set the tone. Zambia's tax-to-GDP ratio had declined by more than half since the early 1970s, to just 16 percent of GDP in 2003.[67] As copper prices rose during the 2000s but tax revenues did not follow suit, the subject became politicized. In early 2008, the government attempted (ultimately unsuccessfully) to introduce a windfall tax of up to 75 percent on mining companies, which required canceling agreements reached with mining companies at privatization.[68] Corporate taxation, particularly of the mines, was a key topic during a presidential election later that year, won by former vice president Rupiah Banda after the death of incumbent Levy Mwanawasa.[69] The Banda administration prioritized strengthening Zambia's tax system and turned up the heat in the run-up to the 2011 election, during which opposition leader Michael Sata stood on an explicit platform of tackling tax avoidance by multinational mining firms.[70] According to one official, "The whole tax regime had an injection in 2010, because we were trying to get rid of [tax] incentives, and we started to [re]negotiate."[71] Another seemed to agree. "There was no specific policy change, it was simply that the minister and cabinet decided to handle this issue. Okay, I suppose you can call that a change in policy."[72]

The specialists' efforts to negotiate and renegotiate tax treaties were obstructed in this context because political decision makers, who were concerned to be seen to increase tax revenues, did not support the tax treaty project. Only when treaties aligned with their political priorities were negotiators able to secure signature and ratification of agreements. This explains why agreements were only signed with strategically important China and with SADC neighbors. Negotiators' long-standing ambitions for new and renegotiated older treaties never saw the light of day, despite completion of negotiations. Even the official version of the 2002 SADC protocol on tax treaties does not have a Zambian ministerial signature.[73] As one official lamented, "If it is new and they are saying 'go for it' it is ratified. If it is old, nobody is interested."[74] According to a prominent tax adviser in a professional services firm, "The treaty with South Africa is very old, it can't be implemented in places. It's 15 years since they renegotiated that treaty. . . . We think cabinet has been lazy, they have not given it a lot of thought."[75] An expatriate technical adviser to the Ministry of Finance stated that "ministers of finance have been reasonably competent, but somewhere in the political system it all disappears."[76]

2011 Onward: A New Attitude toward International Tax?

After the 2011 election, with the change of party administration a new cohort of senior civil servants began their posts at the Treasury, and those who took over the remit for tax treaties did not have the same history of participation in international tax organizations. According to those officials themselves, this fresh perspective and new political impetus, combined with civil society campaigns that drew specific attention to tax treaties, have led to a new approach. Renegotiations were undertaken with the UK, India, Norway, South Africa, Ireland, and the Netherlands (the latter three treaties regarded as substantially problematic). Even the colonial-era treaty with Switzerland, slated for termination in 2014, has since been renegotiated.[77]

"In 2012, with the change of government, this government came in with a different view, they were ready to terminate treaties," said a junior official with experience in both administrations. "We are close to happy [with the renegotiations]. The first thing we did was to repair the damage."[78] The finance ministry official responsible for tax treaties in 2014 appeared skeptical, stating that "there is currently no evidence to show that tax treaties have helped to attract investment into Zambia. . . . So the important advice to third world countries like Zambia will be to demonstrate really how double taxation avoidance can be achieved without signing tax treaties."[79]

The process of renegotiation undertaken by Zambia is intended to stem some of the losses due to abuse of existing tax treaties and to maximize the administrative benefits that Zambia can obtain from the information exchange and mutual assistance provisions of tax treaties.[80] But there is evidence here of a degree of path dependency, as figure 6.2 shows. Despite the clearly skeptical attitude from inside the finance ministry, it is much harder for Zambia to renegotiate or cancel an existing treaty than it is to secure a new one. For example, a tentative attempt by the ZRA to disregard the colonial-era agreement with France failed after the threat of a legal challenge from French businesses in Zambia and from the French government.[81] The newly renegotiated treaty with the UK is a more useful tool for the ZRA's enforcement work, and it includes a broader definition of PE; but in return, Zambia was forced to accept a substantially reduced maximum withholding tax rate on British firms in order to bring the treaty in line with concessions it had offered to China in the 2010 agreement. "It's hard enough competing with Chinese businesses in Africa as it is," a British diplomat explained.[82]

There is a sense from government officials that if the present administration in Zambia were building its treaty network from scratch, it would not conclude

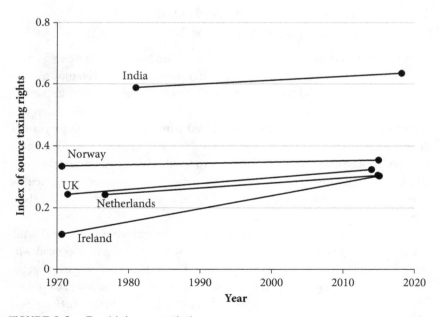

FIGURE 6.2. Zambia's renegotiations

Source: Hearson, "Tax Treaties Explorer."

many treaties at all. Its only fresh agreements it signed between 2012 and 2020 are with other African countries. The agreements with the Seychelles and Mauritius, which had been negotiated and signed under the previous government, are not seen as good deals for Zambia. "The process of approval took too long such that by the time [these] agreements were signed, the agreements were 'out of tune' and therefore lacked the standards we now insist upon," said a senior finance ministry official. "I am not sure if Zambia would remain in good standing with the international community if it decided to annul the treaties (unilaterally or not) with either the UK, Germany, Japan or Canada, for instance. Perhaps we have sold our soul for [having] been aid recipients from countries such as the ones stated above."[83] In 2020, however, Zambia did terminate its treaty with Mauritius.

Conclusion

This chapter looked at a lower-income country that has historically been something of an outlier, with a fluctuating attitude toward tax treaty negotiations. During the 1970s it was a positive outlier, signing more treaties than most of its neighbors, and on worse terms. At this time it did not have specialist bureaucrats to drive the process, and so the decision to negotiate was based on the idea held by political actors that treaties would attract investment, without any clear analysis of the costs and benefits. The process was led by politically appointed nonspecialists, with little technical support or experience, in a context of a high tax-to-GDP ratio that may have reduced the salience of the treaty's costs in the initial period. This meant that negotiation, signature, and ratification were quick, but the quality of negotiation was poor, until an expatriate specialist arrived and caused Zambia to question its approach.

In the late 1990s and 2000s, Zambia had a specialist bureaucracy, which engaged frequently with the international tax community. These officials saw treaties as an important part of the enabling framework for inward investment—not as instruments that would directly attract investment but as tools to ensure foreign investors were taxed according to international rules, and also to increase Zambia's capacity to enforce its tax laws. It was important that older treaties be brought in line with modern standards in order to achieve this. But these objectives were not shared by cabinet ministers, in a context where tough tax politics toward mining companies was of paramount importance. As a consequence, most were not signed or ratified, with the exception of treaties with SADC countries and with China, where specific political pressures existed. It was from 2011 onward that the preferences of bureaucrats and politicians aligned, leading to a rapid wave of negotiations that improved many older treaties but did not undo all of the earlier damage.

VIETNAM AND CAMBODIA

We didn't even know who the Seychelles were. I had to Google it.

—Treaty negotiators, Cambodia

This chapter considers two Southeast Asian countries, Vietnam and Cambodia. In comparison with Zambia, both were late adopters of tax treaties: neither had a single bilateral tax treaty when they began to open up to FDI in the early 1990s. At that time, their attitudes toward investment promotion were not radically different, as illustrated by the tax incentives that both offered to foreign investors and their active BIT negotiation programs. Yet, while Vietnam has signed more tax treaties than almost any other lower-income country, Cambodia has taken a cautious approach, only beginning to sign treaties in 2016. In contrast to conventional explanations of the origins of tax treaties, which view the capital importer as the active pursuer of tax treaties, Cambodia declined requests for tax treaty negotiations from capital-exporting countries and tax havens for many years. Both countries received approaches from numerous capital-exporting countries seeking to enhance opportunities for their multinational investors, and felt competitive pressure to sign tax treaties in order to attract inward investment. Yet for a long time, only Vietnam acquiesced.

What explains this divergence? One difference between the two countries was timing. Vietnam urgently needed to replace its economic dependence on the Soviet Union after the end of the Cold War, and began to negotiate tax treaties in the early 1990s before it had a corporate tax system in place, seeing them as a shortcut to creating a tax regime for foreign investors. This urgency precluded a detailed consideration of a negotiating position, meaning that Vietnam allowed others to determine the content of its treaties. Cambodia, meanwhile, did not face such time pressure, imposing a much lower tax burden on foreign investors to begin with, and depending very little on tax revenue from businesses. By the time Cambodia faced real pressure to negotiate tax treaties, it desperately needed more tax revenue, creating a strong reluctance to sign away taxing rights. In contrast, Vietnam—like 1970's Zambia—had a large reservoir of state income that was unaffected by treaties, in this case from state-owned enterprises.

The consequences of these early choices are visible in the way in which these countries engage with international norms. Vietnamese officials have, since the late 1990s, engaged mostly with the OECD, rather than the UN. While they have become more strategic in their negotiating stance, they are motivated by the idea that all investment, no matter how small, and regardless of the costs or the level of competitive pressure, should be covered by a tax treaty. Vietnam has also used its domestic tax system to take unilateral steps that negate the main supposed investment-promoting benefits of tax treaties. Cambodia, meanwhile, selectively imported technical knowledge from abroad as it prepared to negotiate, strengthening its negotiating position while holding on to some unconventional ideas.

This chapter begins with a comparison of Vietnam's and Cambodia's approaches to international economic cooperation, including tax treaties. It then briefly demonstrates that both countries came under pressure from capital exporters to sign tax treaties. After this, the mechanisms within Vietnam and Cambodia are considered separately.

Comparative Context

Vietnam and Cambodia are neighboring countries in Southeast Asia. Both had somewhat closed economies until the beginning of the 1990s, when they began to open up to FDI. As figure 7.1 shows, FDI flows into Vietnam and Cambodia have been similar on a per capita basis since the early 1990s. One major difference between the two is the large role of state-owned enterprises and state investment in Vietnam's economy, in comparison with Cambodia, which has a much smaller state sector and relies much more on foreign enterprises for its economic growth. As a result, total investment per capita measured by gross fixed capital formation in Vietnam has been double that in Cambodia.

Tax treaties are a general exception to the pattern of participation in international agreements that we can observe for the two countries. Cambodia has usually followed closely behind Vietnam, participating in other forms of agreement within a few years (table 7.1). In contrast, the gap for tax treaties is a quarter of a century. While it is true that Cambodia has concluded fewer BITs than Vietnam, it had nonetheless signed twenty-six by 2017.[1] Yet Vietnam and Cambodia are

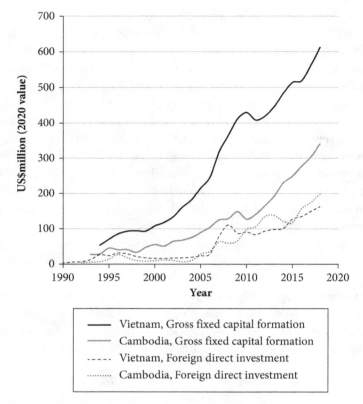

FIGURE 7.1. Investment statistics per capita, Vietnam and Cambodia

Source: World Bank, "World Development Indicators," World Bank Open Data, 2020, http://data.worldbank.org.

TABLE 7.1. Timing of some key milestones in economic integration

EVENT	VIETNAM	CAMBODIA
First investment law	1987	1994
First BIT	1990	1994
First DTT	1992	2016
Joins ASEAN	1995	2000
Joins WTO	2007	2004

Source: IBFD, "IBFD Tax Research Platform," 2020, http://research.ibfd.org/; Margaret Slocomb, An Economic History of Cambodia in the Twentieth Century (Singapore: NUS Press, 2010), 273–75; Pamela Sodhy, "Modernization and Cambodia," Journal of Third World Studies 21, no. 1 (2004): 153; UNCTAD, "International Investment Agreements Navigator," accessed August 10, 2015, http://investmentpolicyhub.unctad.org/IIA.

TABLE 7.2. Treaty-making activity: Cumulative treaties signed

YEARS	BITS SIGNED		DTTS SIGNED	
	CAMBODIA	VIETNAM	CAMBODIA	VIETNAM
Up to 1992	0	12	0	2
1993–97	6	37	0	32
1998–2002	13	45	0	40
2003–7	18	52	0	47
2008–12	21	64	0	62
2013–17	26	66	5	77

Source: UNCTAD, "International Investment Agreements Navigator"; IBFD, "IBFD Tax Research Platform."

polar opposites when it comes to their attitudes toward tax treaties. By 2017, Vietnam had signed seventy-seven tax treaties, while Cambodia did not sign any until 2016. Table 7.2 compares the cumulative number of tax treaties that both countries have signed since 1990 with the number of BITs.

To explain why the numbers of tax treaties signed by these two countries vary so much, this chapter uses secondary literature and field visits to Vietnam and Cambodia. Eleven semi-structured interviews were conducted in Vietnam (in total, four government officials, nine private sector stakeholders, and two others took part in interviews), and five in Cambodia (with two government officials and three private sector stakeholders). In both countries, the government officials responsible for tax treaty policy and negotiations were included in the sample. Sampling was largely purposive, with interviews arranged in advance through email. Government contacts were obtained through an OECD technical adviser who had been active in both countries, private sector contacts through the websites of private sector advisory firms, and other contacts through local NGOs. A small number of additional snowball-sampled interviews were arranged during field visits. In Vietnam, a government-industry consultation meeting on tax treaty interpretation was also observed. In Cambodia, both the lack of any tax treaties at the time of fieldwork and the embryonic state of the country's tax advisory sector reduced the number of potential interviewees available.

Competition for Outward Investment Opportunities in Cambodia and Vietnam

The competitive pressure on Vietnam and Cambodia is reflected in the growing number of treaties signed by countries within the ASEAN region, with which

Cambodia and Vietnam compete for foreign investment and trade. Vietnam and the Philippines have used tax incentives to compete for high-tech manufacturers, for example, while Cambodia, Laos, and Myanmar compete in lower-technology sectors.[2] In both of the case study countries, there was evidence of what appears to be a strategic interaction between lower-income countries, whereby one ASEAN country's signature of tax treaties creates pressure on another.

This is not, however, the only form of strategic interaction driving treaty diffusion. Since opening up, Cambodia has received multiple requests for tax treaties from both Asian and European countries (about ten, according to one government source). Among the countries that, as one official said, "have been writing many times in the past" are Malaysia, Thailand, Korea, China, and Japan.[3] At least two of these countries have made formal requests in person via their ambassadors.[4] Requests have also been received from European countries and more than once from the Seychelles. "We don't even know who they are," said one official, referring to the latter. "I had to Google it," said another.[5]

Vietnam has already signed a treaty with the Seychelles, despite no investment flowing between the two, according to its own statistics. Its large network of treaties signals to other countries that they will receive a positive response if they request negotiations, and many treaties have been initiated from the other country. "Normally when we negotiate with other countries, they decide when we negotiate," confirmed Nguyen Duc Thinh, the head of the International Taxation Department of the General Department of Taxation (GDT), interviewed in 2015.[6] While this confirms that the phenomenon of competition for outward investment described in chapter 3 is still relevant to the present day, the rest of this chapter focuses on decisions made in the lower-income countries.

Vietnam

Following the *doi moi* reforms of 1986, Vietnam's government began to open the country to FDI, passing a liberal investment law that was unusual in that it protected investors from subsequent changes in laws, as well as from expropriation.[7] Furthermore, the new investment regime offered inward investors a tax holiday of up to eight years and a reduced tax rate thereafter.[8] Progress in expanding political and economic relations with the rest of the world was initially slow after 1987, but came to be felt more urgently within the Vietnamese Communist Party when the fall of the Soviet Union left it marginalized.[9] This is thought to have been one of the drivers of Vietnam's willingness to relinquish its military involvement in Cambodia through the Paris peace accords signed in

1991, which in turn led to some thawing of relations with members of ASEAN, although it would take some time to establish trust.[10]

Vietnam threw itself into economic integration even before its domestic legal framework—including its tax laws—had caught up. From 1990 onward it signed BITs at a ferocious pace of around six per year, with European and Southeast Asian countries as partners in roughly equal numbers. A surge in FDI in Vietnam in 1996 followed the lifting of the US trade embargo in 1994, which paved the way for Vietnam to finally join the ASEAN community in 1995, and eventually the WTO in 2007.[11] The ASEAN and WTO logos still light up the main road from Hanoi's Nội Bài International Airport to the city center today.

Vietnam was no slouch when it came to tax treaties, either. It signed its first treaty in 1992, picking up the same, faster pace as for BITs soon afterward (table 7.2). The nineteen tax treaties signed by Vietnam between 1992 and 1995 already covered half of its inward investment, and by 1997 it had concluded a total of thirty-two treaties, now covering two-thirds of all its inward investment.[12] In 1997, Vietnam formally expressed positions on the provisions of the OECD model tax treaty for the first time, reserving the right to include numerous beneficial clauses in its own treaties that are excluded from the OECD model.[13] Figure 7.2 shows how the content of Vietnam's tax treaties changed over time, by comparing them with this declared negotiating position. There appear to be two distinct periods of negotiation: treaties signed between 1992 and 1998 were much more heterogeneous in their content and generally less reflective of Vietnam's own preferences. From 2000 onward, most treaties included 60–90 percent of the clauses that Vietnam had indicated in its negotiating position. While treaties with OECD member countries since 2000 have not tended to be as reflective of Vietnam's negotiating position as others, the same structural break can be seen from 2000 onward, suggesting stronger negotiating by Vietnam. Two specific examples of this structural break are as follows:

- Vietnam's position includes an additional paragraph 7 in article 5 of its tax treaties, giving it the right to tax companies that are "dependent agents" of foreign multinationals. This provision appeared in only half of Vietnam's 1990s treaties, but it was included in all of those signed since 2000.
- It also set out a position in favor of the right to levy a withholding tax on technical service fee payments to foreign contractors, which the model treaties do not permit. It was included in only a quarter of Vietnam's 1990s treaties, but is in more than half of those signed from 2000 onward.

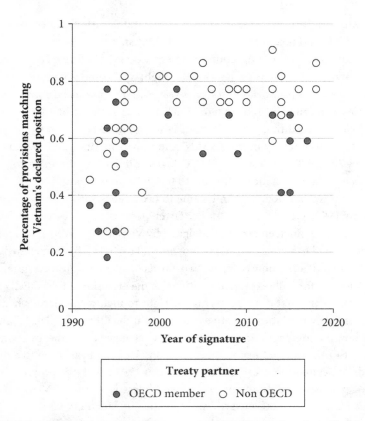

FIGURE 7.2. Vietnam's tax treaties scored against its declared position in reservations to the OECD model treaty

Source: Martin Hearson, "Tax Treaties Explorer," 2020, http://treaties.tax.

A Treaty Network Driven by Competition for Inward Investment

Interviews with current and former Vietnamese officials indicate that an intense desire to attract inward investment explains many of these early decisions. According to Thinh, three factors drove Vietnam's prolific negotiation of tax treaties and its willingness to make big concessions in the 1990s.[14] First, tax treaties and other economic agreements were ways of establishing political and economic relationships with other countries at a time when an economic embargo on Vietnam was still in place in the United States. This weakened Vietnam's negotiating strength. Second, by ensuring that all foreign investment was covered by tax treaties, Vietnam aimed to shortcut the development of domestic corporate tax laws, which would take considerable time at a point when there was a pressing need for inward investment. A third factor driving Vietnam's enthusiasm for tax treaties was a desire to have tax-sparing agreements with capital-exporting countries. Like Zambia in the 1970s, Vietnam in the 1990s was using generous tax incentives to try to attract inward investment; tax-sparing provisions in tax treaties ensured that foreign investors could benefit from the incentives in full. "This was our most vital condition for negotiating a DTA at this time. . . . We had to step back [from other negotiating preferences] a lot because the tax sparing was so vital," said Thinh.[15]

Vietnam's weak position, combined with its lack of experience negotiating, meant that it made concessions that it would not now make. An official who had been involved in these early negotiations explained that Vietnam began its negotiations using the OECD model because it had not heard of the UN model.[16] Thinh concurred: "During that time our negotiating partners were from the OECD and it was urgent to open our door and so we had to accept [OECD model treaty provisions]. . . . When we were beginning to negotiate DTAs, we didn't have so much experience. When the countries came to negotiate with us they forced us to use the OECD model."[17]

As figure 7.2 indicates, however, it was not only with OECD members that Vietnam gave away large amounts of taxing rights. Among the pre-2000 treaties, aside from those with OECD countries, two are considerably less good deals than average for Vietnam. These are with Taiwan and Singapore, by far its two biggest sources of investment outside the OECD.

The Low Importance of Fiscal Cost

Vietnamese officials paid little attention to the costs of treaties they negotiated at this time because raising corporate tax from foreign investors was not a priority. "In Vietnam they don't care much about corporate income tax, it's VAT," one former civil servant explained to me.[18] The country's tax system in the early years of its economic liberalization was complicated and discriminatory, incorporating taxes on turnover, profits, and profit disbursements. It was also administered inefficiently and somewhat arbitrarily by inexperienced and corrupt tax administrators.[19] While this frustrated foreign-owned companies, they benefited greatly because they were exempted from turnover tax and taxed on their profits at a lower headline rate than domestic firms (25 percent compared with a maximum of 45 percent for domestic firms); furthermore, generous tax incentives in the Investment Law meant that most would not become liable for this tax for some time, if at all.[20]

As a result of this tax system, tax revenue from FDI was relatively small, as low as 0.02 percent of GDP in 1991, rising with the stock of FDI to 1.2 percent in 1997.[21] But while tax revenue from foreign companies may have been low, Vietnam raised considerable revenue elsewhere.[22] A paper coauthored by the head of tax policy in the Ministry of Finance notes that, despite difficulties in the administration of the tax system, Vietnam's tax-to-GDP ratio in the 1990s was much higher than other ASEAN countries that would have been expected to have greater "taxability" because of higher per-capita income and a greater industrial share in the economy.[23]

In part, this was because effective tax rates on domestic-owned firms in Vietnam were much higher than the rates in these other countries, exceeding 60 percent once turnover and profit taxes were taken into account.[24] In addition, structural economic differences provided more tax revenue—in particular, the large share of state-owned enterprises in the economy, and the presence of the high-tax oil and gas sector (although revenue from the latter amounted to only around 2 to 3 percent of GDP).[25] In 2000, tax revenue from foreign-owned firms still made up only 5 percent of total corporate income tax revenue, while more than four times as much came from state-owned enterprises.[26] A new tax system promulgated in 1999 simplified the country's tax structure and made it less discriminatory. Foreign-owned firms now paid 33 percent tax on their profits, the same as domestic firms, but they still benefited from generous reductions lasting as long as ten years.[27]

Treaty Negotiators: Limited Capacity but High Autonomy

When Vietnam began to negotiate tax treaties, its negotiators had little prior exposure to the international tax community.[28] Absent technical knowledge and negotiating experience, their approach to concluding tax treaties was incoherent. In the late 1990s, however, "some OECD experts came to Vietnam to talk about the DTAs," according to Thinh.[29] Vietnamese officials became a regular fixture at the OECD's annual Global Forum on Tax Treaties during the 2000s, sending a delegation of two to four persons each time.[30] In contrast, Vietnam did not attend annual meetings of the UN Tax Committee until 2017.[31]

While government officials outside the GDT still reproduce the tax treaties myth,[32] this is not the only logic at work within the GDT itself. Rather, Vietnam has adopted the policy that all investors, no matter how small, should be covered by a tax treaty. "Even if it is a small amount of investment it is still worth it," according to Thinh. This contributes to one business representative's view that "Vietnam's negotiations have been on a 20-year roll."[33] While Thinh and his colleagues want all investors to be covered by a treaty, it is very clear, from interviews and from their approach to applying tax treaties, that this is because they want to apply an international standard to all existing inward investors, not merely to encourage new inward investment.

Among private sector tax practitioners with experience dealing with the GDT, Thinh was described as the driving force behind decisions related to tax treaties.[34] He also suffered from a lack of experienced support: according to a former employee within the International Tax Department, in 2015 Thinh was the only member who had been in his post for more than five years, out of a staff of twelve.[35] According to one European tax lawyer who has worked in the region for over a decade, "It's all about people. If Vietnam didn't have Mr Thinh they wouldn't have any tax treaties."[36] A former official from the Department of Trade stated, "The legacy of signing agreements all the time is set in momentum, and it keeps on going. . . . Sometimes it just happens because someone gets in the routine."[37]

It is notable, however, that the GDT's authority does not extend to being able to implement its desire to renegotiate treaties. The country has accepted an offer from the Netherlands to renegotiate in order to add an anti-abuse clause to that treaty, but while some lower-income countries have faced difficulties persuading higher-income countries to renegotiate treaties that are a good deal for the latter, Vietnam does not appear to have tried. As in Zambia, the main reason relates to internal bureaucratic politics. According to Thinh: "Nowadays . . . we would like to renegotiate. From our side, it's not easy because there would be questions from the other ministries and agencies. They would ask why we should want to. For example, we really want to renegotiate with France, because we don't have an interest article, but the other ministries would say 'everything is fine, why do you want to do this?'"

The Legacy of Past Negotiations

Today, it is much less clear what Vietnam stands to gain from its tax treaty negotiations. In 2005, it decided to abolish withholding tax on profits remitted by foreign investors as dividends, and reduce withholding taxes on interest, royalties, and service fees to very low rates.[38] This dramatic move made its tax system much more attractive but also undercut the main supposed investment-promotion tool of its tax treaties. As Vietnam also no longer prioritizes tax-sparing clauses within its treaties,[39] the tax treaty provisions that might be expected to have the biggest investment-promoting effect are no longer of relevance to investors in Vietnam.

Furthermore, when I visited in 2015, Vietnam's application of its tax treaties was directly undermining the benefits that investors might have hoped to gain.

We can see this by looking at the example of Vietnam's approach to PE, the threshold test that establishes when a foreign company operating in Vietnam becomes liable to pay income tax on its profits. In almost all tax treaties, a company must have a physical presence in a country for a certain period of time to meet this test, subject to some exceptions. In contrast, the criteria in Vietnamese law were much more broad, simply that most companies "who do business in Vietnam or earn income in Vietnam" were liable to income tax.[40] In theory, therefore, any investors who were sensitive to their tax liability should have regarded a tax treaty with Vietnam as an important curb on what many regarded as its aggressive approach to taxation. But Vietnam had chosen to interpret the PE provisions of its treaties in unconventional ways that, according to a typical statement from the VBF (which represents overseas investors), "made the application of DTA[s] of foreign enterprises impossible, effectively it obliterate[s] the legitimate benefit of enterprises."[41] Vietnamese negotiators seemed to want to eat their cake and have it, simultaneously demonstrating their support for the policy project of disseminating OECD standards through tax treaties, and ignoring those standards where they prevented Vietnam from taxing as it would like.

For example, a common difference between the two main models on which tax treaties are based is the provision for a "services PE." Under the OECD model, which favors capital exporters, a foreign company providing services in Vietnam must have a fixed place of business in the country, such as a registered office, to be taxable. Vietnam has expressed a position on the OECD model stating that in its treaties it will seek to include a provision from the UN model that lowers this threshold by permitting it to tax such a company simply if its employees are physically present for a certain period, even without a "fixed place of business." Although more than two-thirds of Vietnam's treaties in force include this service PE provision, it is omitted from many of its older treaties and from treaties covering almost two-thirds of its inward FDI. Vietnam's response to this unsatisfactory situation was to take the position that, absent a service PE provision in a treaty, it was at liberty to tax service providers without any minimum threshold, the exact opposite of how tax treaties are usually interpreted.[42]

The inconsistency between negotiation and administration priorities was not a result of inconsistency between parts of the bureaucracy, because decisions on both were made by the GDT. Vietnam's tax administration is decentralized, and according to tax advisers, its local offices do not have the knowledge to apply tax treaty provisions effectively.[43] They rely on circulars issued by the GDT in Hanoi. Senior officials at a consultation meeting between VBF members and the Ministry of Finance in August 2015 repeated the line in these circulars.[44] Investors' lack of confidence in the independence of the courts meant that no tax treaty case had ever been tried in a court, despite the clear frustration from many investors and their advisers.[45] Administrative appeals, according to tax advisers, were always settled by the International Tax department, which drafted the circulars against which the appeals were directed. "The Deputy Director of the GDT signs off rulings," said a tax adviser. "If there's a dispute you can escalate it to the deputy Minister of Finance, but ultimately it will just go back to Mr Thinh."[46] The result of this system was that companies did not avail themselves of benefits to which they were entitled according to the treaty. "A lot of companies could claim [reduced taxation] under treaties, but they don't. It's too much hassle," stated one interviewee, while another went as far as to state, "I am not aware of foreign investors obtaining treaty benefits."[47]

The consequence of Vietnam's position was that investors paradoxically had *less* certainty under treaties than without them and, worse, that Vietnam's treaties *created* double taxation rather than eliminating it. This latter effect came about because treaty partners generally refused to give their outward investors a credit against tax paid in Vietnam if, in their view, Vietnam should not have the right to levy tax under the treaty (in the absence of a treaty, they would be likely to give a credit in the circumstances described here). Following a US$1 billion investment by Samsung in the country, businesses from Korea, covered by one of Vietnam's earliest and most regretted—by the GDT—treaties, invoked a dispute settlement procedure in the treaty to try to challenge some of these interpretation issues, because they did not expect domestic remedies to make a difference.[48] Disputes were also triggered by Samsung's Dutch and Japanese suppliers. Large sums were involved.[49]

Vietnam: Conclusion

During the 1990s, Vietnam had sought tax treaties to bring in inward investment, establishing political and economic relations with countries following economic liberalization and the fall of the Soviet Union, and making up for its lack of a domestic tax code. The tax costs they created were not anticipated by officials in this early period, and thus caused problems later when companies expected to benefit from these treaty provisions. A main priority in this early period was tax-sparing clauses, but in other areas Vietnam was negotiating without a clear sense of the specific provisions that were important to retain its tax base, because raising tax revenue was not a priority.

Since 2000, greater technical knowledge within the GDT means that Vietnam has negotiated on a much more consistent, assured basis with a wide range of countries including many where there is neither competitive pressure nor a prospect of inward investment. Accompanying this technical knowledge is the idea that all investment, no matter how small, should be covered by a tax treaty. When I visited in 2015, the office within the GDT that negotiates and applies tax treaties appeared unwilling to reconcile this belief with the reality of administering tax treaties, interpreting them in ways that rendered them largely ineffective. As one tax lawyer put it, "They should be looking into the OECD interpretations if they're serious. As it is, it's [tax treaties] just window dressing."[50]

Cambodia

Cambodia's current political era begins with the Paris peace accord in 1991 that formally ended conflict between its warring factions, and the involvement of eighteen other countries in its domestic affairs.[51] Private enterprises had not been recognized by the Cambodian state under the Khmer Rouge, and private property rights were not restored until 1989.[52] On September 21, 1993, Cambodia's new constitution was adopted by its newly elected Constituent Assembly, and an elected government took office. Policymaking in this era was predominantly dictated by outside experts, especially when Cambodia agreed to a Structural Adjustment package in 1994.[53]

The new government in 1994 established for the first time a formal tax system based on self-assessment, replacing what had previously been an "estimated" regime, in which tax officials calculated a firm's estimated profit and then "negotiated" with the taxpayer.[54] But it was not until 1997 that a Western-style tax system was introduced, with taxes on profits and withholding taxes on certain types of payments. Before this, tax treaties may have made little difference.

In August 1994, Cambodia signed its first BIT, with Malaysia, and passed the Cambodian Investment Law, which offered investors in certain sectors generous incentives including an eight-year corporate income tax holiday (the same as Vietnam) and an exemption from tax on dividend payments.[55] There was a setback in investment promotion in July 1997, when the Cambodian People's Party (CPP) instigated a coup. Combined with the Asian financial crisis, this temporarily slowed inward investment in Cambodia; but with successful elections in 1998 placing the CPP in power on a more legitimate basis, Cambodia's integration into the global political economy continued.[56]

In 2004, Cambodia began to seriously consider the idea of signing tax treaties and started work to develop a negotiating model.[57] In 2008, an international tax bureau, tasked with treaty negotiations, was formed within the newly created GDT. But it was not until 2014 that Cambodia opened talks. By 2015, it had completed the first round of negotiations with Vietnam and Thailand and was in correspondence with Brunei, Laos, and Singapore.[58] Agreements were signed in

2016 with China and Singapore, in 2017 with Brunei, Indonesia and Thailand, and subsequently with Vietnam and Korea.

Peer Pressure

All the interviewees situated a shift by Cambodia into negotiating mode in the context of its historical reluctance to sign tax treaties. It is clear that Cambodia has felt pressure to sign tax treaties for some time, not because investors face great obstacles created by double taxation but because it had become increasingly isolated within the region as the only country without a DTT (table 7.3).

In 2008, ASEAN members signed an Economic Community blueprint, which stated that members will "work towards establishing an effective network of bilateral agreements on avoidance of double taxation among ASEAN countries."[59] Though Cambodia was still reluctant, the momentum this created among its neighbors such as Laos and Myanmar—direct competitors for investment—was the final straw. "It's an international tax trend, our neighbours are signing them," said a government official.[60] Tax advisers in the private sector concur. "The government had no intention of signing tax treaties. But now that Myanmar is open, they are considering if we have got behind," said one.[61] Another agreed: "They're under a lot of pressure from everywhere because they hesitated for a very long time. They have considered a lot and they don't want to do it, but because of the pressure from the private sector and government—even Myanmar is doing it now—Cambodia is the only one left."[62]

TABLE 7.3. Tax treaties signed by ASEAN member states

COUNTRY	TAX TREATIES SIGNED		
	1997	2007	2017
Brunei*	0	8	26
Cambodia	0	0	5
Indonesia	51	73	80
Laos	2	6	13
Malaysia	63	88	100
Myanmar	1	7	10
Philippines	35	44	50
Singapore	44	73	106
Thailand	39	66	73
Vietnam	32	47	77

Source: IBFD, "IBFD Tax Research Platform."

*Three treaties concluded prior to Brunei's independence from the United Kingdom are excluded.

Cambodian officials emphasize that their own capacity development has been slow, and believe that Laos and Myanmar have made a mistake by negotiating treaties at a similar stage of capacity development rather than forming a firm position based on more detailed technical knowledge first.[63]

Importance of Fiscal Costs

A comparison of tax performance in Cambodia and Vietnam (figure 7.3) may help explain why Cambodian officials took a different attitude toward tax treaties. In 1995, the first year for which data are available, Cambodia raised tax revenue amounting to as little as 5.3 percent of its GDP and was highly aid-dependent, receiving twice as much government revenue through aid than through taxation.[64] Revenue from corporate taxation was negligible. More than half of its government tax revenue came from trade taxes, a disproportionately high amount compared with other lower-income countries.[65] Cambodia's corporate income tax rate at this time was 20 percent, low in comparison with other countries in the region, and in practice foreign investors could pay much less, as a result of eight-year tax holidays that were followed by a permanent 9 percent preferential tax rate. They were also exempt from withholding taxes on certain dividend, interest, and royalty payments. With such generous treatment for foreign investors already in the domestic tax code, tax treaties were not a high priority.

Increasing corporate tax revenue became an important priority for the Cambodian government in the late 1990s. A World Bank report from 1998 notes that "Cambodia's current revenue-to-GDP ratio is very low by international standards. . . . The Law on Investment is one of the most critical impediments to improved revenue mobilization. . . . The combination of the Law and the [implementing] Regulations has eliminated any room for the business income tax to be a policy instrument in the revenue mobilization effort."[66]

Cambodia began to target reforms to its business tax law and administration, and tax revenue from businesses steadily began to increase, by tenfold as a share of GDP between 1996 and 2016. By the mid-2000s, taxes on businesses made up 15 percent of total tax take, and by 2016 almost a quarter. The Cambodian government had become dependent on taxes on businesses, while its private sector was also heavily penetrated by foreign investment: this would increase demand for tax treaties but make the revenue costs especially significant. According to one interviewee, a GDT study conducted in around 2013 estimated the impact of reduced withholding tax rates, were Cambodia to sign a treaty with Vietnam, at between US$5 million and US$6 million per year.[67] If correct, this would have been a cost of around 2 percent of Cambodia's total tax revenue from businesses—from just one part of one treaty.

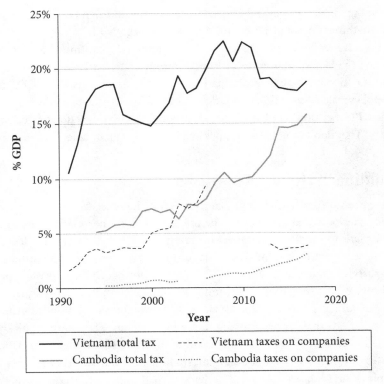

FIGURE 7.3. Selected tax statistics from Vietnam and Cambodia

Source: ICTD/UNU-WIDER, "Government Revenue Dataset," UNU-WIDER, 2020, https://www.wider.unu.edu/project /government-revenue-dataset.

Contrast Cambodia with Vietnam. For the latter, tax revenue from businesses was also an important part of government revenues during the 1990s, but with two important differences. First, overall tax revenues were much higher, mostly between 18 and 20 percent of GDP. Second, much of this tax revenue came from state-owned enterprises, joint ventures, and locally owned businesses. As we saw earlier, FDI represented a much smaller share of total investment, and hence of the tax base. Vietnam also taxed foreign investors more heavily than did Cambodia. The result was that tax treaties made a bigger difference to investors in Vietnam, and had smaller costs to the government as a share of total revenue.

This comparison is supported by interview evidence. Edwin Vanderbruggen, a Dutch tax lawyer practicing across Southeast Asia who advised the GDT on its tax treaty policy, noted that concern about lost revenue was uppermost in the Cambodian officials' minds. In contrast to BITs, he said, tax treaties have an immediate upfront cost. "[The Cambodians] had no understanding of how tax treaties worked, but they did understand that you can't sign tax treaties and not lose anything. They had a very small tax base to begin with."[68]

Tax advisers in the private sector also attributed the continued reticence, including the lack of allocation of human resources to tax treaties until around 2014, to an institutional preoccupation with their fiscal costs. "The GDT is the tax policymaker, execution and judge. When the government set their own revenue KPIs they don't look into the long term, that's why they don't sign," stated one.[69] "They don't want to move quick and incur a lot of loopholes," said another.[70]

Building Technical Knowledge

As the pressure on Cambodia to sign treaties rose, it proceeded to develop a treaty policy cautiously, taking ten years before entering into negotiations, and put in place plans to monitor the impact on revenue of its first few treaties. The final push leading to the opening of negotiations was created by the appointment of a new director general (DG) at the GDT. "When the former DG Sin Yay was replaced by Kong Vibol, this gave it a new impetus. He's much more international," said one.[71] Another agreed that "the previous DG was quite narrow-minded. After the change of DG they started looking into a lot of issues. They started quickly on DTAs but it took a lot of time for them to understand. I thought it was just a matter of time."[72] But Cambodia's international tax bureau still had only four people in 2011, one of whom was studying abroad, and one of whom was actually dedicated to other work. "We had very few human resources, and those human resources were not fit for the job," said one of the civil servants interviewed, who is in a management position within the international tax bureau. He added, "The very day I started, I didn't know what a DTA was."[73]

In this context, external advisers had considerable influence. From the beginning, Cambodia has relied on outside experts with greater expertise than its own staff. Vanderbruggen was hired as a full-time adviser in 2006, to develop a model treaty for use in negotiations.[74] Cambodia also received technical assistance from Australian and Japanese experts (the first a former treaty negotiator) as well as the OECD, Asian Development Bank, and World Bank, and its officials have attended numerous external training courses.[75]

Cambodian officials have identified several areas where treaties that use the conventional rules of international taxation were likely to have a significant impact on the country's revenues, and where they wanted to pursue an unconventional approach. Three of these are the taxation of foreign airlines, insurance companies, and international coach travel.[76] Cambodia currently levies a tax on half the gross value of tickets sold for flights to and from the country, on the gross value of insurance premiums paid by Vietnamese residents, and on the busy coach routes between Ho Chi Minh City, Phnom Penh, and Bangkok. Officials wanted its treaties to permit this to continue. The model treaties, however, state that businesses should be taxed only on their net profits, not gross income, in these circumstances. Airlines are specifically exempted from taxation in operating countries unless they have a PE that generates profits (yet, as a government official wryly observed, state subsidies mean that most airlines flying to Cambodia make a loss, so there is no net profit for Cambodia to tax[77]); the UN model makes an exception for companies selling insurance premiums, treating them as having a PE, while no such exception applies in the OECD model; the international travel article makes no mention of coach companies, which means they can be taxed only if they fall under the conventional PE article.

Cambodian officials have negotiated very well so far (figure 7.4). Its agreements with Thailand, Singapore and Korea compare especially favorably with those signed by Vietnam, when it was also at an early stage of its negotiating history. Cambodia's agreement with China leaves fewer taxing rights intact than Vietnam's, but this is unsurprising given that China has become a far tougher negotiator since it signed with Vietnam in 1995.[78] Nonetheless, Cambodia's negotiators have struggled to maintain their unconventional positions in the face of overwhelming technical consensus that these positions contravene the acceptable standards of the model treaties. According to Vanderbruggen, who drafted Cambodia's model tax treaty,

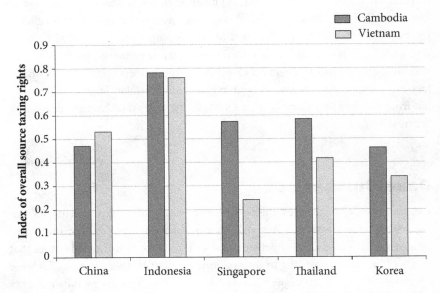

FIGURE 7.4. Cambodia's and Vietnam's negotiations compared

Source: Hearson, "Tax Treaties Explorer."

"I said, 'you cannot be the only country in the world that goes against the OECD, UN and ASEAN model [treaties].'"[79] Said a negotiator, "Your counterpart just tells you that this is not the international standard."[80] For this reason none of Cambodia's treaties allow it to tax airlines from the treaty partners in the way that it wanted to retain. It appears to have had more success on insurance, since it can refer to the authority of the UN model in support of its position. As for coach travel, Cambodia drafted alternative wording in its model treaty, which appears to have been secured in its negotiations with Vietnam and Thailand, the two countries with which it was most relevant.

Cambodia: Conclusion

Cambodia was not late to sign tax treaties because of a lack of competitive pressure. Rather, it actively resisted this pressure in terms of both comparing itself with competitor countries and accepting requests from potential treaty partners to open negotiations. The lack of treaties is also not a result of a reticence to conclude economic agreements with other countries, or of an unwillingness to use its tax system to attract investment, something that international organizations suggested it did too much of. In the early years, there was little need for tax treaties, while the later reluctance to negotiate seems to have resulted from an acute awareness of their fiscal costs, at a time when the government had become dependent on its relatively low revenues from taxes on businesses. It was only once Cambodia's direct competitors had all concluded some tax treaties that government officials reached the conclusion that the costs of not signing treaties exceeded those of doing so. The basis on which this decision was made came not from evidence, such as seeing a positive effect on investment among their competitors (who in fact the Cambodian negotiators believe had made mistakes in signing treaties), but from a feeling that Cambodia could not be the only ASEAN member with no tax treaties.

Case Comparison

Vietnam and Cambodia are outliers—positive and negative, respectively. Vietnam has one of the widest treaty networks of any lower-income country, motivated by a combination of tax competition and an assurance to inward investors that they will be taxed according to international standards. Its earlier treaties were effectively blank checks, signed before Vietnam had properly established a tax regime and certainly before it had developed a comprehensive negotiating position. Government officials were prioritizing the use of tax treaties to overcome other deficiencies that might discourage inward investment, without first forming a complete understanding of the implications of the agreements they were signing. A large pool of revenue from state-owned enterprises meant that, in the trade-off between investment promotion and the fiscal costs of tax treaties, the latter was much less of a concern to policymakers. Today, with revenue raising from foreign companies a higher priority and much more experience of negotiating and applying treaties, Vietnam's GDT is trying to undo some of its earlier mistakes. The binding nature of its treaties combined with politics within government means that it has been forced to do this via unconventional interpretation that contravenes the same international standards that, in principle, it supports through its treaty negotiations.

Cambodia, in contrast, has been a model of how countries should approach treaty negotiation. By the time it was ready to consider tax treaties, corporate tax revenue—and in particular from foreign-owned companies—had become an important part of government revenues, which made the tax costs a more significant concern. Having resisted invitations to begin negotiations for years, Cambodia opened discussions only after a decade-long period of capacity building and policy development, avoiding the mistakes that Vietnam and Zambia had made. It identified particular areas where international standards would impose undesirable tax costs, and although its negotiators came up against the power of the model treaties and the consensus within the tax community, it has managed to carve a distinctive path that protects its interests, at least partially.

HISTORICAL LEGACIES IN A RAPIDLY CHANGING WORLD

If you're not at the table, you're on the menu.

—Slogan used by campaigners for an intergovernmental tax body
at the United Nations

The landscape of global economic governance is changing, moving away from that which characterized most of the negotiations discussed in this book. As power shifts away from the OECD countries, the institutions of the liberal economic order face an existential threat.[1] As Richard Eccleston has argued, "The extent and nature of international cooperation [are] increasingly dependent on the foreign economic policy priorities of China and other emerging powers."[2] Lower-income countries are becoming more organized, but they are also more clearly divided, with the interests of large emerging markets and lower-income countries not always aligned. As we saw in chapters 6 and 7, low-income countries now face their toughest demands when negotiating tax treaties with China.

The multilateral institutions of global tax governance are not immune from this shifting terrain. The usual forum for debates about the organizational infrastructure of global tax governance is the United Nations' Financing for Development process. This is the highest political level at which the status of the UN Tax Committee—responsible among other things for drafting the UN model tax treaty—is discussed. Calls from the G77 group of lower-income countries to upgrade the committee to a full intergovernmental body have been a regular part of this process since 2002, but they reached a new peak in 2015 when a summit in Addis Ababa nearly fell apart. G77 members were adamant that the committee be upgraded, while OECD member states were implacably opposed. With development aid at risk if the conference collapsed, the lower-income countries eventually capitulated.[3]

The slogan quoted above has gone mainstream. In 2015, it featured on a banner unfurled by protesters at the United Nations, but by the time of a conference in the UN's New York headquarters in 2018 it had been appropriated by Pascal Saint-Amans, the director of the OECD's Centre for Tax Policy and Administration. In 2013, the OECD opened up its corporate tax franchise to the G20 members, inviting emerging markets to participate in all its tax work on an equal footing. The result is that a small but discernible Chinese imprint, for example, is visible on the latest drafts of the OECD's transfer pricing guidelines.[4] Since 2016, all lower-income countries have since been invited to participate in an Inclusive Framework covering the implementation of the OECD's anti-tax-avoidance package (known as base erosion and profit shifting, or BEPS); more than one hundred countries, among them the UK, Vietnam, and Zambia, have joined. Others, such as Cambodia, remain skeptically on the outside. While campaigners initially criticized the Inclusive Framework because its mandate was limited to the implementation of standards developed by the OECD and G20, it has become the vehicle through which new policy challenges, notably the controversy about the application of international tax norms to the digital economy, are being addressed. That particular challenge appears to have irreconcilably broken the consensus among OECD members that has lasted for over a century, leaving them less united—and hence more vulnerable—than ever before.[5]

This book therefore comes at a time of great change, and of potential opportunities and risks for lower-income countries. They face a strategic dilemma. On the one hand, the opening at the OECD offers the possibility to shape the tools of international tax cooperation, especially the model treaties, in ways that allow lower-income countries to benefit from participation in the tax treaty regime without needing to give up so much tax revenue. Cancellations, renegotiations, and policy reviews across lower-income countries, together with the entry of new political actors into the politics of tax treaties, suggest the potential to stake out a new, more assertive position. On the other hand, as Tsilly Dagan has suggested, there is good reason to fear that lower-income countries will be the losers from apparently inclusive tax cooperation.[6] In what follows, I reflect on the implications for this situation of historical North-South politics, and sound a note of caution.

How We Got Here: A Brief Summary

The term "double taxation agreement" conveys an idea that is powerful but misleading: that the purpose of the bilateral foundations of the international tax regime is to resolve a problem created by competing claims to tax inward cross-border investment, which will deter that investment. Tsilly Dagan argues that this logic is a myth, and as this book has shown, many actors in the process, including negotiators themselves, agree with her. Most notably, the United Kingdom's international tax officials in the 1970s, responsible for a huge program of negotiations, shared this view. Members of the international tax community abhor double taxation but recognize that even in the absence of a treaty it is unlikely to exist to a degree that will deter large amounts of investment in lower-income countries. Nonetheless, it is axiomatic that the conclusion of tax treaties is the appropriate way for a modern fiscal state to behave, because they embody a set of standards that have been elaborated by experts from the most advanced economies in a technocratic Parisian environment. Behind this apparently depoliticized front, however, we find a century of activity by officials from capital-exporting states to cement a bias in their favor into the international tax regime's multilateral core.

As actors in lower-income countries—fledgling fiscal states—have gained technical knowledge, they have been infused with this bias toward the OECD-centric approach. Vietnam, an unusually prolific negotiator, ensured that all its investors were covered by a tax treaty, even where there was little competitive pressure on it to do so. The way in which it applied those treaties, however, undermined any benefits that investors might have expected to gain from them. Zambia's international tax specialists negotiated and renegotiated agreements that they saw as a priority, but struggled until 2011 to persuade political veto players to sign and ratify them. As Cambodia succumbed to the inevitable logic of competition through tax treaties, its officials had to balance the need for support from external technical advisers with their advice that treaty provisions outside of the international models are not viable.

Meanwhile, the tax treaties myth prevails among actors who do not have this same technical knowledge. To them, signing tax treaties is one of the things that a country wishing to compete for investment does, even though there is not a solid evidence base to support this view. The choice of treaty partners illustrates this point: positive outliers such as Zambia and Vietnam, in negotiations during the 1970s and 1990s, respectively, signed treaties with countries where there was little prospect that the treaty would lead to enhanced investment. These countries' high tax-to-GDP ratios insulated negotiators from more intense scrutiny of their choices, whereas in Cambodia and later in Zambia, the priority to raise more tax revenue from companies has contributed to more cautious approaches.

Negotiations by countries with limited technical expertise and a competition-driven mentality also produced results in terms of the content of their agreements that illustrated the bounded rationality of their negotiating stance. When Zambia's and Vietnam's negotiations were motivated by competition, they also signed away taxing rights that their present negotiators regret. Had they fully appreciated the agreements they were signing, past negotiators might also have been more reluctant to give away so much.

Different ideas produced different priorities over what to negotiate with whom, and why. This is not to say, however, that material factors did not also play a role, as clearly they did. Ideas constructed preferences that sometimes had their origins in material interests. In particular, the UK case and other anecdotal evidence support the idea that higher-income countries actively pursue tax treaties with lower-income countries because this improves the competitive position of their own multinationals. Yet, in the UK, two competing ideas about how treaties would achieve this shaped the country's negotiating priorities. In some instances, the UK turned down an agreement in the face of strong competitive pressure, because it undermined the broader project embodied by the OECD model. Furthermore, even if rational interests did explain the actions of capital exporters, we also need to explain the willingness of capital importers to negotiate. This brings us back to the ideational mechanisms discussed above.

Changes in ideas and negotiating capabilities offer one explanation for differences in negotiating outcomes over time; another is changing priorities. The tax-sparing clauses that were popular in tax treaties from the 1970s to the 1990s provided benefits directly to companies rather than eliminating double taxation. There is some positive evidence to suggest that these clauses stimulate investment in lower-income countries, yet they are not part of the modern tax standards package, and tax specialists have an ambivalent relationship with them. The OECD suggested in 1998 that there was "an emerging consensus on the need for a re-evaluation," claiming that "the basic assumption underlying tax sparing is invalid,"[7] an argument that is much stronger with the move by most OECD countries toward exempting the foreign profits of multinationals from further tax. Yet tax-sparing clauses were an important part of the balance of costs and benefits by lower-income countries at the time many agreements still in force today were negotiated. Furthermore, while tax-sparing clauses clearly motivated some of the particular negotiations considered in the case studies, they by no means explain all. Indeed, UK negotiators regarded tax-sparing clauses as an adjunct to the main function of tax treaties and fought off pressure to sign with Brazil that was largely motivated by the desire for tax sparing. When Zambia negotiated with the UK, and Vietnam negotiated with the United States, both dropped their demands for tax sparing in order to secure an agreement.

This historical account tells us that the global power shift that is currently under way is not enough to change the North-South politics of global tax governance, at least not overnight. The sections that follow consider why this might be the case. The established powers have a strong first-mover advantage baked into multilateral institutions that, for the time being at least, show no sign of losing their dominant position. This advantage is both material, in the content of soft and hard law, and ideational, through the consensus that prevails in an international tax community dominated by practitioners from the Global North, as well as in the nonexpert discourse about tax treaties, which still centers on the tax treaties myth. Even if powerful non-OECD states were to destabilize these existing instruments and ideas, it is not clear that their long-term interests will align with those of low-income countries.

Overcoming the First-Mover Advantage

As we saw in chapter 2, the story of lower-income countries' participation in the original League of Nations points to the need for some caution about the possibilities for change from the current openings. At the League, the first movers' agenda-setting power circumscribed subsequent discussions, limiting the options that lower-income countries could pursue. Had lower-income countries been in the room in 1925 rather than in 1928, the model tax treaties might have looked different. It is much harder to overturn an established consensus than to influence it in the first place. Similarly, had the United Nations rather than the OEEC/OECD picked up the league's work after the Second World War, the more lower-income-country-friendly settlement found in the Mexico Draft might have gained more currency. By the twenty-first century, the hegemonic position enjoyed by the OECD model, as a template both for bilateral treaties and for domestic laws, is difficult for all but the most self-confident emerging markets to challenge. As Eduardo Baistrocchi suggests, OECD tax standards benefit from network effects: any alternative would need to overcome their widespread use by other countries and hence by multinational companies, which creates a powerful incentive to conform.[8] This analysis supports the historical institutionalist case that institutions created from decisions in the past condition the possibilities for action in the present.

Lower-income countries have tried to overcome the bias in the international tax regime at two levels: bilateral and multilateral. In the bilateral setting, a number have sought to renegotiate their tax treaties, strengthening their taxing rights and protecting them against tax avoidance. The results are mixed at best. Figure 8.1 gives the outcomes of 114 renegotiations by lower-income countries, comparing the overall source taxing rights permitted by the original treaty and the renegotiation. Distance above (below) the line shows how much the renegotiation improved (reduced) the balance of taxing rights from the perspective of the lower-income country. The outcomes vary significantly, and the original content of the treaty is a strong predictor of the renegotiated treaty that replaces it.

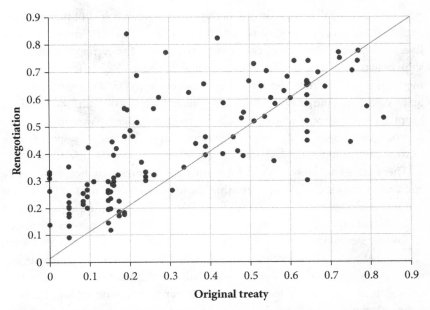

FIGURE 8.1. Tax treaty negotiations by lower-income countries measured using the overall index of source taxing rights

Source: Martin Hearson, "Tax Treaties Explorer," 2020, http://treaties.tax.

As chapter 6 illustrated, Zambia's renegotiations did generally strengthen its taxing rights, but the improvements to each treaty were relatively small, with give and take characterizing the renegotiation. In contrast, the most dramatic improvement by an African country, Rwanda's treaty with Mauritius, was obtained by first canceling, then renegotiating the treaty. This illustrates a point made throughout this book's empirical chapters that lower-income countries often underestimate their power, since their treaty partners may have a greater desire to obtain and maintain a treaty than they realize. This is certainly the case for Mauritius, whose position as an offshore financial center relies in large part on its network of tax treaties. The data set compares treaties against a fairly modest yardstick, and no lower-income country has succeeded in negotiating a tax treaty with a major capital-exporting state on any basis other than the OECD model or equivalent.

What about the multilateral track? Lower-income countries were only given a seat at the OECD table in 2016, but they have long been able to participate in the UN tax committee's deliberations. Beyond the modest improvements to the OECD model that the UN model has embodied since its publication in 1980, the committee has little else to show in terms of tangible tools to help lower-income countries counteract the bias in the international tax system. No doubt interventions such as negotiation manuals and capacity-building programs can help, but they also perpetuate the notion of good practice embodied in the OECD-UN complex. At the level of personnel, this should not be surprising, given the overlapping memberships between UN and OECD committees highlighted in chapter 4. At committee meetings, the social interactions between members from OECD countries are also quite visible, in comparison with less networked members from lower-income countries. At the time of writing, the UN committee's subgroup working on transfer pricing includes three former OECD secretariat staff who were responsible for its work on that topic, all of whom subsequently moved into the private sector.

There are signs, however, that lower-income countries are becoming more effective in their use of the opportunities provided by the UN. In 2017 the new committee elected an African cochair for the first time. According to participants in the discussions, this was because the committee's seven African members united around the same one member.[9] Members from OECD countries, who have always caucused ahead of UN committee meetings, did the same, and the stalemate was resolved through the election of two joint chairs for the first time. Just before this, the committee agreed to include an article permitting withholding taxes on technical services—an issue that has animated bilateral negotiations as early as 1972—into the UN model, where it finally appeared in 2017.

As for the OECD's new Inclusive Framework, the initial signs suggest that changes in institutional form have given lower-income countries some formal scope to participate, but that the OECD's de facto control over discussions has not been relaxed. According to conversations with several representatives of lower-income countries who have participated in the Inclusive Framework, as well as other participants and observers, lower-income countries' interventions are politely listened to but not taken on board if they differ from the existing consensus. "Everybody knows that developing countries can say their position, but proposals are put by the developed countries," according to one,[10] while another concurred that "we feel that everything is predetermined from the G20 and the OECD. . . . They say it is on an equal footing, but that is not true."[11] One former delegate from an OECD country suggests that this dynamic is less nationally derived and more because of "a group of friends meeting each other every couple of months."[12] Effective influence in the OECD committees, this person suggested, depended on going to the same restaurant and drinking wine in the same Parisian apartment as the most influential committee members.

There is some indication that this situation may be subject to change. Both the G20 emerging market countries and the ATAF—which had observer status on behalf of African countries—have claimed some success in shaping OECD standards during the BEPS project, although these changes are certainly only marginal and incremental.[13] Discussions in the Inclusive Framework on the only major outstanding BEPS agenda item, the digital economy, have moved from implementation to standard setting. A policy paper drafted by India, Ghana, and Colombia on behalf of the Intergovernmental Group of 24 lower-income countries was noted by the head of the OECD secretariat to have played a role in shaping the agenda for discussions, which at the time of writing have yet to reach any outcome.[14]

These developments confirm that preexisting institutions created among a core of countries do lock peripheral states into participation in regimes that do not reflect their interests, and entrench interstate power dynamics. Lower-income countries may be able to overcome these lock-in effects, but opportunities for change are likely to be incremental.[15] They also demonstrate that the level of influence lower-income countries can exert within those boundaries is not predetermined. One variable that seems to determine latitude for change is the capacity of lower-income countries' representatives to organize into caucuses and work together. Here the OECD representatives have clear advantages: the status quo is a long-standing consensus among them; they form a social group whose shared understanding of the normative and technical basis of cooperation is maintained through regular informal, as well as formal, interactions.

One side effect of the increased intensity of multilateral bargaining involving lower-income countries, however, is the beginning of a new counterhegemonic intersubjective understanding of the international tax regime that emphasizes its unfairness. Consider a PowerPoint slide from a Ghanaian negotiator—now the cochair of the UN Tax Committee: "International tax rules . . . [are] not in [the] interest of developing countries."[16] This echoes a written statement from Chinese tax officials: "For a long time, in their competition with developing countries for more tax resources (tax base), developed countries have obtained most of the benefits generated by MNEs [multinational enterprises] by relying on their dominant position in formulating the rules and superiority in technology and intangible property, while developing countries have obtained a very small share of the profits."[17] This new discourse was also on display at a meeting of French-speaking African tax officials attended by the author in 2018. According to one participant whose country had joined the OECD, "They arranged everything first and then invited us into the Inclusive Framework. But there are nonetheless some opportunities for African countries there."[18]

Resisting the Logic of Appropriateness

The development of this new discourse among technocrats matters because confrontation in the international tax regime takes place in the technical sphere. Indeed, the politicization of corporate tax policy is often framed by members of the tax community as a risk in itself: it signals policy instability and decisions that prioritize dogmatic principles over economic efficiency. This may in part explain OECD countries' preference for limiting discussion of international tax rules to its technocratic CFA and a UN committee of experts whose members participate only in a personal capacity. Just as the institutional setting of the OECD is higher-income countries' home turf, so for the time being is the "expert" sphere. Lower-income countries need to build knowledge on their own terms, rather than simply assimilating knowledge originating in the North.

Of the cases described in this book, Cambodia illustrates most vividly how this might work. Over a decade, Cambodia's General Directorate of Taxes developed the institutional knowledge and capacity it needed to negotiate tax treaties, relying on expert advice but being ready to challenge it when necessary. The result: Cambodia's treaties are among the most expansive in the taxing rights that they retain—measured using the index of overall source taxing rights, Cambodia has the most sovereignty-preserving treaty network of any lower-income country. Crucially, its treaties include some provisions important to Cambodia that break the mold, in small but important ways.

Looking elsewhere, there is some small evidence of a shift in the center of gravity. The UN's inclusion of an article on technical service fees in its model convention, forty-five years after such articles began to become part of lower-income countries' negotiation platforms, underscores this, as do the data showing an increased prevalence of this article in treaties signed by lower-income countries (figure 8.2). As we saw in chapter 1, tax treaties signed by lower-income countries are also including more generous PE clauses as time goes on, increasing the circumstances in which they are able to levy taxes on the profits made locally by foreign companies. There are some caveats to both of these changes, however. First, they are occurring predominantly within treaties signed between lower-income countries. Tax treaties signed between OECD members and lower-income countries are no more generous in their PE definition now than in the 1970s, on average. Many OECD members still resist articles concerning technical service fees. The UK is a notable example: in the course of researching this book I encountered one example of a country that capitulated to the UK on this issue, and three that had walked away from negotiations because of it. Even where OECD countries agree to include such an article, they naturally extract other concessions in return. The second caveat is that these changes are still taking place within the existing tax treaty paradigm. Overall, tax treaties signed by OECD countries are becoming more, not less, restrictive in the limitations they impose on the taxing rights of lower-income countries.

To look for examples of countries breaking more significantly with the established norms of the international tax regime, we must look beyond tax treaties.

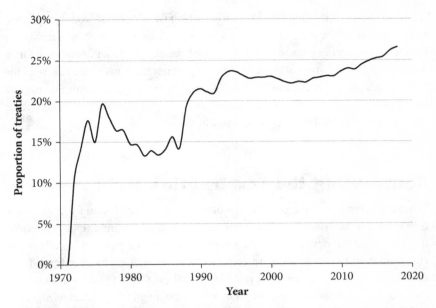

FIGURE 8.2. Cumulative proportion of lower-income countries' treaties including a technical service fee withholding tax clause

Source: Hearson, "Tax Treaties Explorer."

Rwanda, for example, when introducing a broadly OECD-compliant income tax code in 2018, included a provision permitting it to impose a tax surcharge on payments of royalties and technical service fees exceeding 2 percent of a firm's turnover, thus limiting its vulnerability to tax avoidance.[19] The international tax consensus dictates that, so long as these payments can be justified, they should not be penalized in the tax system. India and China, meanwhile, have pushed ahead with interventions that chip away in other ways, laying claim to a much bigger share of the tax base than OECD norms permit.[20] Lower-income countries are also beginning to innovate by introducing new taxes on the digital economy that break with consensus.[21]

The OECD's work on the digital economy, while not driven primarily by lower-income countries, has broken new ground, with an agreement to pursue solutions that "go beyond" the underlying norms and open up the distributional discussion that was previously off limits, with the intention of shifting the balance of taxing rights toward greater source taxation.[22] This shift has been driven by political pressures across higher-income and lower-income countries, which are so great as to threaten the previously stable consensus. According to the US Treasury's deputy assistant secretary for international tax affairs, speaking in February 2019, "The world risks an accelerating trend towards unilateral actions that would jeopardize the coherence of the international tax system."[23] If, indeed, we are observing the beginnings of a more organized lower-income country bloc that demands reform, experience in other areas of global economic governance, such as the failure of the Doha round at the WTO and the Copenhagen climate change summit, suggests that its initial impact will be a period of unilateralism and stalemate, rendering existing global institutions of cooperation ineffective.

Confronting the Tax Treaties Myth

What about the political accountability of negotiators? One lesson from this book is that for any new discourse about the international tax regime to gain traction, it needs to extend beyond the technocratic sphere to the political one. This can empower negotiators reticent to rock the boat, as well as insulate them from making decisions based on the prevailing social norms of the transnational tax community. In interviews, I noticed a new cohort of highly skilled, knowledgeable, and experienced tax negotiators from lower-income countries who vocally expressed critical opinions about the current state of the tax treaty regime.

There is some evidence that the international tax regime more generally has escalated as a political concern in lower-income countries. In 2015, a high-level panel chaired by former South African president Thabo Mbeki published its report on illicit financial flows (IFFs), which was endorsed by the African Union council. The report noted that "double taxation agreements can contain provisions that are harmful to domestic resource mobilization and can be used to facilitate illicit financial outflows. We recommend that African countries review their current and prospective double taxation conventions, particularly those in place with jurisdictions that are significant destinations of IFFs, to ensure that they do not provide opportunities for abuse."[24]

Much more energy has been generated around the issue of tax treaty abuse than on the unfairness built into tax treaties by design. An exception is perhaps the debate over the status of the UN Tax Committee, discussed earlier in this chapter. Foreign ministries and finance ministries of lower-income countries, as well as their tax authorities, appear to be concerned that the existing committee's work to date had not displayed the ambition that they were increasingly seeking. This is why the G77 group of lower-income countries set out "the need to fully upgrade the [UN] Tax Committee into an intergovernmental body."[25]

But lifting discussion about tax treaties from the technical to the political sphere brings with it the attendant risks of slipping further into a cycle of negotiations that are not grounded in a coherent analysis of costs and benefits. A clear message from this book is that a competent team of negotiators can only go so far if they are embedded within a government machine pervaded by the logic of tax competition. Indeed, two negotiators from African countries interviewed in 2018 gave examples of negotiations that had been undermined by senior government ministers who were keen to ink an agreement with the other country as quickly as possible and who acted over the heads of their negotiation teams.[26] Catherine Ngina Mutava collected numerous further examples.[27] Many lower-income countries continue to sign tax treaties because of a perception that they must keep up with their competitors and neighbors. Cambodia's eventual, admittedly reluctant, capitulation to the logic propounded within ASEAN is one example of this, following the example of Zambia's SADC-inspired treaties.

The political pressures do not all operate in one direction, however. As the Zambia case showed, the politicization of multinational companies' tax affairs, widespread over the past decade, can put a brake on negotiations. In Ghana, for example, opposition parties threatened to hold up the ratification of four treaties through the country's parliament in 2018.[28] Kenya's government failed to win the court case brought against its treaty with Mauritius, which was struck down on the grounds that the ratification had not followed proper procedure, despite the permanent secretary to the Treasury's defense of it in evidence. The finding was on a technicality, and the court upheld the broader constitutionality of the treaty's content and the process of ratification, concurring that as an "agreement" it was not subject to the same strictures as a treaty.[29] The political impact of the court case, which for the first time brought tax treaties into the domain of public debate, cannot be underestimated.

Concerns in higher-income countries have also placed pressure on governments of higher-income countries to reconsider their negotiating approach. An unprecedented vote in the UK's parliament on its treaty with Lesotho in 2018 was the first time that a tax treaty has not been waved through by its lawmakers. Both Ireland and the Netherlands conducted reviews into the economic impact of their treaty networks on lower-income countries, after which they offered renegotiations to lower-income countries identified as adversely affected.[30] The European Commission is among the organizations urging major capital-exporting nations to conduct such analyses and has produced a toolkit of suggestions for how they might do so.[31]

New Allies and New Enemies

While Cambodia, Zambia, and Vietnam will need to punch above their weight to shape the contours of the international tax regime, the same is not true for some emerging markets. China has already begun to shape the international tax regime, pushing the OECD toward adapting its transfer pricing rules to absorb some Chinese characteristics.[32] The OECD has been replaced by a G20-OECD complex in which countries including Saudi Arabia, South Africa, and India now have seats at the top table. Yet, as the contours of the global economy shift, it is far from clear that countries such as these share the same interests as Cambodia, Vietnam, and Zambia. Indeed, it is possible that we will see the formation of a higher-income-country–emerging market bloc, making it harder, not easier, for lower-income countries to shift the center of gravity of the tax treaty regime. These fears are grounded in both bilateral and multilateral developments.

At the bilateral level, many of the least generous tax treaties being signed by lower-income countries are with emerging markets that are becoming capital exporters. Among the countries that have signed the most treaties with lower-income countries this century, Turkey, Mauritius, and China appear to be the most aggressive negotiators, with the most residence-based treaties, followed by Middle Eastern states with sovereign wealth funds, Kuwait and the United Arab Emirates (table 8.1). Turkey's position in this table surprised its negotiators when I informed them at a European Commission workshop in 2018. China's bulldozing approach can be seen from Cambodia's tax treaties: while treaties with ASEAN members stand out for their uniform source-based nature, its agreement with China is anomalous, at the other end of the spectrum. Uganda, at least, has left its treaty with China unratified because of its one-sided terms. Lower-income countries cannot rely on large emerging markets that have more clout with international tax rulemaking to carve out changes to model treaties that will benefit them.

TABLE 8.1.   The ten countries that have signed the most tax treaties with lower-income countries since 2000

COUNTRY	INDEX OF OVERALL SOURCE TAXING RIGHTS—AVERAGE	NUMBER OF TREATIES
Turkey	0.31	14
Mauritius	0.37	17
China	0.38	17
Kuwait	0.42	23
United Arab Emirates	0.42	31
Portugal	0.43	13
South Africa	0.46	14
Iran	0.49	14
Qatar	0.52	18
Saudi Arabia	0.53	14

Source: Martin Hearson, "Tax Treaties Explorer," 2020, http://treaties.tax.

In particular, China's advocacy in multilateral forums appears to be aimed not at generating *general* benefits for all lower-income countries but at carving out *special* benefits for China. Rhetorically, China has presented itself as a champion of lower-income-country concerns. A Chinese State Administration of Taxation web page approvingly quotes a Chinese academic observing that "the formulation of the global tax rules has long been dominated by developed countries, with appeals of developing countries not taken into full consideration."[33] It goes on to document concerns common to a wide range of lower-income countries. Yet China's most significant break with OECD rules to date, which grabs a bigger share of the multinational tax base, is based on the "location specific advantages" that it argues make firms more profitable in China than elsewhere. This will benefit China at the expense of lower-income countries as well as OECD members, as demonstrated by the official view that China's market premium is "unique in the world and inimitable by other small and medium-sized developing countries."[34]

A Call for New Research

This book points toward the need to question some of the priorities and assumptions that have characterized thinking about international tax up to now. It is not just policymakers who have been influenced by the seductive logic behind so-called Double Taxation Agreements and the other institutions of the international tax regime. Previous studies addressing this question have tended to assume that tax treaties are primarily the product of capital-importing states' desire to stimulate investment, principally by eliminating double taxation. Convergence on the Western-dominated institutions of international tax cooperation is still often characterized as based on rational calculation that the costs in terms of investment from not conforming exceed those in terms of tax revenue from participation. Critical accounts in the legal literature frequently disagree, arguing that lower-income countries would do better to keep at a distance from the OECD and its model tax treaty, but they are at a loss to explain why they have not done so. Lower-income countries are losing out because they arrived late on the scene, but it is as much ideas as institutions that are path dependent. Rational calculation alone often cannot explain why actors in lower-income countries have come to the conclusion that it is a good idea to sign tax treaties as they have done, and analysis focused on interest groups fails to account for divisions *within* particular types of actors, including inside government. This book's detailed empirical research shows that the way the problem and the solution are constructed differs depending on an actor's technical expertise.

A first direction for future scholarship is therefore toward an understanding of the causal role played by ideas about corporate taxation. Too often, international tax cooperation has been a technocratic area of policy, with decisions made far from the more boisterous world of tax-and-spend politics. Yet it is in this more political domain that it belongs, and many lower-income countries have found that a failure to combine the technical capacity of negotiators with political buy-in to the negotiation strategy has led to poor, incoherent decision making that comes back to haunt them. We could say the same about the decisions made by higher-income countries that led to their post-financial-crisis travails: the current wave of politicization of corporate taxation—and in some countries, of tax treaties themselves—is really a backlash against decades of decisions made by technocrats and politicians that hollowed out the tax base, obscured from the full view of stakeholders.[35] In lower-income countries, which rely heavily on taxation from multinational companies, these decisions, which have bound subsequent governments into tax treaties, tax incentives, stability agreements with mining companies, and so on, do not only undermine the state's ability to provide the public services expected by its citizens. They also compromise tax morale, and with it the nascent fiscal contract between citizens and the state.

A second direction for future research is toward a more grounded theorizing of the relationship between the Global North and the Global South in international tax cooperation. Literature on tax cooperation in international relations and international political economy has been almost entirely focused on tax avoidance, tax evasion, and tax havens, all areas where economic actors gain from the limits of international tax cooperation.[36] The conclusion of this book, similar to that reached by Tsilly Dagan, is that more cooperation is not necessarily a good thing: if international tax rules worked perfectly, the outcome for lower-income countries would still be unsatisfactory, because the rules are biased by design.[37]

Consider the notion of tax competition, which is at the heart of how we theorize the motivations for cooperation. Economics and international political economy have long focused on the "race to the bottom," thought to result from competition between states for *inward* investment. The role of competition between capital-*exporting* states, which seek to increase opportunities for their outward investors, was rarely considered. Yet the truth is not too far from the allegations of the Russian and Polish delegates to the United Nations in the early 1950s (chapter 2): cooperation to relieve double taxation creates a favorable tax environment that promotes the expansion of multinationals from major capital-exporting states. As the headquarters of multinational companies have become more mobile, pitting those states against each other to attract multinationals' headquarters, competition for outward investment has intensified, and international organizations have raised concerns about the spillover effects on lower-income countries.[38] Tax treaties are just one example of an increasingly complex story of tax competition among capital exporters, which may now be the most significant obstacle to more effective tax cooperation.[39] To understand what these countries want when they negotiate a tax treaty, we need a more sophisticated model of their preferences that takes into account the use of international tax rules to provide financial advantages to mobile capital, rather than simply to maximize revenue. The focus in academic and policy discourse on competition among capital importers merely contributes to the tax treaties myth.

Even if we were to accept a significant role for inward investment-promoting tax competition, and for the double taxation problem itself, it does not necessarily follow that the consensus across the OECD-derived model tax treaties, which systematically shift the burden of double tax relief onto lower-income countries, is the inevitable solution. Again, some tax officials, on gaining sufficient understanding of tax treaties to realize this, question the standard treaty articles. But there has not been a concerted push to challenge the hegemonic status of the de facto settlement between higher-income and lower-income countries that is embodied by the OECD model. Here we need to better understand the strategic dilemmas and collective action problems faced by lower-income countries themselves. Why have they failed to maximize the gains possible from existing multilateral institutions, and within the parameters set by the model treaties for bilateral negotiations? Is it meaningful to think about a monolithic bloc of "lower-income countries" given that powerful emerging markets are among the toughest negotiators with lower-income countries and pursue their own agendas in multilateral forums? The approach here, a "thick description" that captures how these issues are understood by negotiators and policymakers, has demonstrated that academics' assumptions about the answers to these questions do not always hold.

This book was written at a time when international tax, and increasingly tax treaties themselves, has become uniquely politicized, creating more interest from actors in lower-income countries in questioning the rules of the tax cooperation game. The timing is not entirely coincidental, and some of the analysis herein has contributed to public debates about the choices made by higher-income and lower-income countries over their tax treaties. Yet historical perspectives on the origins of lower-income countries' tax treaty networks are sorely lacking. During fieldwork in Uganda, civil servants were surprised that I knew much more about their country's past negotiations with the UK than they did. After I presented chapter 5 of this book to a group of African revenue officials, a revenue authority commissioner approached me to say how surprised he was to learn of higher-income countries' own motivations for concluding tax treaties with lower-income countries.

This lack of historical perspective needs to be addressed for a number of reasons. First, many lower-income countries, including Zambia and Vietnam, signed treaties with their biggest sources of investment soon after independence or opening up. The result is that the taxation of much of their foreign investment is governed by agreements on terms reached by negotiators who may have had much less knowledge and experience than their current successors, reaching trade-offs that were specific to the economic and political climate of the day. Second, a negotiated tax treaty is sticky: the consequences for a country's reputation of terminating a treaty may be more significant than not negotiating it in the first place, as a Zambian negotiator lamented.[40] Lower-income countries are subject to "policy drift," whereby domestic and international politics make it tough to alter their historically negotiated treaties, even as the economic context changes around them, potentially making the treaties costly in ways that could not have been anticipated.[41] Third, negotiating positions are determined by precedent, with subsequent negotiations starting from the terms that a country has offered in the past.

Consider the 1973 UK-Kenya tax treaty, with which this book began. It was a Kenyan priority, as in many of the case studies in this book, to secure a tax-sparing clause so that British firms could benefit fully from Kenyan tax incentives. Such a clause is no longer necessary, as the UK has ceased taxing most of the foreign-source profits of British multinationals. The tough negotiation over the taxation of service fees occurred before the internet age had revolutionized the tax planning possible using such payments. On this basis, it might be a sensible strategy for Kenya to go back to the drawing board on this treaty, as it had originally done in the 1970s. The treaties it tore up then were biased against it because they had been imposed under colonial rule. Its treaties today are also biased, but this is a consequence of a hegemony of ideas, not colonization. This hegemony operates differently at the expert and nonexpert levels, but the effect is the same: an imbalanced tax treaty system that serves the interests of OECD member states and multinational firms, to the detriment of development.

APPENDIX
List of Interviews and Meetings Observed

TABLE A.1. Interviews

INTERVIEW NUMBER	YEAR	SETTING	NUMBER OF INTERVIEWEES	COUNTRY INCOME GROUP	TYPE OF INTERVIEWEE
1	2013	Telephone^	1	High	International organization / former civil servant
2	2013	Field visit	1	Upper-middle	Civil servant
3	2013	Field visit	1	Upper-middle	Civil servant
4	2013	Int'l meeting	1	Upper-middle	Civil servant
5	2013	Int'l meeting	1	Upper-middle	Civil servant
6	2013	Int'l meeting^	2	Lower-middle	Civil servant
7	2013	Int'l meeting*	1	Low	Civil servant
8	2013	Field visit	1	Lower-middle	Civil servant
9	2013	Field visit	1	High	Private sector
10	2013	Int'l meeting	1	Low	Civil servant
11	2013	Int'l meeting*	1	Low	Civil servant
12	2013	Int'l meeting*	1	High	Private sector
13	2013	Int'l meeting	1	High	Civil servant
14	2013	Int'l meeting	1	High	Civil servant
15	2013	Int'l meeting	1	Upper-middle	Civil servant
16	2013	Int'l meeting	1	Upper-middle	Civil servant
17	2013	Int'l meeting	1	Upper-middle	Civil servant
18	2013	Int'l meeting	1	High	Civil servant
19	2013	Int'l meeting*	1	High	Civil servant
20	2013	Int'l meeting	3	Low	Civil servant
21	2014	Field visit	1	High	Civil servant
22	2014	Int'l meeting	1	Low	Technical adviser / former civil servant
23	2014	Field visit	1	Lower-middle	Civil servant
24	2014	Field visit	1	Lower-middle	Civil servant
25	2014	Field visit	1	Low	Civil servant
26	2014	Field visit	1	Low	Private sector
27	2014	Field visit	2	Low	Private sector
28	2014	Field visit	3	Low	Civil servant
29	2014	Field visit	1	Low	Academic/private sector

(continued)

TABLE A.1. (continued)

INTERVIEW NUMBER	YEAR	SETTING	NUMBER OF INTERVIEWEES	COUNTRY INCOME GROUP	TYPE OF INTERVIEWEE
30	2014	Field visit	1	Low	Private sector
31	2014	Field visit	1	Low	Civil servant
32	2015	Field visit	2	International organization	International organization / former civil servant
33	2015	Field visit	1	International organization	International organization / former civil servant
34	2015	Field visit	2	High	Civil servant
35	2015	Field visit	2	High	Civil servant
36	2015	Int'l meeting	1	Upper-middle	Civil servant
37	2015	Field visit	1	Upper-middle	Private sector
38	2015	Field visit	2	High	Private sector
39	2015	Field visit	1	High	Civil servant
40	2015	Int'l meeting*	1	International organization	Academic/ international organization
69	2017	Int'l meeting	1	Lower-middle	Civil servant
71	2017	Int'l meeting	1	Lower-middle	Civil servant
72	2018	Int'l meeting	1	Upper-middle	Civil servant
73	2018	Int'l meeting	2	Lower-middle	Civil servant
74	2018	Int'l meeting	1	High	Civil servant
75	2018	Int'l meeting	1	Low	Civil servant
ZAMBIA					
41	2014	Email	1	Lower-middle	Civil servant
42	2014	Telephone	1	Lower-middle	Technical adviser / private sector
43	2014	Field visit^	1	Lower-middle	Civil servant
44	2014	Field visit	1	Lower-middle	Civil servant
45	2014	Field visit	1	Lower-middle	Civil servant
46	2014	Field visit	2	High	Civil servant
47	2014	Field visit	1	International organization	International organization
48	2014	Field visit	1	Lower-middle	Private sector
49	2014	Field visit	1	Lower-middle	Civil servant
50	2014	Field visit	2	Lower-middle	Private sector
51	2014	Field visit	1	Lower-middle	Technical adviser
52	2014	Email	1	Lower-middle	Technical adviser / private sector

TABLE A.1. (continued)

INTERVIEW NUMBER	YEAR	SETTING	NUMBER OF INTERVIEWEES	COUNTRY INCOME GROUP	TYPE OF INTERVIEWEE
VIETNAM					
53	2014	Field visit	1	International organization	International organization
54	2015	Field visit	3	Lower-middle	Private sector
55	2015	Field visit	2	Lower-middle	Civil servant
56	2015	Field visit	1	Lower-middle	Private sector
57	2015	Field visit	1	Lower-middle	Civil servant
58	2015	Telephone	1	Lower-middle	Private sector
59	2015	Field visit	1	Lower-middle	Civil servant
60	2015	Field visit	1	Lower-middle	Private sector
61	2015	Field visit	1	Lower-middle	Private sector
62	2015	Field visit	2	Lower-middle	Private sector
63	2015	Telephone	1	High	Civil servant
70	2017	Int'l meeting	1	Lower-middle	Civil servant
CAMBODIA					
64	2015	Field visit	1	Lower-middle	Civil servant
65	2015	Field visit	1	Lower-middle	Civil servant
66	2015	Telephone	1	Lower-middle	Technical adviser / private sector
67	2015	Field visit	1	Lower-middle	Private sector
68	2015	Field visit	1	Lower-middle	Private sector

*Informal conversation.

^Subject interviewed more than once but recorded here as one interview.

TABLE A.2.   Meetings observed

DATE	LOCATION	ORGANIZING BODY
2012	Geneva	United Nations Committee of Experts on International Cooperation in Tax Matters
2013	New York	United Nations Economic and Social Council (ECOSOC)
2013	Geneva	United Nations Committee of Experts on International Cooperation in Tax Matters
2014	Geneva	United Nations Committee of Experts on International Cooperation in Tax Matters
2015	Paris	OECD Task Force on Tax and Development
2017	Geneva	United Nations Committee of Experts on International Cooperation in Tax Matters
2018	New York	Platform for Collaboration on Tax
2018	Podgorica, Montenegro	European Commission
2018	Rust, Austria	Institute for Austrian and International Tax Law
2018	Antananarivo, Madagascar	Organisation Internationale de la Francophonie

Notes

PROLOGUE

1. Office for National Statistics, "Foreign Direct Investment Involving UK Companies: Outward," February 2020, https://www.ons.gov.uk/businessindustryandtrade/business/businessinnovation/datasets/foreigndirectinvestmentinvolvingukcompaniesoutwardtables.

2. Cited in Sunita Jogarajan, *Double Taxation and the League of Nations* (Cambridge: Cambridge University Press, 2018), 172, https://doi.org/10.1017/9781108368865.

3. D. Hopkins, telegram, January 27, 1972, Inland Revenue IR40/17623, National Archives, London.

4. Minutes of a meeting with representatives of the Confederation of British Industry, March 15, 1972, Inland Revenue IR40/18109, National Archives, London.

5. United Kingdom–Kenya double taxation agreement, 1973.

6. Minutes of UK-Kenya tax treaty negotiation meeting, January 25–29, 1972, Nairobi, Inland Revenue IR40/17623, National Archives, London.

7. Hopkins, telegram, January 27, 1972.

8. I have used the term "lower-income country" somewhat loosely throughout this book, since countries' relative income varies over time and space. Change over time is vividly illustrated in table 5.1, which lists countries regarded by British negotiators in the 1970s as "developing countries." Several are now members of the OECD. In a treaty negotiation, it is the relative wealth of the two negotiating countries that matters, not where they fit into the global picture. Where statistics are given, I have operationalised "lower-income countries" as those categorised by the World Bank as low or lower-middle income in 2020.

1. THE PROBLEM WITH TAX TREATIES

1. US$2.3 trillion in 2014, estimated in OECD, *Measuring and Monitoring BEPS, Action 11—2015 Final Report*, OECD/G20 Base Erosion and Profit Shifting Project (Paris: OECD Publishing, 2015), 102, http://www.oecd-ilibrary.org/taxation/measuring-and-monitoring-beps-action-11-2015-final-report_9789264241343-en.

2. On this, see, for example, Ronen Palan, Richard Murphy, and Christian Chavagneux, *Tax Havens: How Globalization Really Works* (Ithaca, NY: Cornell University Press, 2010); Peter Dietsch and Thomas Rixen, eds., *Global Tax Governance: What Is Wrong with It and How to Fix It* (Colchester: ECPR Press, 2016); Richard Eccleston and Ainsley Elbra, eds., *Business, Civil Society and the 'New' Politics of Corporate Tax Justice*, Elgar Politics and Business Series (Cheltenham: Edward Elgar, forthcoming); Richard Eccleston, *The Dynamics of Global Economic Governance: The OECD, the Financial Crisis and the Politics of International Tax Cooperation* (Cheltenham: Edward Elgar, 2012); Jeremy Leaman and Attiya Waris, eds., *Tax Justice and the Political Economy of Global Capitalism, 1945 to the Present* (New York: Berghahn Books, 2013).

3. Charles R. Irish, "International Double Taxation Agreements and Income Taxation at Source," *International and Comparative Law Quarterly* 23, no. 2 (1974): 292–316, https://doi.org/10.1093/iclqaj/23.2.292; Tsilly Dagan, "The Tax Treaties Myth," *New York University Journal of International Law and Politics* 32 (2000): 939; Victor Thuronyi, "Tax Treaties

and Developing Countries," in *Tax Treaties: Building Bridges between Law and Economics*, ed. Michael Lang et al. (Amsterdam: IBFD, 2010), 441–58; Kim Brooks and Richard Krever, "The Troubling Role of Tax Treaties," in *Tax Design Issues Worldwide*, ed. Geerten M. M. Michielse and Victor Thuronyi (Alphen aan den Rijn, Netherlands: Kluwer Law International, 2015), 159–78; Dimitri Paolini et al., "Tax Treaties with Developing Countries and the Allocation of Taxing Rights," *European Journal of Law and Economics* 42, no. 3 (December 28, 2016): 383–404, https://doi.org/10.1007/s10657-014-9465-9.

4. Ilene Grabel, *When Things Don't Fall Apart: Global Financial Governance and Developmental Finance in an Age of Productive Incoherence* (Cambridge, MA: MIT Press, 2017); Ngaire Woods, "Global Governance after the Financial Crisis: A New Multilateralism or the Last Gasp of the Great Powers?," *Global Policy* 1, no. 1 (January 2010): 51–63, https://doi.org/10.1111/j.1758-5899.2009.0013.x; Kristen Hopewell, "Different Paths to Power: The Rise of Brazil, India and China at the World Trade Organization," *Review of International Political Economy* 22, no. 2 (March 4, 2015): 311–38, https://doi.org/10.1080/09692290.2014.927387; Lauge N. Skovgaard Poulsen, *Bounded Rationality and Economic Diplomacy: The Politics of Investment Treaties in Developing Countries* (Cambridge: Cambridge University Press, 2015).

5. I am grateful to Javier Garcio-Bernardo for this statistic, calculated using the International Monetary Fund's Coordinated Direct Investment Survey and a list of treaties compiled from the International Bureau of Fiscal Documentation. The figure is an average value for the period 2014 to 2018. Javier Garcio-Bernardo, email message to author, September 21, 2020.

6. Dagan, "Tax Treaties Myth," 941.

7. Brooks and Krever, "Troubling Role of Tax Treaties," 160.

8. Fabian Barthel and Eric Neumayer, "Competing for Scarce Foreign Capital: Spatial Dependence in the Diffusion of Double Taxation Treaties," *International Studies Quarterly* 56, no. 4 (December 2012): 645–60, https://doi.org/10.1111/j.1468-2478.2012.00757.x.

9. Typical examples can be found in Embassy of the Republic of Kenya, "Trade and Investment," accessed November 19, 2012, http://www.kenyaembassy.com/economycommerce.html; Zimbabwe Investment Authority, "Exploring Investments in Zimbabwe," accessed November 19, 2012, http://www.zimottawa.com/files/investing_in_zimbabwe.pdf.

10. Martin Hearson and Jalia Kangave, "A Review of Uganda's Tax Treaties and Recommendations for Action" (International Centre for Tax and Development Working Paper 50, Institute of Development Studies, Brighton, UK, 2016), 11.

11. Ministerio de Economía y Finanzas de Peru, "Sobre Los Convenios Para Evitar La Doble Tributación Para Promover La Inversión y Evitar La Evasión Fiscal Internacional," May 15, 2001, http://www.mef.gob.pe/index.php?option=com_content&view=article&id=2199%3Asobre-los-convenios-para-evitar-la-doble-tributacion-para-promover-la-inversion-y-evitar-la-evasion-fiscal-internacional&catid=297%3Apreguntas-frecuentes&Itemid=100143&lang=es.

12. Kurt Weyland, *Bounded Rationality and Policy Diffusion: Social Sector Reform in Latin America* (Princeton, NJ: Princeton University Press, 2007); Lauge N. Skovgaard Poulsen, "Bounded Rationality and the Diffusion of Modern Investment Treaties," *International Studies Quarterly* 58, no. 1 (2014): 1–14, https://doi.org/10.1111/isqu.12051.

13. Lauge N. Skovgaard Poulsen and Emma Aisbett, "When the Claim Hits: Bilateral Investment Treaties and Bounded Rational Learning," *World Politics* 65, no. 2 (2014): 273–313; Srividya Jandhyala, Witold J. Henisz, and Edward D. Mansfield, "Three Waves of BITs: The Global Diffusion of Foreign Investment Policy," *Journal of Conflict Resolution* 55, no. 6 (August 23, 2011): 1047–73, https://doi.org/10.1177/0022002711414373.

14. Martin Hearson, *Tax Treaties in Sub-Saharan Africa: A Critical Review* (Nairobi: Tax Justice Network Africa, 2015); Catherine Ngina Mutava, "Review of Tax Treaty Prac-

tices and Policy Framework in Africa" (International Centre for Tax and Development Working Papers 102, Institute of Development Studies, Brighton, UK, 2019), https://opendocs.ids.ac.uk/opendocs/handle/20.500.12413/14900.

15. For example, Katrin McGauran, *Should the Netherlands Sign Tax Treaties with Developing Countries?* (Amsterdam: SOMO, 2013); Mike Lewis, *Sweet Nothings: The Human Cost of a British Sugar Giant Avoiding Taxes in Southern Africa* (London: ActionAid UK, 2013); ActionAid, *Mistreated: The Tax Treaties That Are Depriving the World's Poorest Countries of Vital Revenue* (London: ActionAid UK, 2016).

16. IMF, "Spillovers in International Corporate Taxation" (IMF Policy Paper, Washington, DC, 2014), 24.

17. Organisation Internationale de la Francophonie, "LIC Ministers Demand Their Fair Share of Global Tax Revenues," press note, 2014, http://www.oecd.org/dac/OIF%20Recommendations.pdf.

18. ATAF, "The Place of Africa in the Shift towards Global Tax Governance: Can the Taxation of the Digitalised Economy Be an Opportunity for More Inclusiveness" (Pretoria: African Tax Administration Forum, 2019), 15.

19. Sanjay Kumar Mishra, "Letter to Alexander Trepelkov," Ministry of Finance, Government of India, 2012, https://www.un.org/esa/ffd/wp-content/uploads/2014/10/ICTM2012_LetterIndia.pdf.

20. Martin Hearson, "Measuring Tax Treaty Negotiation Outcomes: The ActionAid Tax Treaties Dataset" (International Centre for Tax and Development Working Paper 47, Institute of Development Studies, Brighton, UK, 2016); Wim Wijnen and Jan de Goede, *The UN Model in Practice, 1997–2013* (Amsterdam: International Bureau of Fiscal Documentation, 2013).

21. ICTD/UNU-WIDER, "Government Revenue Dataset," UNU-WIDER, 2018, https://www.wider.unu.edu/project/government-revenue-dataset.

22. Mick Moore, Wilson Prichard, and Odd-Helge Fjeldstad, *Taxing Africa: Coercion, Reform and Development*, African Arguments (London: Zed Books, 2018); Ricardo Fenochietto and Carola Pessino, *Understanding Countries' Tax Effort* (Washington, DC: International Monetary Fund, 2013).

23. UNCTAD, "International Tax and Investment Policy Coherence," in *World Investment Report, 2015* (Geneva: United Nations Conference on Trade and Development, 2015), 175–218, http://unctad.org/en/PublicationChapters/wir2015ch5_en.pdf; ICTD/UNU-WIDER, "Government Revenue Dataset."

24. Those that have ratified the Vienna Convention on the law of treaties.

25. For example, the term appears eleven times in a special issue of the *Bulletin for International Taxation*, the house journal of tax treaty specialists, introducing the 2011 update to the UN model treaty (UN Model 2011 Special Issue 2012).

26. Thomas Rixen, "Bilateralism or Multilateralism? The Political Economy of Avoiding International Double Taxation," *European Journal of International Relations* 16, no. 4 (December 2010): 589–614, https://doi.org/10.1177/1354066109346891.

27. Elliott Ash and Omri Marian, *The Making of International Tax Law: Empirical Evidence from Natural Language Processing*, Legal Studies Research Paper Series 2019–02 (Irvine: University of California, 2019).

28. It also makes reference to the aims to "prevent certain types of discrimination as between foreign investors and local taxpayers, and to provide a reasonable element of legal and fiscal certainty." United Nations, *Model Double Taxation Convention between Developed and Developing Countries*, 2017 ed. (New York: United Nations, 2017), iv.

29. OECD, *Model Tax Convention on Income and on Capital* (Paris: OECD Publishing, 2014), 7.

30. Hearson, "Measuring Tax Treaty Negotiation Outcomes."

31. Hearson and Kangave, "Review of Uganda's Tax Treaties and Recommendations for Action."

32. Petr Janský and Marek Šedivý, "Estimating the Revenue Costs of Tax Treaties in Developing Countries," *World Economy*, December 7, 2018, https://doi.org/10.1111/twec .12764; see also ActionAid, *Mistreated*.

33. OECD, *Tax Sparing: A Reconsideration* (Paris: OECD Publishing, 1998).

34. Hearson and Kangave, "Review of Uganda's Tax Treaties and Recommendations for Action."

35. Sebastian Beer and Jan Loeprick, "Too High a Price? Tax Treaties with Investment Hubs in Sub-Saharan Africa," *International Tax and Public Finance*, advance online publication, July 31, 2020.

36. Irish, "International Double Taxation Agreements and Income Taxation at Source"; Reuven S. Avi-Yonah, "Double Tax Treaties: An Introduction," in *The Effect of Treaties on Foreign Direct Investment*, ed. Karl P. Sauvant and Lisa E. Sachs (New York: Oxford University Press, 2009), 99–106, https://doi.org/10.1093/acprof:oso/9780195388534.003 .0004; Thuronyi, "Tax Treaties and Developing Countries"; Pasquale Pistone, "Tax Treaties with Developing Countries: A Plea for New Allocation Rules and a Combined Legal and Economic Approach," in *Tax Treaties: Building Bridges between Law and Economics*, ed. Michael Lang et al. (Amsterdam: IBFD, 2010), 413–40; Allison Christians, "Tax Treaties for Investment and Aid to Sub-Saharan Africa: A Case Study," *Brooklyn Law Review* 15, no. 1999 (2005): 639–700.

37. Dagan, "Tax Treaties Myth"; Irish, "International Double Taxation Agreements and Income Taxation at Source," 316.

38. PWC, *Evolution of Territorial Tax Systems in the OECD* (Washington, DC: Prepared for the Technology CEO Council, 2013).

39. Dagan, "Tax Treaties Myth."

40. John F. Avery Jones, "Are Tax Treaties Necessary?," *Tax Law Review* 53, no. 1 (1999): 1–38; Heather Self, "Some Treaty Issues for Developing Countries" (Queen Mary University guest lecture, London, January 30, 2014); Ariane Pickering, *Why Negotiate Tax Treaties?* (New York: United Nations, 2013).

41. Francis Weyzig, "Tax Treaty Shopping: Structural Determinants of Foreign Direct Investment Routed through the Netherlands," *International Tax and Public Finance* 20, no. 6 (2013): 910–37, https://doi.org/10.1007/s10797-012-9250-z; Vincent Arel-Bundock, "The Unintended Consequences of Bilateralism: Treaty Shopping and International Tax Policy," *International Organization* 71, no. 2 (2017): 349–71, https://doi.org/10.1017 /S0020818317000108.

42. Eduardo Baistrocchi, "The Use and Interpretation of Tax Treaties in the Emerging World: Theory and Implications," *British Tax Review* 28, no. 4 (2008): 352.

43. Karl P. Sauvant and Lisa E. Sachs, eds., *The Effect of Treaties on Foreign Direct Investment* (Oxford: Oxford University Press, 2009).

44. Fabian Barthel, Matthias Busse, and Eric Neumayer, "The Impact of Double Taxation Treaties on Foreign Direct Investment: Evidence from Large Dyadic Panel Data," *Contemporary Economic Policy* 28, no. 3 (December 30, 2009): 366–77, https://doi.org/10 .1111/j.1465-7287.2009.00185.x; Arjan Lejour, "The Foreign Investment Effects of Tax Treaties" (CPB Netherlands Bureau for Economic Analysis Discussion Paper 265, 2014).

45. Paul L. Baker, "An Analysis of Double Taxation Treaties and Their Effect on Foreign Direct Investment," *International Journal of the Economics of Business* 21, no. 3 (September 2, 2014): 341–77, https://doi.org/10.1080/13571516.2014.968454; Beer and Loeprick, "Too High a Price?"

46. Ronald B. Davies, Pehr-Johan Norbäck, and Ayça Tekin-Koru, "The Effect of Tax Treaties on Multinational Firms: New Evidence from Microdata," *World Economy* 32, no. 1

(January 2009): 77–110, https://doi.org/10.1111/j.1467-9701.2009.01158.x; Peter Egger and Valeria Merlo, "Statutory Corporate Tax Rates and Double-Taxation Treaties as Determinants of Multinational Firm Activity," *FinanzArchiv: Public Finance Analysis* 67, no. 2 (June 1, 2011): 145–70, https://doi.org/10.1628/001522111X588754; Bruce A. Blonigen, Lindsay Oldenski, and Nicholas Sly, "The Differential Effects of Bilateral Tax Treaties," *American Economic Journal: Economic Policy* 6 (2014): 1–18, https://doi.org/10.1257/pol.6.2 .1; Julia Braun and Daniel Fuentes, *A Legal and Economic Analysis of Double Taxation Treaties between Austria and Developing Countries* (Vienna: Vienna Institute for International Dialogue and Cooperation, 2014).

47. Davies, Norbäck, and Tekin-Koru, "Effect of Tax Treaties on Multinational Firms."

48. Sunghoon Hong, "Tax Treaties and Foreign Direct Investment: A Network Approach," *International Tax and Public Finance* 25, no. 5 (October 2018): 1277–320, https://doi.org/10 .1007/s10797-018-9489-0; Kunka Petkova, Andrzej Stasio, and Martin Zagler, "On the Relevance of Double Tax Treaties," *International Tax and Public Finance*, September 21, 2019, https://doi.org/10.1007/s10797-019-09570-9; Maarten van 't Riet and Arjan Lejour, "Optimal Tax Routing: Network Analysis of FDI Diversion," *International Tax and Public Finance* 25, no. 5 (October 2018): 1321–71, https://doi.org/10.1007/s10797-018-9491-6.

49. OECD, *Tax Sparing*, 5.

50. Céline Azémar, Rodolphe Desbordes, and Jean-Louis L. Mucchielli, "Do Tax Sparing Agreements Contribute to the Attraction of FDI in Developing Countries?," *International Tax and Public Finance* 14, no. 5 (September 15, 2007): 543–62, https://doi.org/10.1007 /s10797-006-9005-9; Céline Azémar and Andrew Delios, "Tax Competition and FDI: The Special Case of Developing Countries," *Journal of the Japanese and International Economies* 22, no. 1 (March 2008): 85–108, https://doi.org/10.1016/j.jjie.2007.02.001; James R. Hines Jr., "'Tax Sparing' and Direct Investment in Developing Countries," in *International Taxation and Multinational Activity*, ed. James R. Hines Jr. (Chicago: University of Chicago Press, 2000), 39–72; Céline Azémar and Dhammika Dharmapala, "Tax Sparing Agreements, Territorial Tax Reforms, and Foreign Direct Investment," *Journal of Public Economics* 169 (January 1, 2019): 89–108, https://doi.org/10.1016/j.jpubeco.2018.10.013.

51. Michael Lennard, "The UN Model Tax Convention as Compared with the OECD Model Tax Convention—Current Points of Difference and Recent Developments," *Asia-Pacific Tax Bulletin*, no. 1 (2009): 4–11.

52. Oladiwura Ayeyemi Eyitayo-Oyesode, "Source-Based Taxing Rights from the OECD to the UN Model Conventions: Unavailing Efforts and an Argument for Reform," *Law and Development Review* 13, no. 1 (2020): 220, https://doi.org/10.1515/ldr-2018-0073.

53. Wijnen and de Goede, *UN Model in Practice, 1997–2013*; Wim Wijnen, Jan de Goede, and Andrea Alessi, "The Treatment of Services in Tax Treaties," *Bulletin for International Taxation* 66, no. 1 (2012): 27–38; Hearson, "Measuring Tax Treaty Negotiation Outcomes."

54. Kim Brooks, "Canada's Evolving Tax Treaty Policy toward Low-Income Countries," in *Globalization and Its Tax Discontents: Tax Policy and International Investments*, ed. Richard Krever (Toronto: University of Toronto Press, 2010), 187–211; Kim Brooks, "Tax Treaty Treatment of Royalty Payments from Low-Income Countries: A Comparison of Canada and Australia's Policies," *EJournal of Tax Research* 5, no. 2 (2007): 168–97.

55. Irish, "International Double Taxation Agreements and Income Taxation at Source," 301.

56. Veronika Dauer and Richard Krever, "Choosing between the UN and OECD Tax Policy Models: An African Case Study," *EUI Working Papers*, Florence: European University Institute, 2012, 17.

57. Jinyan Li, "The Great Fiscal Wall of China: Tax Treaties and Their Role in Defining and Defending China's Tax Base," *Bulletin for International Taxation* 66, no. 9 (2012): 452–79.

58. Eduardo Baistrocchi, "The International Tax Regime and the BRIC World: Elements for a Theory," *Oxford Journal of Legal Studies* 33, no. 4 (December 1, 2013): 733–66, https://doi.org/10.1093/ojls/gqt012.

59. Honey Lynn Goldberg, "Conventions for the Elimination of International Double Taxation: Toward a Developing Country Model," *Law & Policy in International Business* 15 (1983): 833–909, quoted on 907.

60. Thomas Rixen and Peter Schwarz, "Bargaining over the Avoidance of Double Taxation: Evidence from German Tax Treaties," *FinanzArchiv: Public Finance Analysis* 65, no. 4 (December 1, 2009): 442–71, https://doi.org/10.1628/001522109X486589; Richard Chisik and Ronald B. Davies, "Asymmetric FDI and Tax-Treaty Bargaining: Theory and Evidence," *Journal of Public Economics* 88, no. 6 (June 2004): 1119–48, https://doi.org/10.1016/s0047-2727(03)00059-8; Rixen, "Bilateralism or Multilateralism?"

61. Martin Hearson, "When Do Developing Countries Negotiate Away Their Corporate Tax Base?," *Journal of International Development* 30, no. 2 (2018): 233–55.

62. Wijnen and de Goede, *UN Model in Practice, 1997–2013*; Dauer and Krever, "Choosing between the UN and OECD Tax Policy Models."

63. Rixen and Schwarz, "Bargaining over the Avoidance of Double Taxation"; Chisik and Davies, "Asymmetric FDI and Tax-Treaty Bargaining"; Johannes Becker and Clemens Fuest, "The Nexus of Corporate Income Taxation and Multinational Activity," *FinanzArchiv: Public Finance Analysis* 68, no. 3 (September 2012): 231–51, https://doi.org/10.1628/001522112X653822; Claudio M. Radaelli, "Game Theory and Institutional Entrepreneurship: Transfer Pricing and the Search for Coordination International Tax Policy," *Policy Studies Journal* 26, no. 4 (1998): 603–19; Thomas Rixen, *The Political Economy of International Tax Governance* (New York: Palgrave Macmillan, 2008).

64. Baistrocchi, "Use and Interpretation of Tax Treaties in the Emerging World"; Barthel and Neumayer, "Competing for Scarce Foreign Capital"; Arel-Bundock, "The Unintended Consequences of Bilateralism."

65. Andrew Moravcsik, "Taking Preferences Seriously: A Liberal Theory of International Politics," *International Organization* 51, no. 4 (October 1, 1997): 518, https://doi.org/10.1162/002081897550447. For example, the way in which "veto points" in the treaty-making process may give particular influence to certain groups is considered in chapter 5. See Edward D. Mansfield and Helen V. Milner, *Votes, Vetoes, and the Political Economy of International Trade Agreements* (Oxford: Princeton University Press, 2012); George Tsebelis, *Veto Players: How Political Institutions Work* (New York: Russell Sage Foundation, 2002).

66. Gene M. Grossman and Elhanan Helpman, "Protection for Sale," *American Economic Review* 84, no. 4 (1994): 833–50.

67. Grossman and Helpman, "Protection for Sale"; Pablo M. Pinto, *Partisan Investment in the Global Economy: Why the Left Loves Foreign Direct Investment and FDI Loves the Left* (Cambridge: Cambridge University Press, 2013).

68. Nathan M. Jensen, "Domestic Institutions and the Taxing of Multinational Corporations," *International Studies Quarterly* 57, no. 3 (September 24, 2013): 440–48, https://doi.org/10.1111/isqu.12015.

69. Jason C. Sharman, "Offshore and the New International Political Economy," *Review of International Political Economy* 17, no. 1 (2010): 8–9, https://doi.org/10.1080/09692290802686940.

70. Norwegian Government Commission on Capital Flight from Poor Countries, *Tax Havens and Development: Status, Analyses and Measures* (Oslo: Government Commission on Capital Flight from Poor Countries, 2009).

71. Mutava, *Review of Tax Treaty Practices and Policy Framework in Africa*.

72. Bruce A. Blonigen and Ronald B. Davies, "The Effects of Bilateral Tax Treaties on U.S. FDI Activity," *International Tax and Public Finance* 11, no. 5 (September 2004): 601–22,

https://doi.org/10.1023/B:ITAX.0000036693.32618.00; Daniel L. Millimet and Abdullah Kumas, "It's All in the Timing: Assessing the Impact of Bilateral Tax Treaties on U.S. FDI Activity," in *The Effect of Treaties on Foreign Direct Investment*, ed. Karl P. Sauvant and Lisa E. Sachs (New York: Oxford University Press, 2009), https://doi.org/10.1093/acprof:oso /9780195388534.003.0022.

73. Javier Garcia-Bernardo et al., "Uncovering Offshore Financial Centers: Conduits and Sinks in the Global Corporate Ownership Network," *Scientific Reports* 7 (June 2017): 1–18, https://doi.org/10.1038/s41598-017-06322-9.

74. Martin Hearson and Richard Brooks, *Calling Time: Why SABMiller Should Stop Dodging Taxes in Africa* (London: ActionAid UK, 2010), 24.

75. Irish, "International Double Taxation Agreements and Income Taxation at Source," 300–301.

76. Irish, 309.

77. Dagan, "Tax Treaties Myth," 939.

78. Festus Aukonobera, "Uganda," in *The Impact of the OECD and UN Model Conventions on Bilateral Tax Treaties*, ed. Michael Lang, Pasquale Pistone, and Josef Schuch (Cambridge: Cambridge University Press, 2012), 1084.

79. Natalia Quinones Cruz, "Colombia," in *The Impact of the OECD and UN Model Conventions on Bilateral Tax Treaties*, ed. Michael Lang, Pasquale Pistone, and Josef Schuch (Cambridge: Cambridge University Press, 2012), 204–5.

80. Mutava, *Review of Tax Treaty Practices and Policy Framework in Africa*, 10.

81. ATAF, "Place of Africa in the Shift towards Global Tax Governance," 9.

82. Linda Weiss, "Bringing Domestic Institutions Back In," in *States in the Global Economy: Bringing Domestic Institutions Back In*, ed. Linda Weiss (Cambridge: Cambridge University Press, 2007), 1–34; Theda Skocpol, "Bringing the State Back In: Strategies of Analysis in Current Research," in *Bringing the State Back In*, ed. Peter B. Evans, Dietrich Rueschemeyer, and Theda Skocpol (Cambridge: Cambridge University Press, 1985), 3–38, https:// doi.org/10.1017/CBO9780511628283.002; Deborah A. Bräutigam, "Introduction: Taxation and State-Building in Developing Countries," in *Taxation and State-Building in Developing Countries*, ed. Deborah Brautigam, Odd-Helge Fjeldstad, and Mick Moore (Cambridge: Cambridge University Press, 2008), 1–33, https://doi.org/10.1017/CBO9780511490897 .001; Nicholas Kaldor, "Will Underdeveloped Countries Learn to Tax?," *Foreign Affairs* 41, no. 2 (1963): 410–19.

83. Interview 9. See table A.1 in the appendix for a list of interviews conducted for this book.

84. Daniel Kahneman and Amos Tversky, "Prospect Theory: An Analysis of Decision under Risk," *Econometrica* 47, no. 2 (1979): 263–91, https://doi.org/10.2307/1914185; Weyland, *Bounded Rationality and Policy Diffusion*; Poulsen, *Bounded Rationality and Economic Diplomacy*.

85. Eric M. Zolt, "Tax Treaties and Developing Countries" (Law-Econ Research Paper 18–10, UCLA School of Law, 2018).

86. Arel-Bundock, "Unintended Consequences of Bilateralism"; Barthel and Neumayer, "Competing for Scarce Foreign Capital."

87. Eleni Tsingou, "Club Governance and the Making of Global Financial Rules," *Review of International Political Economy* 22, no. 2 (2014): 225–56, https://doi.org/10.1080 /09692290.2014.890952.

88. Peter M. Haas, "Introduction: Epistemic Communities and International Policy Coordination," *International Organization* 46, no. 1 (May 22, 1992): 1–35, https://doi.org /10.1017/S0020818300001442.

89. Lorraine Eden, M. Tina Dacin, and William P. Wan, "Standards across Borders: Crossborder Diffusion of the Arm's Length Standard in North America," *Accounting,*

Organizations and Society 26 (2001): 1–23; Barthel and Neumayer, "Competing for Scarce Foreign Capital"; Kerrie Sadiq, "The Inherent International Tax Regime and Its Constraints on Australia's Sovereignty," *University of Queensland Law Journal* 31, no. 1 (2012): 131–46. An exception is the United States, where domestic political actors have repeatedly blocked participation in OECD initiatives. See Jason C. Sharman, *Havens in a Storm: The Global Struggle for Tax Regulation* (Ithaca, NY: Cornell University Press, 2006); Lukas Hakelberg, "Coercion in International Tax Cooperation: Identifying the Prerequisites for Sanction Threats by a Great Power," *Review of International Political Economy* 23, no. 3 (May 3, 2016): 511–41, https://doi.org/10.1080/09692290 .2015.1127269; Michael C. Webb, "Defining the Boundaries of Legitimate State Practice: Norms, Transnational Actors and the OECD's Project on Harmful Tax Competition," *Review of International Political Economy* 11, no. 4 (August 2004): 787–827, https://doi .org/10.1080/0969229042000279801.

90. Hakelberg, "Coercion in International Tax Cooperation"; Wouter Lips, "Great Powers in Global Tax Governance: A Comparison of the US Role in the CRS and BEPS," *Globalizations* 16, no. 1 (January 2, 2019): 104–19, https://doi.org/10.1080/14747731 .2018.1496558; Rixen, *Political Economy of International Tax Governance*; Claudio M. Radaelli, "Game Theory and Institutional Entrepreneurship: Transfer Pricing and the Search for Coordination International Tax Policy," *Policy Studies Journal* 26, no. 4 (1998): 603–19.

91. Rixen and Schwarz, "Bargaining over the Avoidance of Double Taxation"; Chisik and Davies, "Asymmetric FDI and Tax-Treaty Bargaining"; Rixen, "Bilateralism or Multilateralism?"

92. Tsebelis, *Veto Players*.

93. Sol Picciotto, "Indeterminacy, Complexity, Technocracy and the Reform of International Corporate Taxation," *Social & Legal Studies* 24, no. 2 (2015): 165–84, https://doi .org/10.1177/0964663915572942.

94. Doris A. Fuchs, *Business Power in Global Governance* (Boulder, CO: Lynne Rienner Publishers, 2007).

95. Pepper D. Culpepper, *Quiet Politics and Business Power: Corporate Control in Europe and Japan* (Cambridge: Cambridge University Press, 2010).

96. Thomas Rixen and Lora Anne Viola, "Historical Institutionalism and International Relations: Towards Explaining Change and Stability in International Institutions," in *Historical Institutionalism and International Relations: Explaining Institutional Development in World Politics*, ed. Thomas Rixen, Lora Anne Viola, and Michael Zurn (Oxford: Oxford University Press, 2016), 3–34; Orfeo Fioretos, "Historical Institutionalism in International Relations," *International Organization* 65, no. 2 (April 2011): 367–99, https://doi.org/10 .1017/S0020818311000002.

97. Rixen, *Political Economy of International Tax Governance*; Philipp Genschel and Thomas Rixen, "Settling and Unsettling the Transnational Legal Order of International Taxation," in *Transnational Legal Orders*, ed. T. C. Halliday and G. Shaffer, Cambridge Studies in Law and Society (Cambridge: Cambridge University Press, 2015), 154–86.

98. Picciotto, "Indeterminacy, Complexity, Technocracy and the Reform of International Corporate Taxation"; Allison Christians, "Networks, Norms and National Tax Policy," *Washington University Global Studies Law Review* 9, no. 1 (2010): 1–38; Rasmus Corlin Christensen, "Elite Professionals in Transnational Tax Governance," *Global Networks*, April 23, 2020, https://doi.org/10.1111/glob.12269; Tim Buttner and Matthias Thiemann, "Breaking Regime Stability? The Politicization of Expertise in the OECD G20 Process on BEPS and the Potential Transformation of International Taxation," *Accounting, Economics, and Law: A Convivium* 7, no. 1 (January 2017), https://doi.org/10.1515/ael-2016-0069.

99. Leonard Seabrooke and Duncan Wigan, "Powering Ideas through Expertise: Professionals in Global Tax Battles," *Journal of European Public Policy* 23, no. 3 (2016): 357–74, https://doi.org/10.1080/13501763.2015.1115536.

100. The numbers do not add up to eighty-four because several interviewees had worked in some combination of the public sector, private sector, and international organizations.

101. In practice, most countries send a single delegate, although a few countries had both a committee member and an official observer.

102. Wikileaks, "Public Library of US Diplomacy," accessed June 22, 2015, https://search.wikileaks.org/plusd.

103. Martin Hearson, "Tax Treaties Explorer," 2020, http://treaties.tax; Hearson, "Measuring Tax Treaty Negotiation Outcomes."

2. A HISTORY OF LOWER-INCOME COUNTRIES IN (AND OUT OF) GLOBAL TAX GOVERNANCE

1. Reuven S. Avi-Yonah, *International Tax as International Law* (New York: Cambridge University Press, 2007).

2. Edwin R. A. Seligman, *The Income Tax: A Study of the History, Theory, and Practice of Income Taxation at Home and Abroad* (New York: Macmillan, 1914).

3. Michael J. Graetz and Michael M. O'Hear, "The 'Original Intent' of U.S. International Taxation," *Duke Law Journal* 46, no. 5 (1997): 1020–109, https://doi.org/10.2307/1372916; Sol Picciotto, *International Business Taxation: A Study in the Internationalization of Business Regulation* (London: Weidenfeld & Nicolson, 1992); Jogarajan, *Double Taxation and the League of Nations*.

4. Allison Christians, "Global Trends and Constraints on Tax Policy in the Least Developed Countries," *University of British Columbia Law Review* 42, no. 2 (2010): 239; Miranda Stewart, "Global Trajectories of Tax Reform: The Discourse of Tax Reform in Developing and Transition Countries," *Harvard International Law Journal* 44, no. 1 (2003): 139–90; Odd-Helge Fjeldstad and Mick Moore, "Tax Reform and State-Building in a Globalised World," in *Taxation and State-Building in Developing Countries*, ed. Deborah Brautigam, Odd-Helge Fjeldstad, and Mick Moore (Cambridge: Cambridge University Press, 2008), 235–60, https://doi.org/10.1017/CBO9780511490897.010; Philipp Genschel and Laura Seelkopf, "Did They Learn to Tax? Taxation Trends outside the OECD," *Review of International Political Economy* 23, no. 2 (2016): 316–44, https://doi.org/10.1080/09692290.2016.1174723.

5. Rudolf Goldscheid, "A Sociological Approach to Problems of Public Finance," in *Classics in the Theory of Public Finance*, ed. Richard A. Musgrave and Alan T. Peacock (London: Palgrave Macmillan UK, 1958), 202, https://doi.org/10.1007/978-1-349-23426-4_14.

6. Joseph Schumpeter, "The Crisis of the Tax State," in *Joseph A. Schumpeter: The Economics and Sociology of Capitalism*, ed. Richard A. Swedberg (Princeton, NJ: Princeton University Press, 1991), 100.

7. Edmund Burke, *Reflections on the French Revolution* (London: Dent, 1955), 105.

8. Schumpeter, "Crisis of the Tax State," 116.

9. Mick Moore, "Between Coercion and Contract: Competing Narratives on Taxation and Governance," in *Taxation and State-Building in Developing Countries*, ed. Deborah Brautigam, Odd-Helge Fjeldstad, and Mick Moore (Cambridge: Cambridge University Press, 2008), 34–63, https://doi.org/10.1017/CBO9780511490897.002.

10. Norbert Elias, *The Civilizing Process* (Oxford: Blackwell, 1994).

11. Charles Tilly, *Coercion, Capital, and European States, A.D. 990–1990* (Cambridge, MA: Basil Blackwell, 1992), 85.

12. HMRC, "Taxation: A Brief History," Bicentenary of Income Tax (HMRC website), archived June 5, 2013, http://webarchive.nationalarchives.gov.uk/+/http://www.hmrc.gov.uk/history/index.htm; Seligman, *Income Tax*.

13. Library of Congress, "History of the US Income Tax," Business Reference Services, updated 2012, http://www.loc.gov/rr/business/hottopic/irs_history.html; Seligman, *Income Tax*.

14. Seligman, *Income Tax*.

15. Deborah A. Bräutigam, "Introduction: Taxation and State-Building in Developing Countries," in *Taxation and State-Building in Developing Countries*, ed. Deborah Brautigam, Odd-Helge Fjeldstad, and Mick Moore (Cambridge: Cambridge University Press, 2008), 1–33, https://doi.org/10.1017/CBO9780511490897.001.

16. Moore, "Between Coercion and Contract"; Margaret Levi, *Of Rule and Revenue* (Berkeley: University of California Press, 1988).

17. Schumpeter, "Crisis of the Tax State."

18. Charles Tilly, "Extraction and Democracy," in *The New Fiscal Sociology*, ed. Isaac William Martin, Ajay K. Mehrotra, and Monica Prasad (Cambridge: Cambridge University Press, 2009), 174, https://doi.org/10.1017/CBO9780511627071.011.

19. Isaac William Martin, Ajay K. Mehrotra, and Monica Prasad, "The Thunder of History: The Origins and Development of the New Fiscal Sociology," in *The New Fiscal Sociology*, ed. Isaac William Martin, Ajay K. Mehrotra, and Monica Prasad (Cambridge: Cambridge University Press, 2009), 1–28, https://doi.org/10.1017/CBO9780511627071.002; Bräutigam, "Introduction"; Nicholas Kaldor, "Will Underdeveloped Countries Learn to Tax?," *Foreign Affairs* 41, no. 2 (1963): 410–19.

20. Martin, Mehrotra, and Prasad, "Thunder of History," 14.

21. Charles Tilly, ed., *The Formation of National States in Western Europe* (Princeton, NJ: Princeton University Press, 1975), 42.

22. Peggy B. Musgrave, "Sovereignty, Entitlement, and Cooperation in International Taxation," *Brooklyn Journal of International Law* 26, no. 4 (2000): 1348.

23. Vito Tanzi, "Globalization, Technological Developments, and the Work of Fiscal Termites," *Brooklyn Journal of International Law* 26 (2000): 1261–85; Musgrave, "Sovereignty, Entitlement, and Cooperation in International Taxation"; Victor Thuronyi, "International Tax Cooperation and a Multilateral Treaty," *Brooklyn Journal of International Law* 26 (2000): 1641–81; Peter Dietsch, *Catching Capital: The Ethics of Tax Competition* (New York: Oxford University Press, 2015); Thomas Rixen, "Tax Competition and Inequality: The Case for Global Tax Governance," *Global Governance* 17 (2011): 447–67.

24. Kenneth Neal Waltz, *Theory of International Politics* (Boston: McGraw-Hill, 1979).

25. Nancy H. Kaufman, "Fairness and the Taxation of International Income," *Law & Policy in International Business* 29, no. 2 (1998): 145–203.

26. Allison Christians, "Sovereignty, Taxation, and Social Contract," University of Wisconsin Legal Studies Research Paper, 2008, 12.

27. Graetz and O'Hear, "'Original Intent' of U.S. International Taxation."

28. Thandika Mkandawire, "On Tax Efforts and Colonial Heritage in Africa," *Journal of Development Studies* 46, no. 10 (2010): 1647–69; Seligman, *Income Tax*; Deborah Brautigam, ed., "Building Leviathan: Revenue, State Capacity and Governance," *IDS Bulletin* 33, no. 3 (2002): 10–20.

29. Moore, "Between Coercion and Contract."

30. Christians, "Global Trends and Constraints on Tax Policy in the Least Developed Countries"; Stewart, "Global Trajectories of Tax Reform"; Fjeldstad and Moore, "Tax Reform and State-Building in a Globalised World"; Genschel and Seelkopf, "Did They Learn to Tax?"

31. Mkandawire, "On Tax Efforts and Colonial Heritage in Africa."

32. Victor Thuronyi, "Introduction," in *Tax Law Design and Drafting*, ed. Victor Thuronyi (Washington, DC: International Monetary Fund, 1998), xxiv.

33. Michael Keen, "Taxation and Development—Again," in *Critical Issues in Taxation and Development*, ed. Clemens Fuest and George R. Zodrow (Cambridge, MA: MIT Press, 2013), 13–44.

34. Malcolm Gillis, "Toward a Taxonomy for Tax Reform," in *Tax Reform in Developing Countries*, ed. Malcolm Gillis (Durham, NC: Duke University Press, 1989), 7.

35. Keimei Kaizuka, "The Shoup Tax System and the Postwar Development of the Japanese Economy," *American Economic Review* 82, no. 2 (May 1, 1992): 221.

36. John Williamson, "What Washington Means by Policy Reform," in *Latin American Adjustment: How Much Has Happened?*, ed. John Williamson (Washington, DC: Institute for International Economics, 1990), 10.

37. Stewart, "Global Trajectories of Tax Reform," 169.

38. Sanjeev Gupta et al., "Foreign Aid and Revenue Response: Does the Composition of Aid Matter?," in *Helping Countries Develop: The Role of Fiscal Policy*, ed. Gabriela Inchauste, Sanjeev Gupta, and Benedict Clements (Washington, DC: International Monetary Fund, 2004), 285–305; Ernesto Crivelli et al., "Foreign Aid and Revenue: Still a Crowding Out Effect," *IMF Working Papers* 12 (2012): 186; but see Oliver Morrisey, Wilson Prichard, and Samantha Torrance, "Aid and Taxation: Exploring the Relationship Using New Data" (International Centre for Tax and Development Working Paper 21, Institute of Development Studies, Brighton, UK, 2014).

39. Ernesto Crivelli et al., "Resource Blessing, Revenue Curse? Domestic Revenue Effort in Resource-Rich Countries," *European Journal of Political Economy*, no. 35 (2014): 88–101; Alun H. Thomas and Juan P. Trevino, *Resource Dependence and Fiscal Effort in Sub-Saharan Africa* (Washington, DC: International Monetary Fund, 2013).

40. Stephen Knack, "Sovereign Rents and Quality of Tax Policy and Administration," *Journal of Comparative Economics* 37, no. 3 (2009): 359–71; Richard Auty, *Sustaining Development in Mineral Economies: The Resource Curse Thesis* (London: Routledge, 2002); James A. Robinson, Ragnar Torvik, and Thierry Verdier, "Political Foundations of the Resource Curse," *Journal of Development Economics* 79, no. 2 (2006): 447–68.

41. Andreas Nölke and Arjan Vliegenthart, "Enlarging the Varieties of Capitalism: The Emergence of Dependent Market Economies in East Central Europe," *World Politics* 61, no. 4 (2009): 670–702; Ben Ross Schneider, "Hierarchical Market Economies and Varieties of Capitalism in Latin America," *Journal of Latin American Studies* 41, no. 3 (2009): 553–75.

42. Fenochietto and Pessino, *Understanding Countries' Tax Effort*.

43. ICTD/UNU-WIDER, "Government Revenue Dataset."

44. Alexander Klemm and S. M. Ali Abass, "A Partial Race to the Bottom: Corporate Tax Developments in Emerging and Developing Economies" (IMF Working Paper 12/28, Washington, DC: International Monetary Fund, 2012); Michael Keen and Mario Mansour, "Revenue Mobilization in Sub-Saharan Africa: Challenges from Globalization" (IMF Working Paper 9/157, International Monetary Fund, Washington, DC, 2009); Stewart, "Global Trajectories of Tax Reform"; Fjeldstad and Moore, "Tax Reform and State-Building in a Globalised World."

45. IMF, *Spillovers in International Corporate Taxation*; Peter J. Mullins, "Moving to Territoriality? Implications for the United States and the Rest of the World" (IMF Working Paper 06/161, International Monetary Fund, Washington, DC, 2006).

46. Quoted in Graetz and O'Hear, "'Original Intent' of U.S. International Taxation," 1066.

47. Hillel David Soifer, "The Causal Logic of Critical Junctures," *Comparative Political Studies* 45, no. 12 (2012): 1572–97.

48. Graetz and O'Hear, "'Original Intent' of U.S. International Taxation," 1021; Jogarajan, *Double Taxation and the League of Nations*; Picciotto, *International Business Taxation*; Mitchell Benedict Carroll, *Global Perspectives of an International Tax Lawyer* (Hicksville: Exposition Press, 1978).

49. Graetz and O'Hear, "'Original Intent' of U.S. International Taxation."

50. Jogarajan, *Double Taxation and the League of Nations*, 167–81.

51. Rixen, *Political Economy of International Tax Governance*.

52. Jogarajan, *Double Taxation and the League of Nations*, 58–72, 172.

53. Jogarajan, 108, 112–13.

54. Jogarajan, 165.

55. Jogarajan, 188–89.

56. League of Nations Fiscal Committee, "Report to the Council on the Work of the Tenth Session of the Committee," League of Nations, 1946, C.37.M.37.1946.II.A. (Geneva: United Nations Archive).

57. League of Nations Fiscal Committee.

58. M. W. Morton, "Fiscal Commission Second Session, Report of the United Kingdom Delegate," TNA, 1949, IR40/9959, National Archives, London.

59. M. W. Morton, "Fiscal Commission Third Session, Report of the United Kingdom Delegate," TNA, July 24, 1951, IR40/9959, National Archives, London.

60. United Nations, "Report of the Fiscal Commission (Third Session)," United Nations, 1951, IR40/9959, National Archives, London.

61. United Nations, "Economic Committee: Summary Record of the One Hundred and Sixteenth Meeting," United Nations, 1951, 7, IR40/9959, National Archives, London.

62. United Nations, 5.

63. United Nations, 6.

64. Cited in Robert Marjolin, "Double Taxation in Europe: Resolution Adopted by the Executive Committee of the International Chamber of Commerce (Note by the Secretary-General)," OEEC, November 12, 1954, IR40/19035, National Archives, London.

65. Marjolin.

66. OEEC, "Creation of a Committee of Experts on Taxation (Note Submitted by the Dutch Delegation)," OEEC, July 11, 1955, 2, IR40/19035, National Archives, London.

67. OEEC, 3.

68. OEEC, "Proposal by the Netherlands, Swiss and German Delegations concerning Double Taxation Questions to Be Discussed by a Group of Taxation Experts Which Should Be Set Up within the O.E.E.C.," OEEC, December 9, 1955, 3, IR40/19035, National Archives, London.

69. OEEC, "Draft Report of the Ad Hoc Group of Experts of Fiscal Questions," OEEC, February 15, 1956, 1, IR40/19035, National Archives, London.

70. OECD, *Model Tax Convention on Income and on Capital*.

71. League of Nations Fiscal Committee, "Report to the Council on the Work of the Tenth Session of the Committee."

72. Andean Community Decision 40 of 1971, which was replaced by decision 578 of 2004.

73. Quinones Cruz, "Colombia"; Goldberg, "Conventions for the Elimination of International Double Taxation," 295.

74. Hearson, *Tax Treaties in Sub-Saharan Africa*.

75. Lennard, "UN Model Tax Convention as Compared with the OECD Model Tax Convention."

76. See, for example, the UN model commentary's discussion of changes to Article 7 of the OECD model. United Nations, *Model Double Taxation Convention between Developed and Developing Countries*, 139–40.

77. Dries Lesage, David Mcnair, and Mattias Vermeiren, "From Monterrey to Doha: Taxation and Financing for Development," *Development Policy Review* 28, no. 2 (2010): 155–72, https://doi.org/10.1111/j.1467-7679.2010.00479.x.

78. OEEC, "Interim on the Activities of the Fiscal Committee," OEEC, July 3, 1957, 7, IR40/19035, National Archives, London.

79. OEEC, 6.

80. Hearson, "When Do Developing Countries Negotiate Away Their Corporate Tax Base?"

81. The 1963 OECD Model Convention contains 55,713 words. The 2017 OECD Model Convention and Transfer Pricing Guidelines contains 557,094 words.

82. Robert A. Green, "Antilegalistic Approaches to Resolving Disputes between Governments: A Comparison of the International Tax and Trade Regimes," *Yale Journal of International Law* 23 (1998): 79.

83. Thomas Rixen, "From Double Tax Avoidance to Tax Competition: Explaining the Institutional Trajectory of International Tax Governance," *Review of International Political Economy* 18, no. 2 (2011): 207, https://doi.org/10.1080/09692290.2010.481921.

84. Rixen, "Bilateralism or Multilateralism?" 207.

85. Genschel and Rixen, "Settling and Unsettling the Transnational Legal Order," 163.

86. Eduardo Baistrocchi and Martin Hearson, *A Global Analysis of Tax Treaty Disputes*, ed. Eduardo Baistrocchi (Cambridge: Cambridge University Press, 2017).

87. Avi-Yonah, *International Tax as International Law*.

88. Alberto Vega and Ilja Rudyk, "Explaining Reservations to the OECD Model Tax Convention: An Empirical Approach," *Indret*, no. 4 (2011): 1–19.

89. Avi-Yonah, *International Tax as International Law*.

90. Jogarajan, *Double Taxation and the League of Nations*.

91. For example, the Convention on Mutual Administrative Assistance in Tax Matters, formerly an OECD/Council of Europe instrument but now open to all interested jurisdictions.

92. Ronen Palan, *The Offshore World: Sovereign Markets, Virtual Places, and Nomad Millionaires* (Ithaca, NY: Cornell University Press, 2003); Picciotto, *International Business Taxation*.

93. Rixen, *Political Economy of International Tax Governance*.

94. OECD, *Addressing Base Erosion and Profit Shifting* (Paris: OECD Publishing, 2013), https://doi.org/10.1787/9789264192744-en; IMF, *Spillovers in International Corporate Taxation*.

95. Francis Weyzig, "Tax Treaty Shopping: Structural Determinants of Foreign Direct Investment Routed Through the Netherlands," *International Tax and Public Finance* 20, no. 6 (2013): 910–37, https://doi.org/10.1007/s10797-012-9250-z.

96. Baistrocchi, "Use and Interpretation of Tax Treaties in the Emerging World"; Arel-Bundock, "Unintended Consequences of Bilateralism."

97. OECD, *Report to G20 Development Working Group on the Impact of BEPS in Low Income Countries (Parts 1 and 2)* (Paris: OECD Publishing, 2014).

98. High-Level Panel on Illicit Financial Flows from Africa, *Illicit Financial Flows* (Addis Ababa: United Nations Economic Commission for Africa, 2015).

3. THE COMPETITION DISCOURSE AND NORTH-SOUTH RELATIONS

1. Layna Mosley, "Room to Move: International Financial Markets and National Welfare States," *International Organization* 54, no. 4 (October 1, 2000): 737–73, https://doi.org/10.1162/002081800551352.

2. Klemm and Abass, "Partial Race to the Bottom"; Thomas Plümper, Vera E. Troeger, and Hannes Winner, "Why Is There No Race to the Bottom in Capital Taxation?," *International Studies Quarterly* 53, no. 3 (September 2009): 761–86, https://doi.org/10.1111/j.1468-2478.2009.00555.x; Scott J. Basinger and Mark Hallerberg, "Remodeling the Competition for Capital: How Domestic Politics Erases the Race to the Bottom," *American Political Science Review* 98, no. 2 (June 21, 2004): 261–76, https://doi.org/10.1017/S0003055404001133; Layna Mosley, "Globalisation and the State: Still Room to Move?," *New Political Economy* 10, no. 3 (September 6, 2005): 355–62, https://doi.org/10.1080/13563460500204241.

3. Fuchs, *Business Power in Global Governance.*

4. Lynne Latulippe, "Tax Competition: An Internalised Policy Goal," in *Global Tax Governance: What Is Wrong with It and How to Fix It*, ed. Peter Dietsch and Thomas Rixen (Colchester: ECPR Press, 2016), 77–100.

5. Frank Dobbin, Beth A. Simmons, and Geoffrey Garrett, "The Global Diffusion of Public Policies: Social Construction, Coercion, Competition, or Learning?," *Annual Review of Sociology* 33, no. 1 (August 2007): 449–72, https://doi.org/10.1146/annurev.soc.33.090106.142507.

6. Ruud A. de Mooij and Sjef Ederveen, "Corporate Tax Elasticities: A Reader's Guide to Empirical Findings," *Oxford Review of Economic Policy* 24, no. 4 (2008): 680–97, https://doi.org/10.1093/oxrep/grn033; Lars P. Feld and Jost H. Heckemeyer, "FDI and Taxation: A Meta-Study," *Journal of Economic Surveys* 25, no. 2 (2011): 233–72, https://doi.org/10.1111/j.1467-6419.2010.00674.x.

7. Tidiane Kinda, "The Quest for Non-resource-based FDI: Do Taxes Matter?" (Working Paper 14/15, International Monetary Fund, Washington, DC, 2014); Charles Oman, *Policy Competition for Foreign Direct Investment: A Study of Competition among Governments to Attract FDI* (Paris: OECD Publishing, 2000).

8. Bethuel Kenyanjui Kinuthia, "Determinants of Foreign Direct Investment in Kenya: New Evidence," in *Proceedings of the African International Business and Management Conference* (Nairobi, August 25–27, 2010); Edward Mwachinga, "Results of Investor Motivation Survey Conducted in the EAC," Presentation at regional workshop on tax incentives (Lusaka, February 12–13, 2013).

9. IMF et al., *Supporting the Development of More Effective Tax Systems: A Report to the G-20 Development Working Group by the IMF, OECD, UN and World Bank* (Paris: OECD Publishing, 2011), 20.

10. Charles M. Tiebout, "A Pure Theory of Local Expenditures," *Journal of Political Economy* 64, no. 5 (1956): 416–24.

11. Reuven S. Avi-Yonah, "Globalization, Tax Competition, and the Fiscal Crisis of the Welfare State," *Harvard Law Review* 113, no. 7 (2000): 1573–676, https://doi.org/10.2307/1342445; Wallace E. (Wallace Eugene) Oates, *Fiscal Federalism* (New York: Harcourt Brace Jovanovich, 1972); Kimberly Clausing, "The Nature and Practice of Tax Competition," in *Global Tax Governance: What Is Wrong with It and How to Fix It*, ed. Peter Dietsch and Thomas Rixen (Colchester: ECPR Press, 2016), 27–54.

12. Philipp Genschel and Peter Schwarz, "Tax Competition: A Literature Review," *Socio-Economic Review* 9, no. 2 (March 15, 2011): 339–70, https://doi.org/10.1093/ser/mwr004.

13. Keen and Mansour, "Revenue Mobilization in Sub-Saharan Africa"; Alan Auerbach, "Why Have Corporate Tax Revenues Declined? Another Look" (NBER Working Paper Series, Cambridge, MA, August 2006), https://doi.org/10.3386/w12463; Klemm and Abass, "Partial Race to the Bottom."

14. Basinger and Hallerberg, "Remodeling the Competition for Capital"; Plümper, Troeger, and Winner, "Why Is There No Race to the Bottom in Capital Taxation?"

15. Dietsch, *Catching Capital.*

16. Clausing, "Nature and Practice of Tax Competition."

17. Poulsen, *Bounded Rationality and Economic Diplomacy.*

18. Kahneman and Tversky, "Prospect Theory."

19. Craig Volden, Michael M. Ting, and Daniel P. Carpenter, "A Formal Model of Learning and Policy Diffusion," *American Political Science Review* 102, no. 3 (August 25, 2008): 319–32, https://doi.org/10.1017/S0003055408080271.

20. Kurt Weyland, "Theories of Policy Diffusion - Lessons from Latin American Pension Reform," *World Politics* 57, no. 2 (2005): 280–81, https://doi.org/10.1353/wp.2005.0019.

21. Sushil Bikhchandani, David Hirshleifer, and Ivo Welch, "Learning from the Behavior of Others: Conformity, Fads, and Informational Cascades," *Journal of Economic Perspectives* 12, no. 3 (1998): 151–70; Sushil Bikhchandani, David Hirshleifer, and Ivo Welch, "A Theory of Fads, Fashion, Custom, and Cultural Change as Informational Cascades," *Journal of Political Economy* 100, no. 5 (1992): 992–1026.

22. Jandhyala, Henisz, and Mansfield, "Three Waves of BITs."

23. Poulsen, *Bounded Rationality and Economic Diplomacy.*

24. James G. March and Johan P. Olsen, "The Logic of Appropriateness," in *The Oxford Handbook of Public Policy*, eds. Robert E. Goodin, Michael Moran, and Martin Rein (Oxford: Oxford University Press, 2008), 689–708, https://doi.org/10.1093/oxfordhb/9780199548453.003.0034.

25. Martha Finnemore and Kathryn Sikkink, "International Norm Dynamics and Political Change," *International Organization* 52, no. 4 (1998): 887–917, https://doi.org/10.1162/002081898550789.

26. Dobbin, Simmons, and Garrett, "Global Diffusion of Public Policies."

27. Here we are concerned with the social interactions within organizations as channels for information rather than the role of experts within the organization's secretariat as "teachers," which is considered in chapter 5. See Martha Finnemore, *National Interests in International Society* (Ithaca, NY: Cornell University Press, 1996); Alexandra Gheciu, "Security Institutions as Agents of Socialization? NATO and the 'New Europe,'" *International Organization* 59, no. 4 (2005): 973–1012, https://doi.org/10.1017/S0020818305050332.

28. Xun Cao, "Networks of Intergovernmental Organizations and Convergence in Domestic Economic Policies," *International Studies Quarterly* 53, no. 4 (2009): 1095–130; Xun Cao, "Global Networks and Domestic Policy Convergence: A Network Explanation of Policy Changes," *World Politics* 64, no. 3 (2012): 375–425; Xun Cao, "Networks as Channels of Policy Diffusion: Explaining Worldwide Changes in Capital Taxation, 1998–2006," *International Studies Quarterly* 54, no. 3 (September 6, 2010): 823–54, https://doi.org/10.1111/j.1468-2478.2010.00611.x.

29. Chang Kil Lee and David Strang, "The International Diffusion of Public-Sector Downsizing: Network Emulation and Theory-Driven Learning," *International Organization* 60, no. 4 (2006): 883–909, https://doi.org/10.1017/S002081830606292.

30. Heinrich Von Stackelberg, *Market Structure and Equilibrium* [Marktform Und Gleichgewicht] (Heidelberg: J. Springer, 1934); Benjamin O. Fordham and Victor Asal, "Billiard Balls or Snowflakes? Major Power Prestige and the International Diffusion of Institutions and Practices," *International Studies Quarterly* 51, no. 1 (March 2007): 31–52, https://doi.org/10.1111/j.1468-2478.2007.00438.x.

31. Lee and Strang, "International Diffusion of Public-Sector Downsizing," 887–89.

32. Alexander Baturo and Julia Gray, "Flatliners: Ideology and Rational Learning in the Adoption of the Flat Tax," *European Journal of Political Research* 48, no. 1 (2009): 130–59, https://doi.org/10.1111/j.1475-6765.2008.00830.x.

33. Jensen, "Domestic Institutions and the Taxing of Multinational Corporations."

34. Stephen Bell and Andrew Hindmoor, "The Structural Power of Business and the Power of Ideas: The Strange Case of the Australian Mining Tax," *New Political Economy*

19, no. 3 (May 30, 2013): 470–86, https://doi.org/10.1080/13563467.2013.796452; Tasha Fairfield, *Private Wealth and Public Revenue in Latin America: Business Power and Tax Politics* (New York: Cambridge University Press, 2015).

35. An example is Barthel and Neumayer, "Competing for Scarce Foreign Capital."

36. Jason C. Sharman, "Power and Discourse in Policy Diffusion: Anti-money Laundering in Developing States," *International Studies Quarterly* 52, no. 3 (2008): 635–56, https://doi.org/10.1111/j.1468-2478.2008.00518.x; Sebastian Heilmann and Nicole Schulte-Kulkmann, "The Limits of Policy Diffusion: Introducing International Norms of Anti-money Laundering into China's Legal System," *Governance* 24, no. 4 (October 1, 2011): 639–64, https://doi.org/10.1111/j.1468-0491.2011.01543.x.

37. Giorgia Maffini, ed., *Business Taxation under the Coalition Government* (Oxford: Oxford University Centre for Business Taxation, 2015).

38. Beth A. Simmons and Zachary Elkins, "The Globalization of Liberalization: Policy Diffusion in the International Political Economy," *American Political Science Review* 98, no. 1 (2004): 171–89.

39. Zachary Elkins, Andrew T. Guzman, and Beth A. Simmons, "Competing for Capital: The Diffusion of Bilateral Investment Treaties, 1960–2000," *International Organization* 60, no. 4 (2006): 811–46, https://doi.org/10.1017/s0020818306060279.

40. Interview 22.

41. Interview 33.

42. Interview 11; Mutava, *Review of Tax Treaty Practices and Policy Framework in Africa.*

43. Interview 6.

44. Interview 5.

45. When I related this to negotiators from higher-income countries, many rejected the idea that they had initiated all, or even most, of their treaties with lower-income countries. This disparity may be explained by countries making reciprocal requests as investment flows between them grow, perhaps with the different timing allowing each side to feel that the other has initiated negotiations. There may also be a historical variation whereby lower-income countries had pursued some treaties with European countries in the past, before the negotiators with whom I spoke were in their posts. Finally, it may also be the case that treaty negotiators based in the revenue authority are not always privy to the initial contacts made by foreign affairs or finance ministries, especially if their countries do not have a treaty policymaking process.

46. Interview 5.

47. Interview 7.

48. Interview 9.

49. Interviews 50, 68.

50. Interview 1.

51. Interview 21.

52. Christians, "Tax Treaties for Investment and Aid to Sub-Saharan Africa," 643.

53. Wikileaks, "Public Library of US Diplomacy."

54. US embassy cable 07SKOPJE190, Mon., March 5, 2007.

55. US embassy cable 06ZAGREB1490, Fri., December 15, 2006.

56. US embassy cable 07ZAGREB285, Mon., March 26, 2007.

57. US embassy cable 08DOHA781, Wed., November 5, 2008.

58. Poulsen and Aisbett, "When the Claim Hits"; Poulsen, *Bounded Rationality and Economic Diplomacy.*

59. Hearson and Kangave, "Review of Uganda's Tax Treaties and Recommendations for Action."

60. This illustrates an important difference between tax treaties and BITs: the main function of a BIT lies in the creation of a "credible commitment" by raising the cost of

expropriation for the government, and if a government comes to regret this concession it can escape it only by terminating the treaty; in contrast, if a government becomes concerned with certain costs of a tax treaty, it can (in principle, at least) alter its negotiating stance to retain more taxing rights without negating the entire case for the treaty.

61. One common conclusion is that smaller countries are more likely to compete over corporate tax rates (though not labor or consumption tax rates) than larger countries. More generally, larger economies have higher corporate tax rates than smaller ones. This conclusion is predicted by economic theories that note that smaller economies are more likely to benefit from attracting more foreign investment at a lower tax rate than larger economies.

62. Basinger and Hallerberg, "Remodeling the Competition for Capital."

63. Duane Swank, "Tax Policy in an Era of Internationalization: Explaining the Spread of Neoliberalism," *International Organization* 60, no. 4 (October 25, 2006): 847–82, https://doi.org/10.1017/S0020818306060280. See also David W. Soskice and Peter A. Hall, eds., *Varieties of Capitalism: The Institutional Foundations of Comparative Advantage* (Oxford: Oxford University Press, 2001).

64. Plümper, Troeger, and Winner, "Why Is There No Race to the Bottom in Capital Taxation?"

65. Katerina Linos, "Diffusion through Democracy," *American Journal of Political Science* 55, no. 3 (2011): 678–95, https://doi.org/10.1111/j.1540-5907.2011.00513.x.

66. Tsebelis, *Veto Players.*

67. Interview 35.

68. Allison Christians, "While Parliament Sleeps: Tax Treaty Practice in Canada," *Journal of Parliamentary and Political Law* 10, no. 15 (2016), https://doi.org/10.2139/ssrn.2780874.

69. Interview, anonymized; Hearson and Kangave, "Review of Uganda's Tax Treaties and Recommendations for Action."

70. On partisanship, FDI, and tax policy, see Pablo M. Pinto, *Partisan Investment in the Global Economy: Why the Left Loves Foreign Direct Investment and FDI Loves the Left* (Cambridge: Cambridge University Press, 2013); Pablo M. Pinto and Santiago M. Pinto, "The Politics of Investment Partisanship: And the Sectoral Allocation of Foreign Direct Investment," *Economics & Politics* 20, no. 2 (June 2008): 216–54, https://doi.org/10.1111/j.1468-0343.2008.00330.x; Nathan M. Jensen and René Lindstadt, "Leaning Right and Learning from the Left: Diffusion of Corporate Tax Policy across Borders," *Comparative Political Studies* 45, no. 3 (2012): 283–311, https://doi.org/10.1177/0010414011421313.

71. For example: McGauran, *Should the Netherlands Sign Tax Treaties with Developing Countries?*; Lewis, *Sweet Nothings*; *Business Daily*, "Africa's Tax Officials Watch Uganda Case Keenly," February 23, 2014.

72. Interview 23.

73. Mark S. Manger, *Investing in Protection: The Politics of Preferential Trade Agreements between North and South* (Cambridge: Cambridge University Press, 2009), 19.

74. Remarks at a hearing of the committee on fiscal affairs, June 2015.

75. Interview 4.

76. Interview 6.

77. Interviews 5, 64.

78. Interview 9.

79. Emmanuel Were, "Kenya: France Telecom Entry Eases Tax Burden," *Business Daily*, December 16, 2007.

80. Interview 20.

81. Interviews 5, 6, 65.

82. Fabrizio Gilardi, "Transnational Diffusion: Norms, Ideas, and Policies," in *Handbook of International Relations*, eds. Walter Carlsnaes, Thomas Risse, and Beth A. Simmons (London: SAGE Publications, 2012), 453–77, https://doi.org/10.4135/9781446247587.n18.

83. Dobbin, Simmons, and Garrett, "Global Diffusion of Public Policies," 457.

84. Interviews, anonymized.

85. For example, there is some correspondence related to the UK's desire to open negotiations with India and Latin American countries. A letter from D. L. Pearson in the Ministry of Overseas Development to F. B. Harrison at the Inland Revenue, dated May 16, 1966, states: "We think it would be both impracticable as well as damaging to aid policy to establish and overtly emphasise any direct link between the amount of aid we provide and the forthcomingness of the recipient Government in fiscal (or indeed other) matters." Inland Revenue IR40/16325, National Archives, London.

86. Julia Braun and Martin Zagler, "The True Art of the Tax Deal: Evidence on Aid Flows and Bilateral Double Tax Agreements," *World Economy* 41, no. 6 (2018): 1478–507.

87. US embassy cable 09BOGOTA3359, Thu., November 12, 2009.

88. US embassy cables 07BUENOSAIRES1795, Mon., September 10, 2007, and 07BUENOSAIRES2241, Tue., November 20, 2007.

89. John Njiraini (speech, Strathmore University, Nairobi, September 12, 2013).

90. Baistrocchi, "Use and Interpretation of Tax Treaties in the Emerging World."

91. Dobbin, Simmons, and Garrett, "Global Diffusion of Public Policies," 456.

92. Ann E. Towns, "Norms and Social Hierarchies: Understanding International Policy Diffusion 'From Below,'" *International Organization* 66, no. 2 (April 5, 2012): 179–209, https://doi.org/10.1017/s0020818312000045.

93. Paul J. DiMaggio and Walter W. Powell, "The Iron Cage Revisited: Institutional Isomorphism and Collective Rationality in Organizational Fields," *American Sociological Review* 48, no. 2 (1983): 148, https://doi.org/10.2307/2095101; see also Finnemore and Sikkink, "International Norm Dynamics and Political Change."

94. Sharman, "Power and Discourse in Policy Diffusion," 646.

95. Weyland, "Theories of Policy Diffusion," 270.

96. Annual institute on federal taxation.

97. Pickering, *Why Negotiate Tax Treaties?*, 17.

98. James G. March and Johan P. Olsen, *Rediscovering Institutions: The Organizational Basis of Politics* (New York: Free Press, 1989).

4. THE INTERNATIONAL TAX COMMUNITY AND THE POLITICS OF EXPERTISE

1. Diane M. Ring, "Who Is Making International Tax Policy? International Organizations as Power Players in a High Stakes World" (Boston College Law School Faculty Papers 264, 2010); Christians, "While Parliament Sleeps"; Picciotto, *International Business Taxation*; Maikel Evers, "Tracing the Origins of the Netherlands' Tax Treaty," *Intertax* 41, no. 6 (2013): 375–86; Picciotto, "Indeterminacy, Complexity, Technocracy and the Reform of International Corporate Taxation."

2. See, for example, the introductions to the model treaties: United Nations, *Model Double Taxation Convention between Developed and Developing Countries*; OECD, *Model Tax Convention on Income and on Capital*.

3. Culpepper, *Quiet Politics and Business Power*.

4. Genschel and Rixen, "Settling and Unsettling the Transnational Legal Order," 163.

5. Michael J. Graetz, "Taxing International Income: Inadequate Principles, Outdated Concepts, and Unsatisfactory Policies," *Brooklyn Journal of International Law* 1 (2000): 261–336; Jogarajan, *Double Taxation and the League of Nations*; Picciotto, *International Business Taxation*.

6. League of Nations, *Report of the Committee of Technical Experts on Double Taxation and Tax Evasion* (Geneva: League of Nations, 1927), 6.

7. Seligman, *Double Taxation and International Fiscal Cooperation*, 143–44.

8. Picciotto, *International Business Taxation*, 37.

9. Jeffrey Owens and Mary C. Bennett, "The OECD Model Tax Convention: Why It Works," *OECD Observer2*, October 2008, http://oecdobserver.org/news/archivestory.php /aid/2756/OECD_Model_Tax_Convention.html.

10. Christians, "Networks, Norms and National Tax Policy," 22.

11. Christians, 22.

12. Diane M. Ring, "International Tax Relations: Theory and Implications," *New York University Tax Law Review* 60 (2006): 148; see also Ring, "Who Is Making International Tax Policy?," 681.

13. J. C. Sharman, "Dysfunctional Policy Transfer in National Tax Blacklists," *Governance* 23, no. 4 (October 2010): 637.

14. Thomas Rixen, "Politicization and Institutional (Non-) Change in International Taxation" (WZB Discussion Paper, SP IV 2008-306, Berlin: Wissenschaftszentrum Berlin für Sozialforschung, 2008), 13; Michael C. Webb, "Shaping International Corporate Taxation," in *Global Corporate Power*, ed. Christopher May (Boulder, CO: Lynne Rienner, 2006), 105–26.

15. Peter M. Haas, "Introduction: Epistemic Communities and International Policy Coordination," *International Organization* 46, no. 1 (May 22, 1992): 3, https://doi.org/10 .1017/S0020818300001442.

16. Christians, "Networks, Norms and National Tax Policy"; Ring, "Who Is Making International Tax Policy?"; Buttner and Thiemann, "Breaking Regime Stability?"; Picciotto, "Indeterminacy, Complexity, Technocracy and the Reform of International Corporate Taxation"; Fritz Brugger and Rebecca Engebretsen, "Defenders of the Status Quo: Making Sense of the International Discourse on Transfer Pricing Methodologies," *Review of International Political Economy*, advance online publication, August 27, 2020, http://doi .org/10.1080/09692290.2020.1807386.

17. Andreas Antoniades, "Epistemic Communities, Epistemes and the Construction of (World) Politics," *Global Society* 17, no. 1 (January 14, 2003): 21–38, https://doi.org/10 .1080/0953732032000053980; Mai'a K. Davis Cross, "Rethinking Epistemic Communities Twenty Years Later," *Review of International Studies* 39, no. 1 (April 11, 2012): 1–24, https:// doi.org/10.1017/S0260210512000034.

18. John Kurt Jacobsen, "Much Ado about Ideas: The Cognitive Factor in Economic Policy," *World Politics* 47, no. 2 (1995): 302, https://doi.org/10.2307/2950654.

19. Tsingou, "Club Governance and the Making of Global Financial Rules," 233.

20. Tsingou, 231.

21. Leslie Sklair, "Social Movements for Global Capitalism: The Transnationalist Class in Action," *Review of International Political Economy* 4, no. 3 (1997): 514–38.

22. League of Nations, *Report of the Committee of Technical Experts on Double Taxation and Tax Evasion*, 8.

23. OECD, *Model Tax Convention on Income and on Capital*, 2010 ed. (Paris: OECD Publishing, 2014), 9, http://www.keepeek.com/Digital-Asset-Management/oecd/taxation /model-tax-convention-on-income-and-on-capital-condensed-version-2010_mtc_cond -2010-en.

24. PWC, *Transfer Pricing and Developing Countries: Final Report* (Brussels: European Commission, 2011), 11.

25. H. David Rosenbloom, "Where's the Pony? Reflections on the Making of International Tax Policy," *Canadian Tax Journal* 57, no. 3 (2009): 491.

26. Jeffrey T. Checkel, "International Institutions and Socialization in Europe: Introduction and Framework," *International Organization* 59, no. 4 (2005): 801–26, https://doi .org/10.1017/S0020818305050289.

27. Buttner and Thiemann, "Breaking Regime Stability?"; Matti Ylönen and Teivo Teivainen, "Politics of Intra-firm Trade: Corporate Price Planning and the Double Role of

the Arm's Length Principle," *New Political Economy*, September 12, 2017, 1–17, https://doi.org/10.1080/13563467.2017.1371124.

28. Observation, March 2012. See table A.2 in the appendix for a list of meetings observed.

29. Observation, October 2015.

30. UNICE, "UNICE Comments on US Transfer Pricing Regulations," *Intertax* 21, no. 8 (1993): 380–81.

31. OECD, *Tax Aspects of Transfer Pricing within Multinational Enterprises: The United States Proposed Regulations: A Report* (Paris: OECD Publishing, 1993), vi.

32. Picciotto, "Indeterminacy, Complexity, Technocracy and the Reform of International Corporate Taxation"; Seabrooke and Wigan, "Powering Ideas through Expertise"; Buttner and Thiemann, "Breaking Regime Stability?"

33. Seabrooke and Wigan, "Powering Ideas through Expertise"; Duncan Wigan and Adam Baden, "Professional Activists on Tax Transparency," in *Professional Networks in Transnational Governance*, ed. Leonard Seabrooke and Lasse Folke Henriksen (Cambridge: Cambridge University Press, 2017), 130–46.

34. Interview 40.

35. Interview 1.

36. As illustrated by the annual "Global tax 50" list published by *International Tax Review*.

37. Andrew Abbott, "Linked Ecologies: States and Universities as Environments for Professions," *Sociological Theory* 23, no. 3 (2005): 245–74, https://doi.org/10.1111/j.0735-2751.2005.00253.x; Leonard Seabrooke and Eleni Tsingou, "Revolving Doors and Linked Ecologies in the World Economy: Policy Locations and the Practice of International Financial Reform" (Working paper 260, Centre for the Study of Globalisation and Regionalisation, University of Warwick, 2009).

38. Ole Jacob Sending and Iver B. Neumann, "Banking on Power: How Some Practices in an International Organization Anchor Others," in *International Practices*, ed. Emanuel Adler and Vincent Pouliot (Cambridge: Cambridge University Press, 2011), 231–54.

39. Leonard Seabrooke, "Epistemic Arbitrage: Transnational Professional Knowledge in Action," *Journal of Professions and Organization* 1, no. 1 (March 1, 2014): 49–64, https://doi.org/10.1093/jpo/jot005.

40. Christensen, "Elite Professionals in Transnational Tax Governance."

41. Rex Marshall, Malcolm Smith, and Robert Armstrong, "The Impact of Audit Risk, Materiality and Severity on Ethical Decision Making," *Managerial Auditing Journal* 21, no. 5 (June 14, 2006): 499, https://doi.org/10.1108/02686900610667265.

42. Jane Frecknall-Hughes and Margaret McKerchar, "Historical Perspectives on the Emergence of the Tax Profession: Australia and the UK," *Australian Tax Forum* 28, no. 2 (2013): 282.

43. Christensen, "Elite Professionals in Transnational Tax Governance."

44. Christian Plesner Rossing, "Tax Strategy Control: The Case of Transfer Pricing Tax Risk Management," *Management Accounting Research* 24, no. 2 (June 2013): 175–94, https://doi.org/10.1016/j.mar.2013.04.008.

45. Graetz and O'Hear, "'Original Intent' of U.S. International Taxation," 1073.

46. Graetz and O'Hear, 1070.

47. Mitchell Benedict Carroll, *Global Perspectives of an International Tax Lawyer* (Hicksville: Exposition Press, 1978).

48. Michael C. Durst, "The Two Worlds of Transfer Pricing Policymaking," *Tax Notes*, January 24, 2011.

49. John Snape, *The Political Economy of Corporation Tax: Theory, Values and Law Reform* (Oxford: Hart, 2011), 89.

50. Mike Truman, "Tax Prat of the Year," *Taxation*, February 6, 2013.

51. Interview 37.

52. Association SHERPA et al., *Specific Instance Regarding Glencore International AG and First Quantum Minerals Ltd and Their Alleged Violations of the OECD Guidelines for Multinational Enterprises via the Activities of Mopani Copper Mines Plc in Zambia* (submission to OECD national contact points in Switzerland and Canada, 2011).

53. PWC, *Transfer Pricing and Developing Countries: Final Report*.

54. Seabrooke and Tsingou, "Revolving Doors and Linked Ecologies in the World Economy."

55. Odd-Helge Fjeldstad and Mick Moore, "Revenue Authorities and Public Authority in Sub-Saharan Africa," *Journal of Modern African Studies* 47, no. 1 (March 18, 2009): 1–18, https://doi.org/10.1017/S0022278X08003637.

56. Seabrooke, "Epistemic Arbitrage," 55.

57. Leonard Seabrooke, "Economists and Diplomacy: Professions and the Practice of Economic Policy," *International Journal*, Summer 2011, 629.

58. Checkel, "International Institutions and Socialization in Europe," 804.

59. March and Olsen, "Logic of Appropriateness."

60. Checkel, "International Institutions and Socialization in Europe"; Alastair Iain Johnston, *Social States: China in International Institutions, 1980–2000* (Princeton, NJ: Princeton University Press, 2008).

61. Johnston, *Social States*.

62. Zürn and Checkel, "Getting Socialized to Build Bridges."

63. Johnston, "Conclusions and Extensions"; Jan Beyers, "Conceptual and Methodological Challenges in the Study of European Socialization," *Journal of European Public Policy* 17, no. 6 (2010): 909–20, https://doi.org/10.1080/13501763.2010.487004; Jeffrey M. Chwieroth, "Testing and Measuring the Role of Ideas: The Case of Neoliberalism in the International Monetary Fund," *International Studies Quarterly* 51, no. 1 (March 1, 2007): 5–30, https://doi.org/10.1111/j.1468-2478.2007.00437.x.

64. Sadiq, "Inherent International Tax Regime and Its Constraints on Australia's Sovereignty," 141.

65. Jeffrey M. Chwieroth, "Neoliberal Economists and Capital Account Liberalization in Emerging Markets," *International Organization* 61, no. 2 (April 11, 2007): 443–63, https://doi.org/10.1017/s0020818307070154.

66. For example, interviews 8 and 45.

67. Finnemore, *National Interests in International Society*; Gheciu, "Security Institutions as Agents of Socialization?"; Friedrich Kratochwil and John Gerard Ruggie, "International Organization: A State of the Art on an Art of the State," *International Organization* 40, no. 4 (May 22, 1986): 753, https://doi.org/10.1017/S0020818300027363; André Broome and Leonard Seabrooke, "Shaping Policy Curves: Cognitive Authority in Transnational Capacity Building," *Public Administration* 93, no. 4 (2015): 956–72, https://doi.org/dx.doi.org/10.1111/padm.12179.

68. United Nations, *Manual for the Negotiation of Bilateral Tax Treaties between Developed and Developing Countries 2019* (New York: United Nations, 2019).

69. Interviews 2, 16, 35.

70. Clive Baxter, speaking at a hearing of the fiscal affairs committee of the Danish Parliament, June 2015.

71. Broome and Seabrooke, "Shaping Policy Curves," 960.

72. Claire A. Dunlop, "Policy Transfer as Learning: Capturing Variation in What Decision-Makers Learn from Epistemic Communities," *Policy Studies* 30, no. 3 (June 2009): 289–311, https://doi.org/10.1080/01442870902863869; Haas, "Introduction"; Davis Cross, "Rethinking Epistemic Communities Twenty Years Later"; Antoniades, "Epistemic

Communities, Epistemes and the Construction of (World) Politics"; Anthony R. Zito, "Epistemic Communities, Collective Entrepreneurship and European Integration," *Journal of European Public Policy* 8, no. 4 (2001): 585–603, https://doi.org/10.1080/13501760110064401.

73. John Snape, "Tax Law: Complexity, Politics and Policymaking," *Social & Legal Studies* 24, no. 2 (2015): 155–63, https://doi.org/10.1177/0964663915575969.

74. Pierre Bourdieu, "The Force of Law: Toward a Sociology of the Juridical Field," *Hastings Law Journal* 38, no. 1971 (1987): 817, 828.

75. Snape, "Tax Law," 157.

76. Picciotto, "Indeterminacy, Complexity, Technocracy and the Reform of International Corporate Taxation," 179.

77. Picciotto, 179.

78. Picciotto, 179.

79. Bell and Hindmoor, "Structural Power of Business and the Power of Ideas"; Fairfield, *Private Wealth and Public Revenue in Latin America*.

80. Culpepper, *Quiet Politics and Business Power*, 159.

81. Charles Edward Lindblom, *Politics and Markets: The World's Political and Economic Systems* (New York: Basic Books, 1977), 205.

82. Ash Amin and Ronen Palan, "Towards a Non-rationalist International Political Economy," *Review of International Political Economy* 8, no. 4 (January 2001): 572–73, https://doi.org/10.1080/09692290110081534.

83. Fjeldstad and Moore, "Tax Reform and State-Building in a Globalised World," 258.

84. Fjeldstad and Moore, 258.

85. Stewart, "Global Trajectories of Tax Reform," 170.

86. For example, Jonathan Di John, "The Political Economy of Taxation and Tax Reform in Developing Countries" (Research paper 74, Helsinki: UNU World Institute for Development Economics Research, 2006).

87. Lisa Philipps, "Discursive Deficits: A Feminist Perspective on the Power of Technical Knowledge in Fiscal Law and Policy," *Canadian Journal of Law and Society* 11 (1996): 141.

88. Stewart, "Global Trajectories of Tax Reform," 173.

89. Ring, "Who Is Making International Tax Policy?"; Allison Christians, "Taxation in a Time of Crisis: Policy Leadership from the OECD to the G20," *Northwestern Journal of Law and Social Policy* 5, no. 1 (Spring 2010): 19–40; Eden, Dacin, and Wan, "Standards across Borders."

90. PWC, *Transfer Pricing and Developing Countries*, 4.

91. Huong Vu, *Several Tax Issues* (Hanoi: Vietnam Business Forum, 2014), 1 (errors in the original).

92. Christians, "Taxation in a Time of Crisis"; Christians, "Networks, Norms and National Tax Policy"; Ring, "Who Is Making International Tax Policy?"; Hugh J. Ault, "Reflections on the Role of the OECD in Developing International Tax Norms," *Brooklyn Journal of International Law* 34, no. 3 (2009): 756–81; Arthur J. Cockfield, "The Rise of the OECD as Informal World Tax Organization through National Responses to E-Commerce Tax Challenges," *Yale Journal of Law and Technology* 8 (2005): 136–87.

93. Richard Eccleston, "The OECD and Global Economic Governance," *Australian Journal of International Affairs* 65, no. 2 (2011): 243, https://doi.org/10.1080/10357718.2011.550106.

94. Eccleston, *Dynamics of Global Economic Governance*; Richard Eccleston and Richard Woodward, "Pathologies in International Policy Transfer: The Case of the OECD Tax Transparency Initiative," *Journal of Comparative Policy Analysis: Research and Practice* 16, no. 3 (November 12, 2013): 216–29, https://doi.org/10.1080/13876988.2013.854446; Jason C. Sharman, "Seeing Like the OECD on Tax," *New Political Economy* 17, no. 1 (2012):

37–41; Sharman, *Havens in a Storm*; Lorraine Eden and Robert T. Kudrle, "Tax Havens: Renegade States in the International Tax Regime?," *Law & Policy* 27, no. 1 (2005): 100.

95. Finnemore, *National Interests in International Society*; Gheciu, "Security Institutions as Agents of Socialization?"

96. Finnemore, *National Interests in International Society*, 13.

97. Finnemore, 13.

98. Kratochwil and Ruggie, "International Organization," 773.

99. Charles G. Nelson, "The Role of the OECD in International Economic Negotiations" (Unpublished PhD thesis, Indiana University, 1970), 159–60, quoted in Martin Marcussen, "The OECD in Search of a Role: Playing the Ideas Game," paper presented at the *ECPR Joint Session of Workshops* (Grenoble, 2001), 3.

100. Bengt Jacobsson, "Regulated Regulators: Global Trends of States Transformation," in *Transnational Governance: Institutional Dynamics of Regulation*, ed. Marie-Laure Djelic and Kerstin Sahlin-Andersson (Cambridge: Cambridge University Press, 2006), 205–24.

101. James G. March and Johan P. Olsen, "The Institutional Dynamics of International Political Orders," *International Organization* 52, no. 4 (1998): 961.

102. Marcussen, "OECD in Search of a Role."

103. Sharman, *Havens in a Storm*.

104. Cockfield, "Rise of the OECD as Informal World Tax Organization through National Responses to E-Commerce Tax Challenges," 171.

105. Henry G. Aubrey, *Atlantic Economic Cooperation* (New York: Published for the Council on Foreign Relations by Praeger, 1967), 29.

106. Marcussen, "OECD in Search of a Role," 21, citing Gunnar Sjöstedt, *OECD-Samarbetet: Funktioner Och Effekter*, Stockholm Political Studies (Stockholm: Statsvetens-kapliga institutionen, 1973), 322–23.

107. Scott Sullivan, *From War to Wealth: Fifty Years of Innovation* (Paris: OECD Publishing, 1997), 98.

108. Rianne Mahon and Stephen McBride, "Standardizing and Disseminating Knowledge: The Role of the OECD in Global Governance," *European Political Science Review* 1, no. 1 (March 20, 2009): 83–101, https://doi.org/10.1017/S1755773909000058.

109. In October 2015, an exhaustive list of fifty-nine CTPA staff was compiled through LinkedIn using the keywords "OECD" and "tax." The professional contacts of the individuals whose profiles were returned from this result were also checked to obtain the names of any colleagues who had not been returned by the keyword search.

110. Sharman, *Havens in a Storm*, 50.

111. Christians, "Networks, Norms and National Tax Policy," 22.

112. Marcussen, "OECD in Search of a Role."

113. Rixen, *Political Economy of International Tax Governance*, 2008.

114. Tony Porter and Michael Webb, "The Role of the OECD in the Orchestration of Global Knowledge Networks," *Canadian Political Science Association Annual Meetings*, no. 1 (2007): 6.

115. Lynne Latulippe, "The Expansion of the Bilateral Tax Treaty Network in the 1990s: The OECD's Role in International Tax Coordination," *Australian Tax Forum* 27, no. 4 (2012): 851–84. An example is interview 45.

116. OECD, *Action Plan on Base Erosion and Profit Shifting* (Paris: OECD Publishing, 2013), 87.

117. PWC, *Transfer Pricing and Developing Countries*, 41.

118. Hearson, *Tax Treaties in Sub-Saharan Africa*.

119. Lennard, "UN Model Tax Convention as Compared with the OECD Model Tax Convention—Current Points of Difference and Recent Developments"; Wijnen and de

Goede, *UN Model in Practice, 1997–2013*; Hearson, "Measuring Tax Treaty Negotiation Outcomes."

120. At the UN, committee members act in a personal capacity, while at the OECD they represent their governments.

121. A. Wilkinson, memo to Minister of State, May 5, 1976, Inland Revenue IR40/19025, National Archives, London.

122. Tsebelis, *Veto Players.*

123. Evers, "Tracing the Origins of the Netherlands' Tax Treaty."

124. Cited in Evers, 385.

125. Fairfield, *Private Wealth and Public Revenue in Latin America*, 11.

126. Avi-Yonah, *International Tax as International Law.*

127. Sadiq, "Inherent International Tax Regime and Its Constraints on Australia's Sovereignty," 132.

128. Yariv Brauner, "An International Tax Regime in Crystallization," *Tax Law Review* 56, no. 2 (2003): 259; Baistrocchi, "Use and Interpretation of Tax Treaties in the Emerging World"; Fjeldstad and Moore, "Tax Reform and State-Building in a Globalised World"; Christians, "Global Trends and Constraints on Tax Policy in the Least Developed Countries."

129. Mutava, *Review of Tax Treaty Practices and Policy Framework in Africa.*

130. Interview 5.

131. Interview 35.

132. Interview 25.

133. Interview 22.

134. Interview 27.

135. Interview 22.

136. Latham & Watkins LLP, "Federal Ministry of Finance Publishes Model for Future Double Tax Treaties," *Tax Info*, January 8, 2014.

137. OECD, *Model Tax Convention on Income and on Capital*, 449–90.

138. Itai Grinberg, "The New International Tax Diplomacy," *Georgetown Law Journal* 104, no. 5 (2016): 1137–96.

139. Ault, "Reflections on the Role of the OECD in Developing International Tax Norms," 760.

140. Cockfield, "Rise of the OECD as Informal World Tax Organization through National Responses to E-Commerce Tax Challenges"; Ault, "Reflections on the Role of the OECD in Developing International Tax Norms."

141. Christians, "Networks, Norms and National Tax Policy"; Ring, "Who Is Making International Tax Policy?"

142. Roger Bunting, Peter Fawcett, and Caroline Makasa, *Working Document COMESA Model Double Taxation Agreement and Commentary* (Brussels: ACE International Consultants, 2011); Ian Farrow and Sunita Jogarajan, *ASEAN Tax Regimes and the Integration of the Priority Sectors: Issues and Options* (Sydney: KPMG Australia, 2006); Ian Farrow and Sunita Jogarajan, "ASEAN Tax Regimes: Impediment or Pathway to Greater Integration," in *Brick by Brick: The Building of an ASEAN Economic Community*, ed. Denis Hew (Singapore: Institute of Southeast Asian Studies / ASEAN-Australia Development Cooperation Programme, 2008), 132–43.

143. Interviews, anonymized.

144. Correspondence reviewed in chapter 5.

145. Interview 10.

146. Hearson, *Tax Treaties in Sub-Saharan Africa.*

147. Kenyan High Court, petition number 494 of 2014, documents on file.

148. Christians, "While Parliament Sleeps," 27.

149. Interview, anonymized.

150. Interview, anonymized.

151. Interview, anonymized; Jason R. Connery, Steven R. Lainoff, and Charles W. Cope, "Current Status of U.S. Tax Treaties and International Tax Agreements," *Tax Management International Journal* 42, no. 106 (2013): 1–10.

152. Interviews 25, 34, 35.

153. Interviews 10, 23.

154. Quinones Cruz, "Colombia," 304.

155. Interview 10.

156. Mutava, *Review of Tax Treaty Practices and Policy Framework in Africa.*

5. THE UNITED KINGDOM

1. John F. Avery Jones, "The United Kingdom's Influence on the OECD Model Tax Convention," *British Tax Review* 56, no. 6 (2011): 653; Graetz and O'Hear, "'Original Intent' of U.S. International Taxation."

2. This phrase is used in a discussion of the diffusion of BITs to lower-income countries, in Elkins, Guzman, and Simmons, "Competing for Capital," 822.

3. D. G. Daymond to J. A. Honeyford, January 21, 1957, Foreign and Commonwealth Office FCO371/126504, National Archives, London.

4. "State of play on countries - January 1981," Inland Revenue IR 40/18110, National Archives, London.

5. "State of play on countries - January 1976," Inland Revenue IR 40/18110, National Archives, London.

6. "State of play on countries - January 1981," Inland Revenue IR 40/18110, National Archives, London.

7. "State of play on countries - October 1974," Inland Revenue IR 40/18110, National Archives, London.

8. J. H. Clement to A. C. Gray, November 13, 1978, Inland Revenue IR 40/18110, National Archives, London.

9. "State of play on countries - January 1981," Inland Revenue IR 40/18110, National Archives, London.

10. Handwritten note, "Relations with Thailand," marked "received in archives" in 1969 Foreign and Commonwealth Office FCO 15/972, National Archives, London.

11. D. Montgomery, letter from British embassy, Bangkok, June 5, 1972, Foreign and Commonwealth Office FCO 15/1645, National Archives, London.

12. Untitled note addressed to a Mr Stewart, October 1973, Inland Revenue IR 40/18109, National Archives, London.

13. A. Wilkinson, memo, September 9, 1977, Inland Revenue IR 40/18445, National Archives, London.

14. The other main reason was requests from businesses that were having trouble remitting income from Bangladesh that had been generated before independence, rather than for tax reasons.

15. O'Neill, telegram, November 5, 1976, Inland Revenue IR 40/18445, National Archives, London.

16. "Double Taxation Talks with Bangladesh," July 27–29, 1977, Inland Revenue IR 40/18445, National Archives, London.

17. Minutes of negotiation between Bangladesh and UK, July 27–29, 1977, Inland Revenue IR 40/18445, National Archives, London.

18. Daymond to Honeyford, January 21, 1957.

19. "Double Taxation Relief," report to the Paymaster General, February 25, 1976, Foreign and Commonwealth Office FCO59/1459, National Archives, London.

20. Daymond to Honeyford, January 21, 1957.

21. There are, of course, exceptions. Businesses that incurred taxes on gross fees—for example, withholding taxes on management fees paid out from clients in lower-income countries—would find that, absent a treaty, these tax payments would not qualify for a credit against UK tax, because the UK considered them to be levied on gross income, not profit. In the opposite direction, staff of foreign airlines working in the UK found themselves in some instances taxed by the UK and by their home country.

22. A. J. Lord, memo, Inland Revenue, March 1, 1967, Foreign Commonwealth Office FCO59/1459, National Archives, London.

23. A. Wilkinson, memo to Financial Secretary, April 8, 1976, Inland Revenue IR40/18941, National Archives, London.

24. M. W. Morton, 1949, Fiscal Commission, Second Session [Report of the United Kingdom Delegate], Inland Revenue IR40/9959, National Archives, London.

25. D. Hopkins, memo to A. H. Smallwood, November 9, 1973, Inland Revenue IR40/17190, National Archives, London. Reference to remarks by "Mr Wass representing the Treasury" at a meeting of July 23, 1973.

26. "Double Taxation Relief."

27. C. Hubbard, memo, December 22, 1974, Inland Revenue IR40/19025, National Archives, London.

28. A. C. Davies to A. Lord, December 15, 1971, Inland Revenue IR40/18109, National Archives, London.

29. United Nations, *Tax Treaties between Developed and Developing Countries: First Report*, ed. Ad Hoc Group of Experts on Tax Treaties between Developed and Developing Countries (New York: United Nations, 1969); United Nations, *Tax Treaties between Developed and Developing Countries: Second Report*, ed. Ad Hoc Group of Experts on Tax Treaties between Developed and Developing Countries (New York: United Nations, 1970).

30. Minutes of meetings with Confederation of British Industry on double taxation, 1971–1981, Inland Revenue IR40/18107 to 18111, National Archives, London.

31. Minutes of a meeting with Representatives of the Confederation of British Industry, March 15, 1972, Inland Revenue IR40/18109, National Archives, London.

32. "Double taxation convention talks with Thailand," October 1976, Inland Revenue IR40/18456, National Archives, London.

33. "Tanzania: Double Taxation," Inland Revenue IR40/17624, 1969–87, National Archives, London.

34. Wilkinson, memo to Financial Secretary, April 8, 1976.

35. Remarks by A. Hopkins recorded in Note of Meeting, June 7, 1974, Inland Revenue IR40/18969, National Archives, London.

36. "Double Taxation Relief."

37. E. L. Gomeche to Inland Revenue, June 26, 1970, Inland Revenue IR40/16974, National Archives, London.

38. Communication from the Zambian Ministry of Foreign Affairs, September 12, 1969, Inland Revenue IR40/16974, National Archives, London.

39. Minutes of negotiation between UK and Zambia, May 24–27, 1971, London, Inland Revenue IR40/16974, National Archives, London.

40. J. A. Johnstone to Inland Revenue, July 2, 1971, Inland Revenue IR40/16974, National Archives, London.

41. Note of Meeting, February 20, 1972, Inland Revenue IR40/17190, National Archives, London.

42. J. Gill to A. H. Smallwood, February 15, 1973, Foreign and Commonwealth Office FCO63/1126, National Archives, London.

43. A. H. Smallwood to I. H. Harris, March 15, 1973, Foreign and Commonwealth Office FCO59/973, National Archives, London.

44. D. Kerr, memo, March 27, 1973, Foreign and Commonwealth Office FCO59/973, National Archives, London.

45. A. T. Baillie, memos, November 1, 1972, and April 4, 1973, Foreign and Commonwealth Office FCO59/973, National Archives, London.

46. D. Kerr, memo, March 27, 1973.

47. According to biographies on the UK Parliament website, tenure during the period covered by this chapter was as follows: Dick Taverne, 1968–70; Bernard Jenkin, 1970–72; Terence Higgins, 1972–73; John Gilbert, 1974–75; Robert Sheldon, 1975–79; Nigel Lawson, 1979–81.

48. A. H. Smallwood, memo, December 5, 1975, Inland Revenue IR40/18941, National Archives, London.

49. Anonymous, memo, December 3, 1975, Inland Revenue IR40/18941, National Archives, London.

50. Note of Meeting, May 3, 1976, Inland Revenue IR40/18941, National Archives, London.

51. Memo from Private Secretary to Financial Secretary, October 1974, Inland Revenue IR40/18941, National Archives, London.

52. Anonymous, memo, December 3, 1975.

53. Note of Meeting, May 3, 1976.

54. Baillie, memo, April 4, 1973.

55. For example, as the UK and Brazil reopened negotiations in the early 1970s, a tax manager of RTZ, who was preparing major investments in the country, lobbied officials at the Inland Revenue in London and at the British embassy in Brazil. Note of Meeting, October 13, 1971, Inland Revenue IR40/17189, National Archives, London.

56. CBI (Confederation of British Industry), memo, September 16, 1974, Overseas Development OD42/104, National Archives, London.

57. Minutes of a meeting with Representatives of the Confederation of British Industry, July 4, 1975, Inland Revenue IR40/18109, National Archives, London.

58. Minutes of a meeting with Representatives of the Confederation of British Industry, July 4, 1975.

59. Minutes of a meeting with Representatives of the Confederation of British Industry, July 4, 1975.

60. P. E. Moran to I. P. Gunn, November 24, 1975, Inland Revenue IR40/19097, National Archives, London.

61. The term "firewall" is introduced in Etel Solingen, "Of Dominoes and Firewalls: The Domestic, Regional, and Global Politics of International Diffusion," *International Studies Quarterly* 56, no. 4 (2012): 631–44, https://doi.org/10.1111/isqu.12034.

62. M. J. Powell, "History of Double Taxation Negotiations with Egypt/UAR," November 1, 1968, Inland Revenue IR40/17378, National Archives, London.

63. "Egypt: Double Taxation," Inland Revenue IR40/17378, 1961–74, National Archives, London.

64. Letter from the Egyptian ambassador, March 18, 1969, Inland Revenue IR40/17378, National Archives, London.

65. A.J.C.E. Baillie, November 25 and December 1, 1969, Inland Revenue IR40/17378, National Archives, London.

66. J. L. Sayer to Inland Revenue, December 2, 1969, Inland Revenue IR40/17378, National Archives, London.

67. Letter from British embassy, February 12, 1971, Inland Revenue IR40/17378, National Archives, London.

68. M. J. Wilmshurst to Inland Revenue, October 16, 1970, Inland Revenue IR40/17378, National Archives, London.

69. J. Johnson, memo, March 9, 1972, Inland Revenue IR40/17378, National Archives, London.

70. M. J. Wilmshurst to Inland Revenue, November 2, 1972, Foreign and Commonwealth Office FCO 39/1280, National Archives, London.

71. "CBI Representations on an Egyptian Double Taxation Agreement," January 19, 1976, Inland Revenue IR40/19097, National Archives, London.

72. Note on UK/Egypt double taxation talks, May 1976, Inland Revenue IR40/19097, National Archives, London.

73. Minutes of a Meeting between Inland Revenue and Construction Design Services, September 7, 1976, Inland Revenue IR40/19097, National Archives, London.

74. F. W. Batstone to British embassy, January 4, 1978, Foreign and Commonwealth Office FCO 93/1565, National Archives, London.

75. J. O. Edwardes, memo, April 27, 1979, Inland Revenue IR40/19097, National Archives, London.

76. A. Wilkinson, memo to Minister of State, May 5, 1976, Inland Revenue IR40/19025, National Archives, London.

77. Wilkinson, memo to Minister of State, May 5, 1976.

78. F. Dornelles, recorded in Note of Talks in Brazilia, October 29–31, 1974, Inland Revenue IR40/19025, National Archives, London.

79. Minutes of a meeting with Representatives of the Confederation of British Industry, August 6, 1975, Inland Revenue IR40/19025, National Archives, London.

80. Wilkinson, memo to Minister of State, May 5, 1976.

81. "Brazil Brief 16: Double Taxation Relief Agreement," August 25, 1974, Inland Revenue IR40/19025, National Archives, London.

82. D. Hopkins, memo to A. H. Smallwood, November 9, 1973, Inland Revenue IR40/17190, National Archives, London.

83. "Brazil Brief 16."

84. P. Shore to D. Healey, December 12, 1974, Inland Revenue IR40/19025, National Archives, London.

85. See, for example, F. N. Harvey to A. H. Smallwood, January 12, 1976, Inland Revenue IR40/19025, National Archives, London.

86. A. H. Smallwood, memo, August 7, 1975, Inland Revenue IR40/19025, National Archives, London.

87. P. E. Moran to A. H. Smallwood, September 26, 1975, Inland Revenue IR40/19025, National Archives, London.

88. Wilkinson, memo to Minister of State, May 5 1976; Smallwood, memo, August 7, 1975.

89. Crosland, telegram, May 24, 1976, Inland Revenue IR40/19025, National Archives, London.

90. B. Pollard, telegram, May 26, 1976, Inland Revenue IR40/19025, National Archives, London.

91. Pollard, telegram.

92. B. Pollard, memo, June 4, 1975, Inland Revenue IR40/19025, National Archives, London.

93. Pollard, memo.

94. J. B. Shepherd, memo, July 14, 1992, Inland Revenue IR40/17808, National Archives, London.

95. Delegated Legislation Committee, June 30, 2014.

96. Note addressed to the British High Commission, January 21, 1963, Inland Revenue IR40/14909, National Archives, London.

97. "Historical background to talks," September 13, 1978, Inland Revenue IR40/17629, National Archives, London.

98. Correspondence in Foreign & Commonwealth Office FCO 65/1231, 1972, National Archives, London.

99. The note terminating the Nigeria-UK treaty is dated June 29, 1978. Inland Revenue IR40/17629, National Archives, London.

100. Draft telegram, July 27, 1978, Inland Revenue IR40/17629, National Archives, London.

101. "Taxation brief for Mr Barratt's visit to Nigeria and meeting with the Director of Inland Revenue: December 1978," Inland Revenue IR40/17629, National Archives, London.

102. A. P. Beauchamp to D. O. Olorunlake, May 18, 1979, Inland Revenue IR40/17630, National Archives, London.

103. D. O. Olorunlake to A. P. Beauchamp, April 17, 1979, Inland Revenue IR40/17630, National Archives, London.

104. "Extract from briefing for Chancellor re meeting with Sir David Steel on Tuesday 10/7/79," Inland Revenue IR40/17630, National Archives, London.

105. "Nigeria: Double Taxation," Inland Revenue IR40/17631, 1967–76, National Archives, London.

106. "Taxation brief for Mr Barratt's visit."

6. ZAMBIA

1. IBFD, "IBFD Tax Research Platform," accessed June 20, 2016, http://research.ibfd.org/.

2. Wikileaks, "Public Library of US Diplomacy."

3. Irish, "International Double Taxation Agreements and Income Taxation at Source"; Charles R. Irish, "Transfer Pricing Abuses and Less Developed Countries," *University of Miami Inter-American Law Review* 18, no. 1 (1986): 83–136; Andrew Sardanis, *Zambia: The First Fifty Years* (London: IB Tauris, 2014).

4. M. Knoetze, *Report of the Commissioner of Taxes, 1966/7* (Lusaka: Zambia Department of Taxes, 1968).

5. Irish, "International Double Taxation Agreements and Income Taxation at Source."

6. P. C. Luhanga, *Report of the Commissioner of Taxes, 1970/1* (Lusaka: Zambia Department of Taxes, 1972); D. Chiwenda, *Report of the Commissioner of Taxes, 1971/2* (Lusaka: Zambia Department of Taxes, 1973).

7. Irish, "International Double Taxation Agreements and Income Taxation at Source" contrasts Kenya and Malawi, while Nigeria is discussed in chapter 5 of this book.

8. Oliver S. Saasa, *Zambia's Policies towards Foreign Investment: The Case of the Mining and Non-mining Sectors* (Uppsala: Scandinavian Institute of African Studies, 1987), 30.

9. Two exempted dividends paid to direct investors from tax in the home country entirely.

10. Communication from the Zambian Ministry of Foreign Affairs, September 12, 1969, Inland Revenue IR40/16974, National Archives, London.

11. Kenneth David Kaunda, *Zambia's Economic Revolution: Address at Mulungushi, 19th April, 1968* (Lusaka: Zambia Information Services, 1968).

12. Sardanis, *Zambia*, 67.

13. Antony Martin, *Minding Their Own Business: Zambia's Struggle Against Western Control* (Harmondsworth: Penguin, 1975). Cited in Sardanis, *Zambia*, 55.

14. Ann Seidman, "The Distorted Growth of Import-Substitution Industry: The Zambian Case," *Journal of Modern African Studies* 12, no. 4 (1974): 620.

15. Seidman, 611.

16. Quoted in Sardanis, *Zambia*, 97.

17. Quoted in Sardanis, 97.

18. Zambia Ministry of Development Planning and National Guidance, *Second National Development Plan, January, 1972–December, 1976* (Lusaka: Zambia Ministry of Development Planning and National Guidance, 1971).

19. Wilson Prichard, Alex Cobham, and Andrew Goodall, "The ICTD Government Revenue Dataset" (International Centre for Tax and Development Working Paper 19, Institute of Development Studies, Brighton, UK, 2014).

20. D. Chiwenda, *Report of the Commissioner of Taxes, 1972/3* (Lusaka: Zambia Department of Taxes, 1974), 6.

21. Zambia Ministry of Development Planning and National Guidance, *Second National Development Plan*, 59.

22. L. W. Bwalya, *Report of the Commissioner of Taxes, 1973/4* (Lusaka: Zambia Department of Taxes, 1975).

23. Bwalya, 21–22.

24. Interview 42.

25. Irish, "International Double Taxation Agreements and Income Taxation at Source," 316.

26. Interview 42.

27. Irish, "International Double Taxation Agreements and Income Taxation at Source," 300.

28. Interview 53.

29. Interview 42.

30. Bwalya, *Report of the Commissioner of Taxes, 1973/4*, 12; Chiwenda, *Report of the Commissioner of Taxes, 1971/2*.

31. Irish, "International Double Taxation Agreements and Income Taxation at Source," 300.

32. Robert L. Curry Jr., "Problems in Acquiring Mineral Revenues for Financing Economic Development: A Case Study of Zambia during 1970–78," *American Journal of Economics and Sociology* 43, no. 1 (1984): 42.

33. Dennis L. Dresang and Ralph A. Young, "The Public Service," in *Administration in Zambia*, ed. William Tordoff (Manchester: Manchester University Press, 1980), 86.

34. Dennis L. Dresang, *The Zambia Civil Service: Entrepreneurialism and Development Administration* (Nairobi: East African Pub. House, 1975), 117.

35. Dresang and Young, "Public Service," 86.

36. Andrew Sardanis, in *Zambia: The First Fifty Years*, mentions three different permanent secretaries during this era. The third of these, E. C. Chibwe, permanent secretary from 1971, had become ambassador to West Germany by 1974. Timothy M. Shaw, "The Foreign Policy System of Zambia," *African Studies Review* 19, no. 1 (1976): 55.

37. Irish, "International Double Taxation Agreements and Income Taxation at Source," 300.

38. Ministry of Foreign Affairs of the Republic of Zambia, Untitled Letter, September 12, 1969, Inland Revenue IR40/16974, National Archives, London.

39. See chapter 5.

40. Pro forma sheet dated May 5, 1971, Inland Revenue IR40/16974, National Archives, London.

41. Sardanis, *Zambia*, 59; Dresang, *Zambia Civil Service*, 139–42.

42. Sardanis, *Zambia*, 59; Dresang, *Zambia Civil Service*, 139–42.

43. Curry, "Problems in Acquiring Mineral Revenues for Financing Economic Development," 46.

44. Interview 43.

45. "Income Tax Treaty Negotiations," October 11, 1973, US diplomatic cable ref 1973LUSAKA01854_b. Source: Wikileaks, "Public Library of US Diplomacy."

46. The Zambian negotiation team for the first two rounds is indicated in "Income Tax Treaty Negotiations," July 5, 1974, US cable ref 1974LUSAKA01386_b. Reference to a third round of negotiations is made in "Status of U.S.-Zambia Double Taxation Agreement," January 21, 1975, US cable ref 1975STATE013771_b. Source: Wikileaks.

47. Lise Rakner, *Political and Economic Liberalisation in Zambia, 1991–2001* (Stockholm: Nordic Africa Institute, 2003), 14.

48. Fjeldstad and Moore, "Revenue Authorities and Public Authority in Sub-Saharan Africa."

49. According to Mwenda, the ZRA is not as autonomous in practice as the ideal type might suggest, since the chair of its governing board and its commissioner general are appointed by the president. Kenneth Kaoma Mwenda, "Efficacy of the Institutional and Regulatory Framework for the Administration of Tax Law in Zambia," *Richmond Journal of Global Law and Business* 5, no. 1 (2005): 37–67.

50. OECD, *Investment Policy Review of Zambia (2011 Preliminary Draft)* (Paris: OECD Publishing, 2011), 66.

51. Interview 45.

52. Interview 45.

53. Attendance records on file with the author.

54. Latulippe, "Expansion of the Bilateral Tax Treaty Network in the 1990s," 872.

55. SADC, *Memorandum of Understanding on Co-operation in Taxation and Related Matters* (Pretoria: Southern African Development Community, 2002), 7–8.

56. Roger Bunting, Peter Fawcett, and Caroline Makasa, *A Roadmap for Further Negotiations by COMESA Countries* (Brussels: ACE International Consultants, 2012).

57. Interview 45.

58. UNCTAD and Japan Bank for International Cooperation, *Blue Book on Best Practice in Investment Promotion and Facilitation* (Geneva: United Nations, 2006), 24.

59. Interview 45.

60. Interview 49.

61. Interview 45.

62. Interviews 45, 49.

63. For example, interviews 41 and 47.

64. Interview 45.

65. Interview 49.

66. Interview 49.

67. Prichard, Cobham, and Goodall, "ICTD Government Revenue Dataset."

68. David Manley, *A Guide to Mining Taxation in Zambia* (Lusaka: Zambia Institute for Policy Analysis & Research, 2013), 32.

69. Miles Larmer, *Rethinking African Politics: A History of Opposition in Zambia* (Farnham: Ashgate, 2011), 262.

70. Mutuna Chanda, "Should Zambia Impose Windfall Taxes on Mining Companies?," *BBC News Online*, September 13, 2011, https://www.bbc.co.uk/news/av/world-africa-14898575.

71. Interview 44.

72. Interview 45.

73. SADC, *Memorandum of Understanding on Co-operation in Taxation and Related Matters*.

74. Interview 45.
75. Interview 41.
76. Interview 51.
77. Status of Zambian tax treaties, 2014, Finance Ministry document on file with the author.
78. Interview 44.
79. Interview 41.
80. Interviews 40, 41.
81. Interviews 41, 44, 48.
82. Interview 46.
83. Interview 41.

7. VIETNAM AND CAMBODIA

1. According to Lauge Poulsen, who interviewed a Cambodian BIT negotiator, these treaties were seen "as strategic instruments to comfort investors in post-war environments." Lauge N. Skovgaard Poulsen, "Sacrificing Sovereignty by Chance: Investment Treaties, Developing Countries, and Bounded Rationality" (PhD thesis, London School of Economics, 2011), 145–46.
2. Andrew Charlton, *Incentive Bidding for Mobile Investment: Economic Consequences and Potential Responses* (Paris: OECD Publishing, 2003), 17, https://doi.org/10.1787/864178271805.
3. Interview 65.
4. Interview 65.
5. Interviews 64, 65.
6. Interview 55.
7. Binh Tran-Nam, "Economic Liberalization and Vietnam's Long-Term Growth Prospects," *Journal of the Asia Pacific Economy* 4, no. 2 (January 1999): 248, https://doi.org/10.1080/13547869908724681.
8. *Harvard Law Review*, "Protection of Foreign Direct Investment in a New World Order: Vietnam. A Case Study," 107, no. 8 (1994): 2004, https://doi.org/10.2307/1341765.
9. Martin Gainsborough, "Vietnam and ASEAN: The Road to Membership?," *Pacific Review* 6, no. 4 (January 1993): 381–87, https://doi.org/10.1080/09512749308719061.
10. Gainsborough.
11. Hoang Mai Pham, *Foreign Direct Investment and Development in Vietnam: Policy Implications* (Singapore: Institute of Southeast Asian Studies, 2004), 24.
12. These figures are accurate whether using data on FDI stocks in 1998 or 2011. See Pham, "FDI and Development in Vietnam"; General Statistic Office of Vietnam, "Foreign Direct Investment Projects Licensed by Main Counterparts (Accumulation of Projects Having Effect as of 31/12/2012)," 2014, http://www.gso.gov.vn/default_en.aspx?tabid=471&idmid=3&ItemID=14366. From 1988 to 1998, over half of the FDI in Vietnam had come from five nearby countries—Singapore, Taiwan, Japan, Hong Kong, and Korea—and these five countries still constituted 53 percent of investment stock in Vietnam in 2011.
13. OECD, *Model Tax Convention on Income and on Capital*.
14. Interview 55.
15. Interview 55.
16. Interview 68.
17. Interview 55.
18. Interview 59.
19. Tran-Nam, "Economic Liberalization and Vietnam's Long-Term Growth Prospects."
20. Tran-Nam.

21. Pham, "FDI and Development in Vietnam," 59.

22. Binh Tran-Nam, "Taxation and Economic Development in Vietnam," in *Taxation in ASEAN and China: Local Institutions, Regionalism, Global Systems and Economic Development*, ed. Nolan Cormac Sharkey (Abingdon: Routledge, 2012), 126–46.

23. Ngo Dinh Quang and Nguyen Tien Dung, "Tax Reform in Vietnam," *Vietnam's Socio-Economic Development: A Social Science Review*, no. 10 (1997): 7.

24. Figures cited in Quang and Dung, 9.

25. Quang and Dung, 4.

26. Government figures cited in Martin Rama, Deepak Mishra, and Duc Minh Pham, "Overview of the Tax System in Vietnam," in *Tax Reform in Vietnam: Towards a More Efficient and Equitable System*, ed. Gangadha Prasad Shukla et al. (Washington, DC: World Bank, 2011), 19.

27. Quang and Dung, "Tax Reform in Vietnam," 11.

28. Interview 68.

29. Interview 55.

30. Attendance lists on file with the author.

31. Attendance lists on file with the author.

32. Interview 57.

33. Interview 62.

34. Interviews 54, 56, 61, 66.

35. Interview 54.

36. Interview 66.

37. Interview 59.

38. Tran-Nam, "Taxation and Economic Development in Vietnam," 132.

39. Interview 55.

40. Ministry of Finance, "Guidelines for Fulfilment of Tax Liability of Foreign Entities Doing Business in Vietnam or Earning Income in Vietnam" (Circular 103/2014/TT-BTC, 2014), 2.

41. Vu, *Several Tax Issues*, 7.

42. Public discussion between government officials and industry, Hanoi, August 2015.

43. Interviews 54, 60, 61.

44. The author attended as an observer.

45. Interview 62.

46. Interview 54.

47. Interviews 60, 54.

48. Interviews 55, 62; VBF-MOF consultation.

49. Interview 68.

50. Interview 62.

51. Margaret Slocomb, *An Economic History of Cambodia in the Twentieth Century* (Singapore: NUS Press, 2010), 231.

52. Siphana Sok, "Role of Law and Legal Institutions in Cambodia Economic Development: Opportunities to Skip the Learning Curve" (Doctoral thesis, Bond University, Australia, 2008), 52.

53. Slocomb, *Economic History of Cambodia in the Twentieth Century*, 236; David M. Ayres, *Anatomy of a Crisis: Education, Development, and the State in Cambodia, 1953–1998* (Honolulu: University of Hawaii Press, 2000).

54. Um Seiha, "Cambodia: Tax Revenue Reform Issues, Further Reforms," presentation at *Third IMF High Level Tax Conference for Asian and Pacific Countries* (Tokyo, January 31 to February 3, 2012), 6.

55. Slocomb, *Economic History of Cambodia in the Twentieth Century*, 279–80.

56. Slocomb, 279–80.

57. Interviews 64, 66.

58. Interviews 64, 65.

59. ASEAN, *ASEAN Economic Community Blueprint* (Jakarta: Association of Southeast Asian Nations, 2008), 14.

60. Interview 64.

61. Interview 67.

62. Interview 68.

63. Interviews 64, 65.

64. Martin Godfrey et al., "Technical Assistance and Capacity Development in an Aid-Dependent Economy: The Experience of Cambodia," *World Development* 30, no. 3 (2002): 359.

65. Ronald B. St. John, "The Political Economy of the Royal Government of Cambodia," *Contemporary Southeast Asia* 17, no. 3 (1995): 265–81.

66. World Bank, *Cambodia Country Economic Memorandum* (Washington, DC: World Bank, 1998), 9.

67. Interview 67.

68. Interview 66.

69. Interview 68.

70. Interview 67.

71. Interview 66.

72. Interview 68.

73. Interview 65.

74. Interviews 64, 66.

75. Interviews 64, 65.

76. Interviews 65, 66.

77. Interview 65.

78. Li, "Great Fiscal Wall of China."

79. Interview 66.

80. Interview 65.

8. HISTORICAL LEGACIES IN A RAPIDLY CHANGING WORLD

1. Cornel Ban and Mark Blyth, "The BRICs and the Washington Consensus: An Introduction," *Review of International Political Economy* 20, no. 2 (April 2013): 241–55, https://doi.org/10.1080/09692290.2013.779374; Robert H. Wade, "Emerging World Order? From Multipolarity to Multilateralism in the G20, the World Bank, and the IMF," *Politics & Society* 39, no. 3 (September 2011): 347–78, https://doi.org/10.1177/0032329211415503; Woods, "Global Governance after the Financial Crisis."

2. Eccleston, *Dynamics of Global Economic Governance*, 16.

3. Eliza Anyangwe, "Glee, Relief and Regret: Addis Ababa Outcome Receives Mixed Reception," *Guardian* (US edition), July 16, 2015, https://www.theguardian.com/global-development/2015/jul/16/outcome-document-addis-ababa-ffd3-financing-for-development.

4. Martin Hearson and Wilson Prichard, "China's Challenge to International Tax Rules and Implications for Global Economic Governance," *International Affairs* 94, no. 6 (2018): 1287–307.

5. Rasmus Corlin Christensen and Martin Hearson, "The New Politics of Global Tax Governance: Taking Stock a Decade after the Financial Crisis," *Review of International Political Economy* 26, no. 5 (September 2019): 1068–88, https://doi.org/10.1080/09692290.2019.1625802.

6. Tsilly Dagan, *International Tax Policy: Between Competition and Cooperation* (Cambridge: Cambridge University Press, 2017).

7. OECD, *Tax Sparing*, 21–23.

8. Eduardo Baistrocchi, "Tax Disputes under Institutional Instability: Theory and Implications," *Modern Law Review* 75, no. 4 (July 2012): 547–77, https://doi.org/10.1111/j.1468-2230.2012.00914.x.

9. Interview 69, and informal conversations at the meeting.

10. Interview 72; a point also made by both participants in interview 73.

11. Interview 71.

12. Interview 74.

13. Hearson and Prichard, "China's Challenge to International Tax Rules and Implications for Global Economic Governance"; ATAF, "Place of Africa in the Shift towards Global Tax Governance."

14. OECD, "OECD Tax Talks #11," January 29, 2019, https://www.oecd.org/ctp/tax-talks-webcasts.htm.

15. Rixen, "From Double Tax Avoidance to Tax Competition."

16. Eric Mensah, "Mobilizing Domestic Resources for Development & International Cooperation: Ghana's Perspective," *Presentation at G24 Technical Group Meeting* (Addis Ababa: Intergovernmental Group of 24, February 27–28, 2017).

17. Cited in Jinyan Li, "China and BEPS: From Norm-Taker to Norm-Shaker," *Bulletin for International Taxation* (June/July 2015): 359.

18. Interview 75.

19. Kabona Esiara, "Rwanda Caps Income Tax Outflows to 2pc," East African, September 8, 2018, https://www.theeastafrican.co.ke/business/Rwanda-caps-income-tax-outflows-to-2pc/2560-4750192-lvjpcez/index.html.

20. Hearson and Prichard, "China's Challenge to International Tax Rules and Implications for Global Economic Governance."

21. Solomon Rukundo, "Addressing the Challenges of Taxation of the Digital Economy: Lessons for African Countries" (International Centre for Tax and Development Working Papers, Institute of Development Studies, Brighton, UK, 2020).

22. OECD, "OECD Tax Talks #11."

23. Jennifer McLoughlin, "Digital Services Tax Approach Would Kill OECD Consensus," *Tax Notes International* (Falls Church, VA: Tax Analysts, 2019).

24. High-Level Panel on Illicit Financial Flows from Africa, *Illicit Financial Flows*, 81.

25. Kingsley Mamobolo, "Closing Statement on Behalf of the Group of 77 and China," Third International Conference on Financing for Development, Addis Ababa, July 16, 2015, http://www.g77.org/statement/getstatement.php?id=150716.

26. Interview 73.

27. Mutava, "Review of Tax Treaty Practices and Policy Framework in Africa."

28. Musah Yahaya Jafaru, "Minority Raises Issues with Taxation Agreement with 4 Countries," Graphic Online, May 15, 2018, https://www.graphic.com.gh/news/politics/minority-raises-issues-with-taxation-agreement-with-4-countries.html.

29. Daisy Ogembo, "The Tax Justice Network-Africa v Cabinet Secretary for National Treasury & 2 Others: A Big Win for Tax Justice Activism?" *British Tax Review*, no. 2 (2019): 105–19.

30. High Court of Kenya, Constitutional, Judicial Review and Human Rights Division, Petition 494 of 2014.

31. European Commission, "Toolbox Spill-Over Effects of EU Tax Policies on Developing Countries," Platform/26/2017/EN, June 15, 2017, https://ec.europa.eu/taxation_customs/sites/taxation/files/platform_dta_spillovers_toolbox.docx.pdf.

32. Hearson and Prichard, "China's Challenge to International Tax Rules and Implications for Global Economic Governance."

33. SAT, "Multi-pronged Measures Reflective of Responsible Tax Authorities in China—Overview of Taxes Supporting the Belt and Road Initiative [in Chinese], May 11, 2017, http://www.chinatax.gov.cn/eng/n2367726/c2694305/content.html.

34. Quoted in Li, "China and BEPS."

35. Christensen and Hearson, "New Politics of Global Tax Governance."

36. Martin Hearson, "The Challenges for Developing Countries in International Tax Justice," *Journal of Development Studies* 54, no. 10 (2018): 1932–38, https://doi.org/10.1080/00220388.2017.1309040.

37. Dagan, *International Tax Policy.*

38. IMF, *Spillovers in International Corporate Taxation*; European Commission, "Toolbox Spill-Over Effects of EU Tax Policies on Developing Countries"; see also Andrew Baker and Richard Murphy, "The Political Economy of 'Tax Spillover': A New Multilateral Framework," *Global Policy* 10, no. 2 (2019): 178–92.

39. Lips, "Great Powers in Global Tax Governance"; Hakelberg, "Coercion in International Tax Cooperation."

40. Interview 41.

41. Jacob S. Hacker, "Privatizing Risk without Privatizing the Welfare State: The Hidden Politics of Social Policy Retrenchment in the United States," *American Political Science Review* 98, no. 2 (2004): 243–60, https://doi.org/10.1017/S0003055404001121.

Bibliography

Abbott, Andrew. "Linked Ecologies: States and Universities as Environments for Professions." *Sociological Theory* 23, no. 3 (2005): 245–74. https://doi.org/10.1111/j.0735-2751.2005.00253.x.

ActionAid. *Mistreated: The Tax Treaties That Are Depriving the World's Poorest Countries of Vital Revenue.* London: ActionAid UK, 2016.

Amin, Ash, and Ronen Palan. "Towards a Non-rationalist International Political Economy." *Review of International Political Economy* 8, no. 4 (January 2001): 559–77. https://doi.org/10.1080/09692290110081534.

Antoniades, Andreas. "Epistemic Communities, Epistemes and the Construction of (World) Politics." *Global Society* 17, no. 1 (January 14, 2003): 21–38. https://doi.org/10.1080/0953732032000053980.

Anyangwe, Eliza. "Glee, Relief and Regret: Addis Ababa Outcome Receives Mixed Reception." *Guardian* (US edition), July 16, 2015. https://www.theguardian.com/global-development/2015/jul/16/outcome-document-addis-ababa-ffd3-financing-for-development.

Arel-Bundock, Vincent. "The Unintended Consequences of Bilateralism: Treaty Shopping and International Tax Policy." *International Organization* 71, no. 2 (2017): 349–71. https://doi.org/10.1017/S0020818317000108.

ASEAN. *ASEAN Economic Community Blueprint.* Jakarta: Association of South East Asian Nations, 2008.

Ash, Elliott, and Omri Marian. *The Making of International Tax Law: Empirical Evidence from Natural Language Processing.* Legal Studies Research Paper Series 2019–02. Irvine: University of California, 2019.

Association SHERPA, Berne Declaration, Centre for Trade Policy and Development, L'Entraide missionnaire, and Mining Alerte. *Specific Instance Regarding Glencore International AG and First Quantum Minerals Ltd and Their Alleged Violations of the OECD Guidelines for Multinational Enterprises via the Activities of Mopani Copper Mines Plc in Zambia.* Submission to OECD national contact points in Switzerland and Canada, 2011.

ATAF. "The Place of Africa in the Shift towards Global Tax Governance: Can the Taxation of the Digitalised Economy Be an Opportunity for More Inclusiveness." Pretoria: African Tax Administration Forum, 2019.

Aubrey, Henry G. *Atlantic Economic Cooperation.* New York: Published for the Council on Foreign Relations by Praeger, 1967.

Auerbach, Alan. "Why Have Corporate Tax Revenues Declined? Another Look." NBER Working Paper Series, Cambridge, MA, August 2006. https://doi.org/10.3386/w12463.

Aukonobera, Festus. "Uganda." In *The Impact of the OECD and UN Model Conventions on Bilateral Tax Treaties,* edited by Michael Lang, Pasquale Pistone, and Josef Schuch, 1083–100. Cambridge: Cambridge University Press, 2012.

Ault, Hugh J. "Reflections on the Role of the OECD in Developing International Tax Norms." *Brooklyn Journal of International Law* 34, no. 3 (2009): 756–81.

Auty, Richard. *Sustaining Development in Mineral Economies: The Resource Curse Thesis.* London: Routledge, 2002.

Avery Jones, John F. "Are Tax Treaties Necessary?" *Tax Law Review* 53, no. 1 (1999): 1–38.

———. "The United Kingdom's Influence on the OECD Model Tax Convention." *British Tax Review* 56, no. 6 (2011): 653–83.

Avi-Yonah, Reuven S. "Double Tax Treaties: An Introduction." In *The Effect of Treaties on Foreign Direct Investment*, edited by Karl P. Sauvant and Lisa E. Sachs, 99–106. New York: Oxford University Press, 2009. https://doi.org/10.1093/acprof:oso/9780195388534.003.0004.

———. "Globalization, Tax Competition, and the Fiscal Crisis of the Welfare State." *Harvard Law Review* 113, no. 7 (2000): 1573–676. https://doi.org/10.2307/1342445.

———. *International Tax as International Law.* New York: Cambridge University Press, 2007.

Ayres, David M. *Anatomy of a Crisis: Education, Development, and the State in Cambodia, 1953–1998.* Honolulu: University of Hawaii Press, 2000.

Azémar, Céline, and Andrew Delios. "Tax Competition and FDI: The Special Case of Developing Countries." *Journal of the Japanese and International Economies* 22, no. 1 (March 2008): 85–108. https://doi.org/10.1016/j.jjie.2007.02.001.

Azémar, Céline, Rodolphe Desbordes, and Jean-Louis L. Mucchielli. "Do Tax Sparing Agreements Contribute to the Attraction of FDI in Developing Countries?" *International Tax and Public Finance* 14, no. 5 (September 15, 2007): 543–62. https://doi.org/10.1007/s10797-006-9005-9.

Azémar, Céline, and Dhammika Dharmapala. "Tax Sparing Agreements, Territorial Tax Reforms, and Foreign Direct Investment." *Journal of Public Economics* 169 (January 1, 2019): 89–108. https://doi.org/10.1016/j.jpubeco.2018.10.013.

Baistrocchi, Eduardo. "The International Tax Regime and the BRIC World: Elements for a Theory." *Oxford Journal of Legal Studies* 33, no. 4 (December 1, 2013): 733–66. https://doi.org/10.1093/ojls/gqt012.

———. "Tax Disputes under Institutional Instability: Theory and Implications." *Modern Law Review* 75, no. 4 (July 2012): 547–77. https://doi.org/10.1111/j.1468-2230.2012.00914.x.

———. "The Use and Interpretation of Tax Treaties in the Emerging World: Theory and Implications." *British Tax Review* 28, no. 4 (2008): 352–91.

Baistrocchi, Eduardo, and Martin Hearson. *A Global Analysis of Tax Treaty Disputes.* Edited by Eduardo Baistrocchi. Cambridge: Cambridge University Press, 2017.

Baker, Andrew, and Richard Murphy. "The Political Economy of 'Tax Spillover': A New Multilateral Framework." *Global Policy* 10, no. 2 (2019): 178–92.

Baker, Paul L. "An Analysis of Double Taxation Treaties and Their Effect on Foreign Direct Investment." *International Journal of the Economics of Business* 21, no. 3 (September 2, 2014): 341–77. https://doi.org/10.1080/13571516.2014.968454.

Ban, Cornel, and Mark Blyth. "The BRICs and the Washington Consensus: An Introduction." *Review of International Political Economy* 20, no. 2 (April 2013): 241–55. https://doi.org/10.1080/09692290.2013.779374.

Barthel, Fabian, Matthias Busse, and Eric Neumayer. "The Impact of Double Taxation Treaties on Foreign Direct Investment: Evidence from Large Dyadic Panel Data." *Contemporary Economic Policy* 28, no. 3 (December 30, 2009): 366–77. https://doi.org/10.1111/j.1465-7287.2009.00185.x.

Barthel, Fabian, and Eric Neumayer. "Competing for Scarce Foreign Capital: Spatial Dependence in the Diffusion of Double Taxation Treaties." *International Studies Quarterly* 56, no. 4 (December 2012): 645–60. https://doi.org/10.1111/j.1468-2478.2012.00757.x.

Basinger, Scott J., and Mark Hallerberg. "Remodeling the Competition for Capital: How Domestic Politics Erases the Race to the Bottom." *American Political Science Review* 98, no. 2 (June 21, 2004): 261–76. https://doi.org/10.1017/S0003055404001133.

Baturo, Alexander, and Julia Gray. "Flatliners: Ideology and Rational Learning in the Adoption of the Flat Tax." *European Journal of Political Research* 48, no. 1 (2009): 130–59. https://doi.org/10.1111/j.1475-6765.2008.00830.x.

Becker, Johannes, and Clemens Fuest. "The Nexus of Corporate Income Taxation and Multinational Activity." *FinanzArchiv: Public Finance Analysis* 68, no. 3 (September 2012): 231–51. https://doi.org/10.1628/001522112X653822.

Beer, Sebastian, and Jan Loeprick. "Too High a Price? Tax Treaties with Investment Hubs in Sub-Saharan Africa." *International Tax and Public Finance*, advance online publication, July 31, 2020. https://doi.org/10.1007/s10797-020-09615-4.

Bell, Stephen, and Andrew Hindmoor. "The Structural Power of Business and the Power of Ideas: The Strange Case of the Australian Mining Tax." *New Political Economy* 19, no. 3 (May 30, 2013): 470–86. https://doi.org/10.1080/13563467.2013.796452.

Beyers, Jan. "Conceptual and Methodological Challenges in the Study of European Socialization." *Journal of European Public Policy* 17, no. 6 (2010): 909–20. https://doi.org/10.1080/13501763.2010.487004.

Bikhchandani, Sushil, David Hirshleifer, and Ivo Welch. "Learning from the Behavior of Others: Conformity, Fads, and Informational Cascades." *Journal of Economic Perspectives* 12, no. 3 (1998): 151–70.

——. "A Theory of Fads, Fashion, Custom, and Cultural Change as Informational Cascades." *Journal of Political Economy* 100, no. 5 (1992): 992–1026.

Blonigen, Bruce A., and Ronald B. Davies. "The Effects of Bilateral Tax Treaties on U.S. FDI Activity." *International Tax and Public Finance* 11, no. 5 (September 2004): 601–22. https://doi.org/10.1023/B:ITAX.0000036693.32618.00.

Blonigen, Bruce A., Lindsay Oldenski, and Nicholas Sly. "The Differential Effects of Bilateral Tax Treaties." *American Economic Journal: Economic Policy* 6 (2014): 1–18. https://doi.org/10.1257/pol.6.2.1.

Bourdieu, Pierre. "The Force of Law: Toward a Sociology of the Juridical Field." *Hastings Law Journal* 38, no. 1971 (1987): 805–53.

Braun, Julia, and Daniel Fuentes. *A Legal and Economic Analysis of Double Taxation Treaties between Austria and Developing Countries*. Vienna: Vienna Institute for International Dialogue and Cooperation, 2014.

Braun, Julia, and Martin Zagler. "The True Art of the Tax Deal: Evidence on Aid Flows and Bilateral Double Tax Agreements." *World Economy* 41, no. 6 (2018): 1478–507.

Brauner, Yariv. "An International Tax Regime in Crystallization." *Tax Law Review* 56, no. 2 (2003): 259–328.

Brautigam, Deborah. "Building Leviathan: Revenue, State Capacity and Governance." Edited by Deborah Brautigam. *IDS Bulletin* 33, no. 3 (2002): 10–20.

——. "Introduction: Taxation and State-Building in Developing Countries." In *Taxation and State-Building in Developing Countries*, edited by Deborah Brautigam, Odd-Helge Fjeldstad, and Mick Moore, 1–33. Cambridge: Cambridge University Press, 2008. https://doi.org/10.1017/CBO9780511490897.001.

Brooks, Kim. "Canada's Evolving Tax Treaty Policy toward Low-Income Countries." In *Globalization and Its Tax Discontents: Tax Policy and International Investments*, edited by Richard Krever, 187–211. Toronto: University of Toronto Press, 2010.

——. "Tax Treaty Treatment of Royalty Payments from Low-Income Countries: A Comparison of Canada and Australia's Policies." *EJournal of Tax Research* 5, no. 2 (2007): 168–97.

Brooks, Kim, and Richard Krever. "The Troubling Role of Tax Treaties." In *Tax Design Issues Worldwide*, edited by Geerten M. M. Michielse and Victor Thuronyi, 159–78. Alphen aan den Rijn, Netherlands: Kluwer Law International, 2015.

Broome, André, and Leonard Seabrooke. "Shaping Policy Curves: Cognitive Authority in Transnational Capacity Building." *Public Administration* 93, no. 4 (2015): 956–72. https://doi.org/dx.doi.org/10.1111/padm.12179.

Brugger, Fritz, and Rebecca Engebretsen. "Defenders of the Status Quo: Making Sense of the International Discourse on Transfer Pricing Methodologies." *Review of International Political Economy*, advance online publication, August 27, 2020. https://doi.org/10.1080/09692290.2020.1807386

Bunting, Roger, Peter Fawcett, and Caroline Makasa. *A Roadmap for Further Negotiations by COMESA Countries*. Brussels: ACE International Consultants, 2012.

———. *Working Document COMESA Model Double Taxation Agreement and Commentary*. Brussels: ACE International Consultants, 2011.

Burke, Edmund. *Reflections on the French Revolution*. London: Dent, 1955.

Business Daily. "Africa's Tax Officials Watch Uganda Case Keenly." February 23, 2014.

Buttner, Tim, and Matthias Thiemann. "Breaking Regime Stability? The Politicization of Expertise in the OECD G20 Process on BEPS and the Potential Transformation of International Taxation." *Accounting, Economics, and Law: A Convivium* 7, no. 1 (January 2017). https://doi.org/10.1515/ael-2016-0069.

Bwalya, L. W. *Report of the Commissioner of Taxes, 1973/4*. Lusaka: Zambia Department of Taxes, 1975.

Cao, Xun. "Global Networks and Domestic Policy Convergence: A Network Explanation of Policy Changes." *World Politics* 64, no. 3 (2012): 375–425.

———. "Networks as Channels of Policy Diffusion: Explaining Worldwide Changes in Capital Taxation, 1998–2006." *International Studies Quarterly* 54, no. 3 (September 6, 2010): 823–54. https://doi.org/10.1111/j.1468-2478.2010.00611.x.

———. "Networks of Intergovernmental Organizations and Convergence in Domestic Economic Policies." *International Studies Quarterly* 53, no. 4 (2009): 1095–130.

Carroll, Mitchell Benedict. *Global Perspectives of an International Tax Lawyer*. Hicksville: Exposition Press, 1978.

Chanda, Mutuna. "Should Zambia Impose Windfall Taxes on Mining Companies?" *BBC News Online*, September 13, 2011. https://www.bbc.co.uk/news/av/world-africa-14898575.

Charlton, Andrew. *Incentive Bidding for Mobile Investment: Economic Consequences and Potential Responses*. Paris: OECD Publishing, 2003. https://doi.org/10.1787/864178271805.

Checkel, Jeffrey T. "International Institutions and Socialization in Europe: Introduction and Framework." *International Organization* 59, no. 4 (2005): 801–26. https://doi.org/10.1017/S0020818305050289.

Chisik, Richard, and Ronald B. Davies. "Asymmetric FDI and Tax-Treaty Bargaining: Theory and Evidence." *Journal of Public Economics* 88, no. 6 (June 2004): 1119–48. https://doi.org/10.1016/s0047-2727(03)00059-8.

Chiwenda, D. *Report of the Commissioner of Taxes, 1971/2*. Lusaka: Zambia Department of Taxes, 1973.

———. *Report of the Commissioner of Taxes, 1972/3*. Lusaka: Zambia Department of Taxes, 1974.

Christensen, Rasmus Corlin. "Elite Professionals in Transnational Tax Governance." *Global Networks*, advance online publication, April 23, 2020. https://doi.org/10.1111/glob.12269.

Christensen, Rasmus Corlin, and Martin Hearson. "The New Politics of Global Tax Governance: Taking Stock a Decade after the Financial Crisis." *Review of International Political Economy* 26, no. 5 (September 3, 2019): 1068–88. https://doi.org/10.1080/09692290.2019.1625802.

Christians, Allison. "Global Trends and Constraints on Tax Policy in the Least Developed Countries." *University of British Columbia Law Review* 42, no. 2 (2010): 239–74.

———. "Networks, Norms and National Tax Policy." *Washington University Global Studies Law Review* 9, no. 1 (2010): 1–38.

———. "Sovereignty, Taxation, and Social Contract." University of Wisconsin Legal Studies Research Paper, 2008.

———. "Tax Treaties for Investment and Aid to Sub-Saharan Africa: A Case Study." *Brooklyn Law Review* 15, no. 1999 (2005): 639–700.

———. "Taxation in a Time of Crisis: Policy Leadership from the OECD to the G20." *Northwestern Journal of Law and Social Policy* 5, no. 1 (Spring 2010): 19–40.

———. "While Parliament Sleeps: Tax Treaty Practice in Canada." *Journal of Parliamentary and Political Law* 10, no. 15 (2016). https://doi.org/10.2139/ssrn.2780874.

Chwieroth, Jeffrey M. "Neoliberal Economists and Capital Account Liberalization in Emerging Markets." *International Organization* 61, no. 2 (April 11, 2007): 443–63. https://doi.org/10.1017/s0020818307070154.

———. "Testing and Measuring the Role of Ideas: The Case of Neoliberalism in the International Monetary Fund." *International Studies Quarterly* 51, no. 1 (March 1, 2007): 5–30. https://doi.org/10.1111/j.1468-2478.2007.00437.x.

Clausing, Kimberly. "The Nature and Practice of Tax Competition." In *Global Tax Governance: What Is Wrong with It and How to Fix It*, edited by Peter Dietsch and Thomas Rixen, 27–54. Colchester: ECPR Press, 2016.

Cockfield, Arthur J. "The Rise of the OECD as Informal World Tax Organization through National Responses to E-Commerce Tax Challenges." *Yale Journal of Law and Technology* 8 (2005): 136–87.

Connery, Jason R., Steven R. Lainoff, and Charles W. Cope. "Current Status of U.S. Tax Treaties and International Tax Agreements." *Tax Management International Journal* 42, no. 106 (2013): 1–10.

Crivelli, Ernesto, D. Benedek, Priscilla S. Muthoora, and S. Gupta. "Foreign Aid and Revenue: Still a Crowding Out Effect." *IMF Working Paper* 12/186. Washington, DC: International Monetary Fund, 2012.

Crivelli, Ernesto, Sanjeev Gupta, E. Crivelli, and S. Gupta. "Resource Blessing, Revenue Curse? Domestic Revenue Effort in Resource-Rich Countries." *European Journal of Political Economy*, no. 35 (2014): 88–101.

Culpepper, Pepper D. *Quiet Politics and Business Power: Corporate Control in Europe and Japan*. Cambridge: Cambridge University Press, 2010.

Curry, Robert L., Jr. "Problems in Acquiring Mineral Revenues for Financing Economic Development: A Case Study of Zambia during 1970–78." *American Journal of Economics and Sociology* 43, no. 1 (1984): 37–52.

Dagan, Tsilly. *International Tax Policy: Between Competition and Cooperation*. Cambridge: Cambridge University Press, 2017.

———. "The Tax Treaties Myth." *New York University Journal of International Law and Politics* 32 (2000): 939–96.

Dauer, Veronika, and Richard Krever. "Choosing between the UN and OECD Tax Policy Models: An African Case Study." EUI Working Papers, Florence, European University Institute, 2012.

Davies, Ronald B., Pehr-Johan Norbäck, and Ayça Tekin-Koru. "The Effect of Tax Treaties on Multinational Firms: New Evidence from Microdata." *World Economy* 32, no. 1 (January 2009): 77–110. https://doi.org/10.1111/j.1467-9701.2009.01158.x.

Davis Cross, Mai'a K. "Rethinking Epistemic Communities Twenty Years Later." *Review of International Studies* 39, no. 1 (April 11, 2012): 1–24. https://doi.org/10.1017/S0260210512000034.

Dietsch, Peter. *Catching Capital: The Ethics of Tax Competition.* New York: Oxford University Press, 2015.

Dietsch, Peter, and Thomas Rixen, eds. *Global Tax Governance: What Is Wrong with It and How to Fix It.* Colchester: ECPR Press, 2016.

DiMaggio, Paul J., and Walter W. Powell. "The Iron Cage Revisited: Institutional Isomorphism and Collective Rationality in Organizational Fields." *American Sociological Review* 48, no. 2 (1983): 147–60. https://doi.org/10.2307/2095101.

Dobbin, Frank, Beth A. Simmons, and Geoffrey Garrett. "The Global Diffusion of Public Policies: Social Construction, Coercion, Competition, or Learning?" *Annual Review of Sociology* 33, no. 1 (August 2007): 449–72. https://doi.org/10.1146/annurev.soc.33.090106.142507.

Dresang, Dennis L. *The Zambia Civil Service: Entrepreneurialism and Development Administration.* Nairobi: East African Pub. House, 1975.

Dresang, Dennis L., and Ralph A. Young. "The Public Service." In *Administration in Zambia,* edited by William Tordoff, 68–103. Manchester: Manchester University Press, 1980.

Dunlop, Claire A. "Policy Transfer as Learning: Capturing Variation in What Decision-Makers Learn from Epistemic Communities." *Policy Studies* 30, no. 3 (June 2009): 289–311. https://doi.org/10.1080/01442870902863869.

Durst, Michael C. "The Two Worlds of Transfer Pricing Policymaking." *Tax Notes,* January 24, 2011.

Eccleston, Richard. *The Dynamics of Global Economic Governance: The OECD, the Financial Crisis and the Politics of International Tax Cooperation.* Cheltenham: Edward Elgar, 2012.

———. "The OECD and Global Economic Governance." *Australian Journal of International Affairs* 65, no. 2 (2011): 243–55. https://doi.org/10.1080/10357718.2011.550106.

Eccleston, Richard, and Ainsley Elbra, eds. *Business, Civil Society and the 'New' Politics of Corporate Tax Justice.* Elgar Politics and Business Series. Cheltenham: Edward Elgar, forthcoming.

Eccleston, Richard, and Richard Woodward. "Pathologies in International Policy Transfer: The Case of the OECD Tax Transparency Initiative." *Journal of Comparative Policy Analysis: Research and Practice* 16, no. 3 (November 12, 2013): 216–29. https://doi.org/10.1080/13876988.2013.854446.

Eden, Lorraine, M. Tina Dacin, and William P. Wan. "Standards across Borders: Cross-border Diffusion of the Arm's Length Standard in North America." *Accounting, Organizations and Society* 26 (2001): 1–23.

Eden, Lorraine, and Robert T. Kudrle. "Tax Havens: Renegade States in the International Tax Regime?" *Law & Policy* 27, no. 1 (2005): 100–127.

Egger, Peter, and Valeria Merlo. "Statutory Corporate Tax Rates and Double-Taxation Treaties as Determinants of Multinational Firm Activity." *FinanzArchiv: Public Finance Analysis* 67, no. 2 (June 1, 2011): 145–70. https://doi.org/10.1628/001522111X588754.

Elias, Norbert. *The Civilizing Process.* Oxford: Blackwell, 1994.

Elkins, Zachary, Andrew T. Guzman, and Beth A. Simmons. "Competing for Capital: The Diffusion of Bilateral Investment Treaties, 1960–2000." *International Organization* 60, no. 4 (2006): 811–46. https://doi.org/10.1017/s0020818306060279.

Embassy of the Republic of Kenya. "Trade and Investment." Accessed November 19, 2012. http://www.kenyaembassy.com/economycommerce.html.

Esiara, Kabona. "Rwanda Caps Income Tax Outflows to 2pc." East African, September 8, 2018. https://www.theeastafrican.co.ke/tea/business/rwanda-caps-income-tax-out flows-to-2pc-1402004.

European Commission. "Toolbox Spill-Over Effects of EU Tax Policies on Developing Countries." Platform/26/2017/EN. June 15, 2017. https://ec.europa.eu/taxation_customs/sites/taxation/files/platform_dta_spillovers_toolbox.docx.pdf.

Evers, Maikel. "Tracing the Origins of the Netherlands' Tax Treaty." Intertax 41, no. 6 (2013): 375–86.

Eyitayo-Oyesode, Oladiwura Ayeyemi. "Source-Based Taxing Rights from the OECD to the UN Model Conventions: Unavailing Efforts and an Argument for Reform." Law and Development Review 13, no. 1 (2020): 193–227. https://doi.org/10.1515/ldr-2018 -0073.

Fairfield, Tasha. Private Wealth and Public Revenue in Latin America: Business Power and Tax Politics. New York: Cambridge University Press, 2015.

Farrow, Ian, and Sunita Jogarajan. "ASEAN Tax Regimes: Impediment or Pathway to Greater Integration." In Brick by Brick: The Building of an ASEAN Economic Community, edited by Denis Hew, 132–43. Singapore: Institute of Southeast Asian Studies / ASEAN-Australia Development Cooperation Programme, 2008.

——. ASEAN Tax Regimes and the Integration of the Priority Sectors: Issues and Options. Sydney: KPMG Australia, 2006.

Feld, Lars P., and Jost H. Heckemeyer. "FDI and Taxation: A Meta-Study." Journal of Economic Surveys 25, no. 2 (2011): 233–72. https://doi.org/10.1111/j.1467-6419.2010 .00674.x.

Fenochietto, Ricardo, and Carola Pessino. Understanding Countries' Tax Effort. Washington, DC: International Monetary Fund, 2013.

Finnemore, Martha. National Interests in International Society. Ithaca, NY: Cornell University Press, 1996.

Finnemore, Martha, and Kathryn Sikkink. "International Norm Dynamics and Political Change." International Organization 52, no. 4 (1998): 887–917. https://doi.org/10 .1162/002081898550789.

Fioretos, Orfeo. "Historical Institutionalism in International Relations." International Organization 65, no. 2 (April 2011): 367–99. https://doi.org/10.1017/S00208183 11000002.

Fjeldstad, Odd-Helge, and Mick Moore. "Revenue Authorities and Public Authority in Sub-Saharan Africa." Journal of Modern African Studies 47, no. 1 (March 18, 2009): 1–18. https://doi.org/10.1017/S0022278X08003637.

——. "Tax Reform and State-Building in a Globalised World." In Taxation and State-Building in Developing Countries, edited by Deborah Brautigam, Odd-Helge Fjeldstad, and Mick Moore, 235–60. Cambridge: Cambridge University Press, 2008. https://doi.org/10.1017/CBO9780511490897.010.

Fordham, Benjamin O., and Victor Asal. "Billiard Balls or Snowflakes? Major Power Prestige and the International Diffusion of Institutions and Practices." International Studies Quarterly 51, no. 1 (March 2007): 31–52. https://doi.org/10.1111/j.1468 -2478.2007.00438.x.

Frecknall-Hughes, Jane, and Margaret McKerchar. "Historical Perspectives on the Emergence of the Tax Profession: Australia and the UK." Australian Tax Forum 28, no. 2 (2013): 276–88.

Fuchs, Doris A. Business Power in Global Governance. Boulder, CO: Lynne Rienner Publishers, 2007.

Gainsborough, Martin. "Vietnam and ASEAN: The Road to Membership?" *Pacific Review* 6, no. 4 (January 1993): 381–87. https://doi.org/10.1080/09512749308719061.

Garcia-Bernardo, Javier, Jan Fichtner, Eelke M. Heemskerk, and Frank W. Takes. "Uncovering Offshore Financial Centers: Conduits and Sinks in the Global Corporate Ownership Network." *Scientific Reports* 7 (June 2017): 1–18. https://doi.org/10.1038/s41598-017-06322-9.

General Statistic Office of Vietnam. "Foreign Direct Investment Projects Licensed by Main Counterparts (Accumulation of Projects Having Effect as of 31/12/2012)." 2014. http://www.gso.gov.vn/default_en.aspx?tabid=471&idmid=3&ItemID=14366.

Genschel, Philipp, and Thomas Rixen. "Settling and Unsettling the Transnational Legal Order." In *Transnational Legal Orders*, edited by T. C. Halliday and G. Shaffer, 154–86. Cambridge Studies in Law and Society. Cambridge: Cambridge University Press, 2015.

Genschel, Philipp, and Peter Schwarz. "Tax Competition: A Literature Review." *Socio-Economic Review* 9, no. 2 (March 15, 2011): 339–70. https://doi.org/10.1093/ser/mwr004.

Genschel, Philipp, and Laura Seelkopf. "Did They Learn to Tax? Taxation Trends outside the OECD." *Review of International Political Economy* 23, no. 2 (2016): 316–44. https://doi.org/10.1080/09692290.2016.1174723.

Gheciu, Alexandra. "Security Institutions as Agents of Socialization? NATO and the 'New Europe.'" *International Organization* 59, no. 4 (2005): 973–1012. https://doi.org/10.1017/S0020818305050332.

Gilardi, Fabrizio. "Transnational Diffusion: Norms, Ideas, and Policies." In *Handbook of International Relations*, edited by Walter Carlsnaes, Thomas Risse, and Beth A. Simmons, 453–77. London: SAGE Publications, 2012. https://doi.org/10.4135/9781446247587.n18.

Gillis, Malcolm. "Toward a Taxonomy for Tax Reform." In *Tax Reform in Developing Countries*, edited by Malcolm Gillis, 7–21. Durham, NC: Duke University Press, 1989.

Godfrey, Martin, Chan Sophal, Toshiyasu Kato, and Long Vou. "Technical Assistance and Capacity Development in an Aid-Dependent Economy: The Experience of Cambodia." *World Development* 30, no. 3 (2002): 355–73.

Goldberg, Honey Lynn. "Conventions for the Elimination of International Double Taxation: Toward a Developing Country Model." *Law & Policy in International Business* 15 (1983): 833–909.

Goldscheid, Rudolf. "A Sociological Approach to Problems of Public Finance." In *Classics in the Theory of Public Finance*, edited by Richard A. Musgrave and Alan T. Peacock, 202–13. London: Palgrave Macmillan UK, 1958. https://doi.org/10.1007/978-1-349-23426-4_14.

Grabel, Ilene. *When Things Don't Fall Apart: Global Financial Governance and Developmental Finance in an Age of Productive Incoherence*. Cambridge, MA: MIT Press, 2017.

Graetz, Michael J. "Taxing International Income: Inadequate Principles, Outdated Concepts, and Unsatisfactory Policies." *Brooklyn Journal of International Law* 1 (2000): 261–336.

Graetz, Michael J., and Michael M. O'Hear. "The 'Original Intent' of U.S. International Taxation." *Duke Law Journal* 46, no. 5 (1997): 1020–109. https://doi.org/10.2307/1372916.

Green, Robert A. "Antilegalistic Approaches to Resolving Disputes between Governments: A Comparison of the International Tax and Trade Regimes." *Yale Journal of International Law* 23 (1998): 79.

Grinberg, Itai. "The New International Tax Diplomacy." *Georgetown Law Journal* 104, no. 5 (2016): 1191.

Grossman, Gene M., and Elhanan Helpman. "Protection for Sale." *American Economic Review* 84, no. 4 (1994): 833–50.

Gupta, Sanjeev, Benedict Clements, E. R. Tiongsen, and Alexander Pivovarsky. "Foreign Aid and Revenue Response: Does the Composition of Aid Matter?" In *Helping Countries Develop: The Role of Fiscal Policy*, edited by Gabriela Inchauste, Sanjeev Gupta, and Benedict Clements, 285–305 Washington, DC: International Monetary Fund, 2004.

Haas, Peter M. "Introduction: Epistemic Communities and International Policy Coordination." *International Organization* 46, no. 1 (May 22, 1992): 1–35. https://doi.org/10.1017/S0020818300001442.

Hacker, Jacob S. "Privatizing Risk without Privatizing the Welfare State: The Hidden Politics of Social Policy Retrenchment in the United States." *American Political Science Review* 98, no. 2 (2004): 243–60. https://doi.org/10.1017/S0003055404001121.

Hakelberg, Lukas. "Coercion in International Tax Cooperation: Identifying the Prerequisites for Sanction Threats by a Great Power." *Review of International Political Economy* 23, no. 3 (May 3, 2016): 511–41. https://doi.org/10.1080/09692290.2015.1127269.

Harvard Law Review. "Protection of Foreign Direct Investment in a New World Order: Vietnam. A Case Study." 107, no. 8 (1994): 1995–2012. https://doi.org/10.2307/1341765.

Hearson, Martin. "The Challenges for Developing Countries in International Tax Justice." *Journal of Development Studies* 54, no. 10 (2018): 1932–38. https://doi.org/10.1080/00220388.2017.1309040.

——. "Measuring Tax Treaty Negotiation Outcomes: The ActionAid Tax Treaties Dataset." International Centre for Tax and Development Working Paper 47, Institute of Development Studies, Brighton, UK, 2016.

——. Tax Treaties Explorer (website), 2020. http://treaties.tax.

——. *Tax Treaties in Sub-Saharan Africa: A Critical Review*. Nairobi: Tax Justice Network Africa, 2015.

——. "When Do Developing Countries Negotiate Away Their Corporate Tax Base?" *Journal of International Development* 30, no. 2 (2018): 233–55.

Hearson, Martin, and Richard Brooks. *Calling Time: Why SABMiller Should Stop Dodging Taxes in Africa*. London: ActionAid UK, 2010.

Hearson, Martin, and Jalia Kangave. "A Review of Uganda's Tax Treaties and Recommendations for Action." International Centre for Tax and Development Working Paper 50, Institute of Development Studies, Brighton, UK, 2016.

Hearson, Martin, and Wilson Prichard. "China's Challenge to International Tax Rules and Implications for Global Economic Governance." *International Affairs* 94, no. 6 (2018): 1287–307.

Heilmann, Sebastian, and Nicole Schulte-Kulkmann. "The Limits of Policy Diffusion: Introducing International Norms of Anti-money Laundering into China's Legal System." *Governance* 24, no. 4 (October 1, 2011): 639–64. https://doi.org/10.1111/j.1468-0491.2011.01543.x.

High-Level Panel on Illicit Financial Flows from Africa. *Illicit Financial Flows*. Addis Ababa: United Nations Economic Commission for Africa, 2015. http://www.uneca.org/sites/default/files/PublicationFiles/iff_main_report_26feb_en.pdf.

Hines, James R., Jr. "'Tax Sparing' and Direct Investment in Developing Countries." In *International Taxation and Multinational Activity*, edited by James R. Hines Jr., 39–72. Chicago: University of Chicago Press, 2000.

HMRC. "Taxation: A Brief History." Bicentenary of Income Tax. HMRC website. Archived June 5, 2013. http://webarchive.nationalarchives.gov.uk/+/http://www.hmrc.gov.uk/history/index.htm.

Hong, Sunghoon. "Tax Treaties and Foreign Direct Investment: A Network Approach." *International Tax and Public Finance* 25, no. 5 (October 2018): 1277–320. https://doi.org/10.1007/s10797-018-9489-0.

Hopewell, Kristen. "Different Paths to Power: The Rise of Brazil, India and China at the World Trade Organization." *Review of International Political Economy* 22, no. 2 (March 4, 2015): 311–38. https://doi.org/10.1080/09692290.2014.927387.

IBFD. "IBFD Tax Research Platform." 2020. http://research.ibfd.org/.

ICTD/UNU-WIDER. "Government Revenue Dataset." UNU-WIDER, 2018. https://www.wider.unu.edu/project/government-revenue-dataset.

IMF, OECD, UN, and World Bank. *Supporting the Development of More Effective Tax Systems: A Report to the G-20 Development Working Group by the IMF, OECD, UN and World Bank.* Paris: OECD Publishing, 2011.

International Monetary Fund. "Coordinated Direct Investment Survey." Updated March 13, 2020. https://data.imf.org/?sk=40313609-F037-48C1-84B1-E1F1CE54D6D5.

———. "Spillovers in International Corporate Taxation." IMF Policy Paper, Washington, DC, 2014.

Irish, Charles R. "International Double Taxation Agreements and Income Taxation at Source." *International and Comparative Law Quarterly* 23, no. 2 (1974): 292–316. https://doi.org/10.1093/iclqaj/23.2.292.

———. "Transfer Pricing Abuses and Less Developed Countries." *University of Miami Inter-American Law Review* 18, no. 1 (1986): 83–136.

Jacobsen, John Kurt. "Much Ado about Ideas: The Cognitive Factor in Economic Policy." *World Politics* 47, no. 2 (1995): 283–310. https://doi.org/10.2307/2950654.

Jacobsson, Bengt. "Regulated Regulators: Global Trends of States Transformation." In *Transnational Governance: Institutional Dynamics of Regulation*, edited by Marie-Laure Djelic and Kerstin Sahlin-Andersson, 205–24. Cambridge: Cambridge University Press, 2006.

Jafaru, Musah Yahaya. "Minority Raises Issues with Taxation Agreement with 4 Countries." Graphic Online, May 15, 2018. https://www.graphic.com.gh/news/politics/minority-raises-issues-with-taxation-agreement-with-4-countries.html.

Jandhyala, Srividya, Witold J. Henisz, and Edward D. Mansfield. "Three Waves of BITs: The Global Diffusion of Foreign Investment Policy." *Journal of Conflict Resolution* 55, no. 6 (August 23, 2011): 1047–73. https://doi.org/10.1177/0022002711414373.

Janský, Petr, and Marek Šedivý. "Estimating the Revenue Costs of Tax Treaties in Developing Countries." *World Economy*, December 7, 2018. https://doi.org/10.1111/twec.12764.

Jensen, Nathan M. "Domestic Institutions and the Taxing of Multinational Corporations." *International Studies Quarterly* 57, no. 3 (September 24, 2013): 440–48. https://doi.org/10.1111/isqu.12015.

Jensen, Nathan M., and René Lindstadt. "Leaning Right and Learning from the Left: Diffusion of Corporate Tax Policy across Borders." *Comparative Political Studies* 45, no. 3 (2012): 283–311. https://doi.org/10.1177/0010414011421313.

Jogarajan, Sunita. *Double Taxation and the League of Nations.* Cambridge: Cambridge University Press, 2018. https://doi.org/10.1017/9781108368865.

John, Jonathan Di. "The Political Economy of Taxation and Tax Reform in Developing Countries." Research Paper 74, Helsinki, UNU World Institute for Development Economics Research, 2006.

John, Ronald B. St. "The Political Economy of the Royal Government of Cambodia." *Contemporary Southeast Asia* 17, no. 3 (1995): 265–81.

Johnston, Alastair Iain. "Conclusions and Extensions: Toward Mid-range Theorizing and beyond Europe." *International Organization* 59, no. 4 (2005): 1013–44.

——. *Social States: China in International Institutions, 1980–2000*. Princeton, NJ: Princeton University Press, 2008.

Kahneman, Daniel, and Amos Tversky. "Prospect Theory: An Analysis of Decision under Risk." *Econometrica* 47, no. 2 (1979): 263–91. https://doi.org/10.2307/191 4185.

Kaizuka, Keimei. "The Shoup Tax System and the Postwar Development of the Japanese Economy." *American Economic Review* 82, no. 2 (May 1, 1992): 221–25.

Kaldor, Nicholas. "Will Underdeveloped Countries Learn to Tax?" *Foreign Affairs* 41, no. 2 (1963): 410–19.

Kaufman, Nancy H. "Fairness and the Taxation of International Income." *Law & Policy in International Business* 29, no. 2 (1998): 145–203.

Kaunda, Kenneth David. *Zambia's Economic Revolution: Address at Mulungushi, 19th April, 1968*. Lusaka: Zambia Information Services, 1968.

Keen, Michael. "Taxation and Development - Again." In *Critical Issues in Taxation and Development*, edited by Clemens Fuest and George R. Zodrow (Cambridge, MA: MIT Press, 2013), 13–44.Keen, Michael, and Mario Mansour. "Revenue Mobilization in Sub-Saharan Africa: Challenges from Globalization." Working Paper 9/157, International Monetary Fund, Washington, DC, 2009.

Kinda, Tidiane. "The Quest for Non-resource-based FDI: Do Taxes Matter?" Working Paper 14/15, International Monetary Fund, Washington, DC, 2014.

Kinuthia, Bethuel Kenyanjui. "Determinants of Foreign Direct Investment in Kenya: New Evidence." In *Proceedings of the African International Business and Management Conference*. Nairobi, August 25–27, 2010.

Klemm, Alexander, and S. M. Ali Abass. "A Partial Race to the Bottom: Corporate Tax Developments in Emerging and Developing Economies." IMF Working Paper 12/28, Washington, DC: International Monetary Fund, 2012.

Knack, Stephen. "Sovereign Rents and Quality of Tax Policy and Administration." *Journal of Comparative Economics* 37, no. 3 (2009): 359–71.

Knoetze, M. *Report of the Commissioner of Taxes, 1966/7*. Lusaka: Zambia Department of Taxes, 1968.

Kratochwil, Friedrich, and John Gerard Ruggie. "International Organization: A State of the Art on an Art of the State." *International Organization* 40, no. 4 (May 22, 1986): 753–75. https://doi.org/10.1017/S0020818300027363.

Larmer, Miles. *Rethinking African Politics: A History of Opposition in Zambia*. Farnham: Ashgate, 2011.

Latham & Watkins LLP. "Federal Ministry of Finance Publishes Model for Future Double Tax Treaties." *Tax Info*, January 8, 2014.

Latulippe, Lynne. "The Expansion of the Bilateral Tax Treaty Network in the 1990s: The OECD's Role in International Tax Coordination." *Australian Tax Forum* 27, no. 4 (2012): 851–84.

——. "Tax Competition: An Internalised Policy Goal." In *Global Tax Governance: What Is Wrong with It and How to Fix It*, edited by Peter Dietsch and Thomas Rixen, 77–100. Colchester: ECPR Press, 2016.

League of Nations. *Report of the Committee of Technical Experts on Double Taxation and Tax Evasion*. Geneva: League of Nations, 1927.

League of Nations Fiscal Committee. "Report to the Council on the Work of the Tenth Session of the Committee." League of Nations, 1946. C.37.M.37.1946.II.A. Geneva: United Nations Archive.

Leaman, Jeremy, and Attiya Waris, eds. *Tax Justice and the Political Economy of Global Capitalism, 1945 to the Present*. New York: Berghahn Books, 2013.

Lee, Chang Kil, and David Strang. "The International Diffusion of Public-Sector Downsizing: Network Emulation and Theory-Driven Learning." *International Organization* 60, no. 4 (2006): 883–909. https://doi.org/10.1017/S002081830606292.

Lejour, Arjan. "The Foreign Investment Effects of Tax Treaties." CPB Netherlands Bureau for Economic Analysis Discussion Paper 265, 2014.

Lennard, Michael. "The UN Model Tax Convention as Compared with the OECD Model Tax Convention—Current Points of Difference and Recent Developments." *Asia-Pacific Tax Bulletin*, no. 1 (2009): 4–11.

Lesage, Dries, David Mcnair, and Mattias Vermeiren. "From Monterrey to Doha: Taxation and Financing for Development." *Development Policy Review* 28, no. 2 (2010): 155–72. https://doi.org/10.1111/j.1467-7679.2010.00479.x.

Levi, Margaret. *Of Rule and Revenue*. Berkeley: University of California Press, 1988.

Lewis, Mike. *Sweet Nothings: The Human Cost of a British Sugar Giant Avoiding Taxes in Southern Africa*. London: ActionAid UK, 2013.

Li, Jinyan. "China and BEPS: From Norm-Taker to Norm-Shaker." *Bulletin for International Taxation* 69, no. 6/7 (2015): 355–70.

———. "The Great Fiscal Wall of China: Tax Treaties and Their Role in Defining and Defending China's Tax Base." *Bulletin for International Taxation* 66, no. 9 (2012): 452–79.

Library of Congress. "History of the US Income Tax." Business Reference Services. Updated 2012. http://www.loc.gov/rr/business/hottopic/irs_history.html.

Lindblom, Charles Edward. *Politics and Markets: The World's Political and Economic Systems*. New York: Basic Books, 1977.

Linos, Katerina. "Diffusion through Democracy." *American Journal of Political Science* 55, no. 3 (2011): 678–95. https://doi.org/10.1111/j.1540-5907.2011.00513.x.

Lips, Wouter. "Great Powers in Global Tax Governance: A Comparison of the US Role in the CRS and BEPS." *Globalizations* 16, no. 1 (January 2, 2019): 104–19. https://doi.org/10.1080/14747731.2018.1496558.

Luhanga, PC. *Report of the Commissioner of Taxes, 1970/1*. Lusaka: Zambia Department of Taxes, 1972.

Maffini, Giorgia, ed. *Business Taxation under the Coalition Government*. Oxford: Oxford University Centre for Business Taxation, 2015.

Mahon, Rianne, and Stephen McBride. "Standardizing and Disseminating Knowledge: The Role of the OECD in Global Governance." *European Political Science Review* 1, no. 1 (March 20, 2009): 83–101. https://doi.org/10.1017/S1755773909000058.

Mamobolo, Kingsley. "Closing Statement on Behalf of the Group of 77 and China." Third International Conference on Financing for Development, Addis Ababa, July 16, 2015. http://www.g77.org/statement/getstatement.php?id=150716.

Manger, Mark S. *Investing in Protection: The Politics of Preferential Trade Agreements between North and South*. Cambridge: Cambridge University Press, 2009.

Manley, David. *A Guide to Mining Taxation in Zambia*. Lusaka: Zambia Institute for Policy Analysis & Research, 2013.

Mansfield, Edward D., and Helen V. Milner. *Votes, Vetoes, and the Political Economy of International Trade Agreements*. Oxford: Princeton University Press, 2012.

March, James G., and Johan P. Olsen. "The Institutional Dynamics of International Political Orders." *International Organization* 52, no. 4 (1998): 943–69.

———. "The Logic of Appropriateness." In *The Oxford Handbook of Public Policy*, edited by Robert E. Goodin, Michael Moran, and Martin Rein, 689–708. Oxford: Oxford University Press, 2008. https://doi.org/10.1093/oxfordhb/9780199548453.003.0034.

———. *Rediscovering Institutions: The Organizational Basis of Politics*. New York: Free Press, 1989.

Marcussen, Martin. "The OECD in Search of a Role: Playing the Ideas Game." Paper presented at the *ECPR Joint Session of Workshops*, Grenoble, 2001.

Marjolin, Robert. "Double Taxation in Europe: Resolution Adopted by the Executive Committee of the International Chamber of Commerce (Note by the Secretary-General)." OEEC, November 12, 1954. IR40/19035. National Archives, London.

Marshall, Rex, Malcolm Smith, and Robert Armstrong. "The Impact of Audit Risk, Materiality and Severity on Ethical Decision Making." *Managerial Auditing Journal* 21, no. 5 (June 14, 2006): 497–519. https://doi.org/10.1108/02686900610667265.

Martin, Antony. *Minding Their Own Business: Zambia's Struggle Against Western Control.* Harmondsworth: Penguin, 1975.

Martin, Isaac William, Ajay K. Mehrotra, and Monica Prasad. "The Thunder of History: The Origins and Development of the New Fiscal Sociology." In *The New Fiscal Sociology*, edited by Isaac William Martin, Ajay K. Mehrotra, and Monica Prasad, 1–28. Cambridge: Cambridge University Press, 2009. https://doi.org/10.1017/CBO9780 511627071.002.

McGauran, Katrin. *Should the Netherlands Sign Tax Treaties with Developing Countries?* Amsterdam: SOMO, 2013.

McLoughlin, Jennifer. "Digital Services Tax Approach Would Kill OECD Consensus." *Tax Notes International.* Falls Church, VA: Tax Analysts, February 4, 2019.

Mensah, Eric. "Mobilizing Domestic Resources for Development & International Cooperation: Ghana's Perspective." *Presentation at G24 Technical Group Meeting.* Addis Ababa: Intergovernmental Group of 24, February 27–28, 2017.

Millimet, Daniel L., and Abdullah Kumas. "It's All in the Timing: Assessing the Impact of Bilateral Tax Treaties on U.S. FDI Activity." In *The Effect of Treaties on Foreign Direct Investment*, edited by Karl P. Sauvant and Lisa E. Sachs, 535–657. New York: Oxford University Press, 2009. https://doi.org/10.1093/acprof:oso/9780195388534 .003.0022.

Ministerio de Economía y Finanzas de Peru. "Sobre Los Convenios Para Evitar La Doble Tributación Para Promover La Inversión y Evitar La Evasión Fiscal Internacional." May 15, 2001. http://www.mef.gob.pe/index.php?option=com_content&view=arti cle&id=2199%3Asobre-los-convenios-para-evitar-la-doble-tributacion-para -promover-la-inversion-y-evitar-la-evasion-fiscal-internacional&catid=297%3Ap reguntas-frecuentes&Itemid=100143&lang=es.

Ministry of Finance. *Guidelines for Fulfilment of Tax Liability of Foreign Entities Doing Business in Vietnam or Earning Income in Vietnam*, Circular 103/2014/TT-BTC, 2014.

Mishra, Sanjay Kumar. "Letter to Alexander Trepelkov." Ministry of Finance, Government of India, 2012. https://www.un.org/esa/ffd/wp-content/uploads/2014/10/ICTM2012 _LetterIndia.pdf.

Mkandawire, Thandika. "On Tax Efforts and Colonial Heritage in Africa." *Journal of Development Studies* 46, no. 10 (2010): 1647–69. https://doi.org/10.1080/00220388 .2010.500660.

Mooij, Ruud A. de, and Sjef Ederveen. "Corporate Tax Elasticities: A Reader's Guide to Empirical Findings." *Oxford Review of Economic Policy* 24, no. 4 (2008): 680–97. https://doi.org/10.1093/oxrep/grn033.

Moore, Mick. "Between Coercion and Contract: Competing Narratives on Taxation and Governance." In *Taxation and State-Building in Developing Countries*, edited by Deborah Brautigam, Odd-Helge Fjeldstad, and Mick Moore, 34–63. Cambridge: Cambridge University Press, 2008. https://doi.org/10.1017/CBO9780511490897 .002.

Moore, Mick, Wilson Prichard, and Odd-Helge Fjeldstad. *Taxing Africa: Coercion, Reform and Development.* African Arguments. London: Zed Books, 2018.

Moravcsik, Andrew. "Taking Preferences Seriously: A Liberal Theory of International Politics." *International Organization* 51, no. 4 (October 1, 1997): 513–53. https://doi.org/10.1162/002081897550447.

Morrisey, Oliver, Wilson Prichard, and Samantha Torrance. "Aid and Taxation: Exploring the Relationship Using New Data." International Centre for Tax and Development Working Paper 21, Institute of Development Studies, Brighton, UK, 2014.

Mosley, Layna. "Globalisation and the State: Still Room to Move?" *New Political Economy* 10, no. 3 (September 6, 2005): 355–62. https://doi.org/10.1080/13563460500204241.

———. "Room to Move: International Financial Markets and National Welfare States." *International Organization* 54, no. 4 (October 1, 2000): 737–73. https://doi.org/10.1162/002081800551352.

Mullins, Peter J. "Moving to Territoriality? Implications for the United States and the Rest of the World." IMF Working Paper 06/161, Washington, DC, 2006.

Musgrave, Peggy B. "Sovereignty, Entitlement, and Cooperation in International Taxation." *Brooklyn Journal of International Law* 26, no. 4 (2000): 1335–56.

Mutava, Catherine Ngina. "Review of Tax Treaty Practices and Policy Framework in Africa." International Centre for Tax and Development Working Paper 102, Institute of Development Studies, Brighton, UK, 2019. https://opendocs.ids.ac.uk/opendocs/handle/20.500.12413/14900.

Mwachinga, Edward. "Results of Investor Motivation Survey Conducted in the EAC." Presentation at regional workshop on tax incentives, Lusaka, February 12–13, 2013.

Mwenda, Kenneth Kaoma. "Efficacy of the Institutional and Regulatory Framework for the Administration of Tax Law in Zambia." *Richmond Journal of Global Law and Business* 5, no. 1 (2005): 37–67.

Nelson, Charles G. "The Role of the OECD in International Economic Negotiations." Unpublished PhD thesis, Indiana University, 1970.

Nölke, Andreas, and Arjan Vliegenthart. "Enlarging the Varieties of Capitalism: The Emergence of Dependent Market Economies in East Central Europe." *World Politics* 61, no. 4 (2009): 670–702.

Norwegian Government Commission on Capital Flight from Poor Countries. *Tax Havens and Development: Status, Analyses and Measures*. Oslo: Government Commission on Capital Flight from Poor Countries, 2009.

Oates, Wallace E. (Wallace Eugene). *Fiscal Federalism*. New York: Harcourt Brace Jovanovich, 1972.

Ogembo, Daisy. "The Tax Justice Network-Africa v Cabinet Secretary for National Treasury & 2 Others: A Big Win for Tax Justice Activism?" *British Tax Review* 2019, no. 2 (2019): 105–19.

OECD. *Action Plan on Base Erosion and Profit Shifting*. Paris: OECD Publishing, 2013.

———. *Addressing Base Erosion and Profit Shifting*. Paris: OECD Publishing, 2013. https://doi.org/10.1787/9789264192744-en.

———. *Investment Policy Review of Zambia (2011 Preliminary Draft)*. Paris: OECD Publishing, 2011.

———. *Measuring and Monitoring BEPS, Action 11—2015 Final Report*. OECD/G20 Base Erosion and Profit Shifting Project. Paris: OECD Publishing, 2015. http://www.oecd-ilibrary.org/taxation/measuring-and-monitoring-beps-action-11-2015-final-report_9789264241343-en.

———. *Model Tax Convention on Income and on Capital*. Paris: OECD Publishing, 2014.

———. "OECD Tax Talks #11," January 29, 2019. https://www.oecd.org/ctp/tax-talks-webcasts.htm.

———. *Report to G20 Development Working Group on the Impact of BEPS in Low Income Countries (Parts 1 and 2)*. Paris: OECD Publishing, 2014.

———. *Tax Aspects of Transfer Pricing within Multinational Enterprises: The United States Proposed Regulations: A Report*. Paris: OECD Publishing, 1993.

———. *Tax Sparing: A Reconsideration*. Paris: OECD Publishing, 1998.

OEEC. "Creation of a Committee of Experts on Taxation (Note Submitted by the Dutch Delegation)." OEEC, July 11, 1955. IR40/19035. National Archives, London.

———. "Draft Report of the Ad Hoc Group of Experts of Fiscal Questions." OEEC, February 15, 1956. IR40/19035. National Archives, London.

———. "Interim on the Activities of the Fiscal Committee." OEEC, July 3, 1957. IR40/19035. National Archives, London.

———. "Proposal by the Netherlands, Swiss and German Delegations concerning Double Taxation Questions to Be Discussed by a Group of Taxation Experts Which Should Be Set Up within the O.E.E.C." OEEC, December 9, 1955. IR40/19035. National Archives, London.

Office for National Statistics. "Foreign Direct Investment Involving UK Companies: Outward." February 2020. https://www.ons.gov.uk/businessindustryandtrade/business/businessinnovation/datasets/foreigndirectinvestmentinvolvingukcompaniesoutwardtables.

Oman, Charles. *Policy Competition for Foreign Direct Investment: A Study of Competition among Governments to Attract FDI*. Paris: OECD Publishing, 2000.

Organisation Internationale de la Francophonie. "LIC Ministers Demand Their Fair Share of Global Tax Revenues." Press note, 2014. http://www.oecd.org/dac/OIF%20Recommendations.pdf.

Owens, Jeffrey, and Mary C. Bennett. "The OECD Model Tax Convention: Why It Works." *OECD Observer2*, October 2008. http://oecdobserver.org/news/archivestory.php/aid/2756/OECD_Model_Tax_Convention.html.

Palan, Ronen. *The Offshore World: Sovereign Markets, Virtual Places, and Nomad Millionaires*. Ithaca, NY: Cornell University Press, 2003.

Palan, Ronen, Richard Murphy, and Christian Chavagneux. *Tax Havens: How Globalization Really Works*. Ithaca, NY: Cornell University Press, 2010.

Paolini, Dimitri, Pasquale Pistone, Giuseppe Pulina, and Martin Zagler. "Tax Treaties with Developing Countries and the Allocation of Taxing Rights." *European Journal of Law and Economics* 42, no. 3 (December 28, 2016): 383–404. https://doi.org/10.1007/s10657-014-9465-9.

Petkova, Kunka, Andrzej Stasio, and Martin Zagler. "On the Relevance of Double Tax Treaties." *International Tax and Public Finance*, September 21, 2019. https://doi.org/10.1007/s10797-019-09570-9.

Pham, Hoang Mai. *Foreign Direct Investment and Development in Vietnam: Policy Implications*. Singapore: Institute of Southeast Asian Studies, 2004.

Philipps, Lisa. "Discursive Deficits: A Feminist Perspective on the Power of Technical Knowledge in Fiscal Law and Policy." *Canadian Journal of Law and Society* 11, no. 1 (1996): 141–76.

Picciotto, Sol. "Indeterminacy, Complexity, Technocracy and the Reform of International Corporate Taxation." *Social & Legal Studies* 24, no. 2 (2015): 165–84. https://doi.org/10.1177/0964663915572942.

———. *International Business Taxation: A Study in the Internationalization of Business Regulation*. London: Weidenfeld & Nicolson, 1992.

Pickering, Ariane. *Why Negotiate Tax Treaties?* New York: United Nations, 2013.

Pinto, Pablo M. *Partisan Investment in the Global Economy: Why the Left Loves Foreign Direct Investment and FDI Loves the Left*. Cambridge: Cambridge University Press, 2013.

Pinto, Pablo M., and Santiago M. Pinto. "The Politics of Investment Partisanship: And the Sectoral Allocation of Foreign Direct Investment." *Economics & Politics* 20, no. 2 (June 2008): 216–54. https://doi.org/10.1111/j.1468-0343.2008.00330.x.

Pistone, Pasquale. "Tax Treaties with Developing Countries: A Plea for New Allocation Rules and a Combined Legal and Economic Approach." In *Tax Treaties: Building Bridges between Law and Economics*, edited by Michael Lang, Pasquale Pistone, Josef Schuch, Claus Staringer, Alfred Storck, and Martin Zagler, 413–40. Amsterdam: IBFD, 2010.

Plesner Rossing, Christian. "Tax Strategy Control: The Case of Transfer Pricing Tax Risk Management." *Management Accounting Research* 24, no. 2 (June 2013): 175–94. https://doi.org/10.1016/j.mar.2013.04.008.

Plümper, Thomas, Vera E. Troeger, and Hannes Winner. "Why Is There No Race to the Bottom in Capital Taxation?" *International Studies Quarterly* 53, no. 3 (September 2009): 761–86. https://doi.org/10.1111/j.1468-2478.2009.00555.x.

Porter, Tony, and Michael Webb. "The Role of the OECD in the Orchestration of Global Knowledge Networks." *Canadian Political Science Association Annual Meetings*, no. 1 (2007): 1–16.

Poulsen, Lauge N. Skovgaard. *Bounded Rationality and Economic Diplomacy: The Politics of Investment Treaties in Developing Countries*. Cambridge: Cambridge University Press, 2015.

——. "Bounded Rationality and the Diffusion of Modern Investment Treaties." *International Studies Quarterly* 58, no. 1 (2014): 1–14. https://doi.org/10.1111/isqu.12051.

——. "Sacrificing Sovereignty by Chance: Investment Treaties, Developing Countries, and Bounded Rationality." PhD thesis, London School of Economics, 2011.

Poulsen, Lauge N. Skovgaard, and Emma Aisbett. "When the Claim Hits: Bilateral Investment Treaties and Bounded Rational Learning." *World Politics* 65, no. 2 (2014): 273–313.

Prichard, Wilson, Alex Cobham, and Andrew Goodall. "The ICTD Government Revenue Dataset." International Centre for Tax and Development Working Paper 19, Institute of Development Studies, Brighton, UK, 2014.

Putnam, Robert D. "Diplomacy and Domestic Politics: The Logic of Two-Level Games." *International Organization* 42, no. 3 (1988): 427–60. https://doi.org/10.1017/S0020818300027697.

PWC. *Evolution of Territorial Tax Systems in the OECD*. Washington, DC: Prepared for the Technology CEO Council, 2013.

——. *Transfer Pricing and Developing Countries: Final Report*. Brussels: European Commission, 2011.

Quang, Ngo Dinh, and Nguyen Tien Dung. "Tax Reform in Vietnam." *Vietnam's Socio-Economic Development: A Social Science Review*, no. 10 (1997): 3–16.

Quinones Cruz, Natalia. "Colombia." In *The Impact of the OECD and UN Model Conventions on Bilateral Tax Treaties*, edited by Michael Lang, Pasquale Pistone, and Josef Schuch, 294–307. Cambridge: Cambridge University Press, 2012.

Radaelli, Claudio M. "Game Theory and Institutional Entrepreneurship: Transfer Pricing and the Search for Coordination International Tax Policy." *Policy Studies Journal* 26, no. 4 (1998): 603–19.

Rakner, Lise. *Political and Economic Liberalisation in Zambia, 1991–2001*. Stockholm: Nordic Africa Institute, 2003.

Rama, Martin, Deepak Mishra, and Duc Minh Pham. "Overview of the Tax System in Vietnam." In *Tax Reform in Vietnam: Towards a More Efficient and Equitable System*, edited by Gangadha Prasad Shukla, Duc Minh Pham, Michael Engelschalk, and Tuan Minh Le, 17–32. Washington, DC: World Bank, 2011.

Ring, Diane M. "International Tax Relations: Theory and Implications." *New York University Tax Law Review* 60 (2006): 83–154.

——. "Who Is Making International Tax Policy? International Organizations as Power Players in a High Stakes World." Boston College Law School Faculty Papers 264, 2010.

Rixen, Thomas. "Bilateralism or Multilateralism? The Political Economy of Avoiding International Double Taxation." *European Journal of International Relations* 16, no. 4 (December 2010): 589–614. https://doi.org/10.1177/1354066109346891.

——. "From Double Tax Avoidance to Tax Competition: Explaining the Institutional Trajectory of International Tax Governance." *Review of International Political Economy* 18, no. 2 (2011): 197–227. https://doi.org/10.1080/09692290.2010.481921.

——. *The Political Economy of International Tax Governance.* New York: Palgrave Macmillan, 2008.

——. "Politicization and Institutional (Non-) Change in International Taxation." WZB Discussion Paper, SP IV 2008-306, Berlin, Wissenschaftszentrum Berlin für Sozialforschung, 2008.

——. "Tax Competition and Inequality: The Case for Global Tax Governance." *Global Governance* 17 (2011): 447–67.

Rixen, Thomas, and Peter Schwarz. "Bargaining over the Avoidance of Double Taxation: Evidence from German Tax Treaties." *FinanzArchiv: Public Finance Analysis* 65, no. 4 (December 1, 2009): 442–71. https://doi.org/10.1628/001522109X486589.

Rixen, Thomas, and Lora Anne Viola. "Historical Institutionalism and International Relations: Towards Explaining Change and Stability in International Institutions." In *Historical Institutionalism and International Relations: Explaining Institutional Development in World Politics*, edited by Thomas Rixen, Lora Anne Viola, and Michael Zurn, 3–34. Oxford: Oxford University Press, 2016.

Robinson, James A., Ragnar Torvik, and Thierry Verdier. "Political Foundations of the Resource Curse." *Journal of Development Economics* 79, no. 2 (2006): 447–68.

Rosenbloom, H. David. "Cross-Border Arbitrage: The Good, the Bad and the Ugly." *Taxes* 85, no. 3 (2007): 115–17.

——. "Where's the Pony? Reflections on the Making of International Tax Policy." *Canadian Tax Journal* 57, no. 3 (2009): 489–503.

Rukundo, Solomon. "Addressing the Challenges of Taxation of the Digital Economy: Lessons for African Countries." International Centre for Tax and Development Working Paper, Institute of Development Studies, Brighton, UK, 2020.

Saasa, Oliver S. *Zambia's Policies towards Foreign Investment: The Case of the Mining and Non-mining Sectors.* Uppsala: Scandinavian Institute of African Studies, 1987.

SADC. *Memorandum of Understanding on Co-operation in Taxation and Related Matters.* Pretoria: Southern African Development Community, 2002.

Sadiq, Kerrie. "The Inherent International Tax Regime and Its Constraints on Australia's Sovereignty." *University of Queensland Law Journal* 31, no. 1 (2012): 131–46.

Sardanis, Andrew. *Zambia: The First Fifty Years.* London: IB Tauris, 2014.

Sauvant, Karl P., and Lisa E. Sachs, eds. *The Effect of Treaties on Foreign Direct Investment.* Oxford: Oxford University Press, 2009.

Schneider, Ben Ross. "Hierarchical Market Economies and Varieties of Capitalism in Latin America." *Journal of Latin American Studies* 41, no. 3 (2009): 553–75.

Schumpeter, Joseph. "The Crisis of the Tax State." In *Joseph A. Schumpeter: The Economics and Sociology of Capitalism*, edited by Richard A. Swedberg, 99–140. Princeton, NJ: Princeton University Press, 1991.

Seabrooke, Leonard. "Economists and Diplomacy: Professions and the Practice of Economic Policy." *International Journal* (Summer 2011): 629–42.

——. "Epistemic Arbitrage: Transnational Professional Knowledge in Action." *Journal of Professions and Organization* 1, no. 1 (March 1, 2014): 49–64. https://doi.org/10.1093/jpo/jot005.

Seabrooke, Leonard, and Eleni Tsingou. "Revolving Doors and Linked Ecologies in the World Economy: Policy Locations and the Practice of International Financial Reform." Working paper 260, Centre for the Study of Globalisation and Regionalisation, University of Warwick, 2009.

Seabrooke, Leonard, and Duncan Wigan. "Powering Ideas through Expertise: Professionals in Global Tax Battles." *Journal of European Public Policy* 23, no. 3 (2016): 357–74. https://doi.org/10.1080/13501763.2015.1115536.

Seidman, Ann. "The Distorted Growth of Import-Substitution Industry: The Zambian Case." *Journal of Modern African Studies* 12, no. 4 (1974): 601–31.

Seiha, Um. "Cambodia: Tax Revenue Reform Issues, Further Reforms." Presentation at *Third IMF High Level Tax Conference for Asian and Pacific Countries*. Tokyo, January 31 to February 3, 2012.

Self, Heather. "Some Treaty Issues for Developing Countries." Queen Mary University guest lecture, London, January 30, 2014.

Seligman, Edwin R. A. *Double Taxation and International Fiscal Cooperation: Being a Series of Lectures Delivered at the Académie de Droit International de La Haye.* New York: Macmillan, 1928.

——. *The Income Tax: A Study of the History, Theory, and Practice of Income Taxation at Home and Abroad.* New York: Macmillan, 1914.

Sending, Ole Jacob, and Iver B. Neumann. "Banking on Power: How Some Practices in an International Organization Anchor Others." In *International Practices*, edited by Emanuel Adler and Vincent Pouliot, 231–54. Cambridge: Cambridge University Press, 2011.

Sharman, Jason C. *Havens in a Storm: The Global Struggle for Tax Regulation.* Ithaca, NY: Cornell University Press, 2006.

——. "Offshore and the New International Political Economy." *Review of International Political Economy* 17, no. 1 (2010): 1–19. https://doi.org/10.1080/09692290802686940.

——. "Power and Discourse in Policy Diffusion: Anti-money Laundering in Developing States." *International Studies Quarterly* 52, no. 3 (2008): 635–56. https://doi.org/10.1111/j.1468-2478.2008.00518.x.

——. "Seeing Like the OECD on Tax." *New Political Economy* 17, no. 1 (2012): 37–41.

Shaw, Timothy M. "The Foreign Policy System of Zambia." *African Studies Review* 19, no. 1 (1976): 31–66.

Simmons, Beth A., and Zachary Elkins. "The Globalization of Liberalization: Policy Diffusion in the International Political Economy." *American Political Science Review* 98, no. 1 (2004): 171–89.

Sjöstedt, Gunnar. *OECD-Samarbetet: Funktioner Och Effekter.* Stockholm Political Studies. Stockholm: Statsvetenskapliga institutionen, 1973.

Sklair, Leslie. "Social Movements for Global Capitalism: The Transnational Capitalist Class in Action." *Review of International Political Economy* 4, no. 3 (January 1, 1997): 514–38. https://doi.org/10.1080/096922997347733.

Skocpol, Theda. "Bringing the State Back In: Strategies of Analysis in Current Research." In *Bringing the State Back In*, edited by Peter B. Evans, Dietrich Rueschemeyer, and Theda Skocpol, 3–38. Cambridge: Cambridge University Press, 1985. https://doi.org/10.1017/CBO9780511628283.002.

Slocomb, Margaret. *An Economic History of Cambodia in the Twentieth Century.* Singapore: NUS Press, 2010.

Snape, John. *The Political Economy of Corporation Tax: Theory, Values and Law Reform.* Oxford: Hart, 2011.

——. "Tax Law: Complexity, Politics and Policymaking." *Social & Legal Studies* 24, no. 2 (2015): 155–63. https://doi.org/10.1177/0964663915575969.

Soifer, Hillel David. "The Causal Logic of Critical Junctures." *Comparative Political Studies* 45, no. 12 (2012): 1572–97.

Sok, Siphana. "Role of Law and Legal Institutions in Cambodia Economic Development: Opportunities to Skip the Learning Curve." Doctoral thesis, Bond University, Australia, 2008.

Solingen, Etel. "Of Dominoes and Firewalls: The Domestic, Regional, and Global Politics of International Diffusion." *International Studies Quarterly* 56, no. 4 (2012): 631–44. https://doi.org/10.1111/isqu.12034.

Soskice, David W., and Peter A. Hall, eds. *Varieties of Capitalism: The Institutional Foundations of Comparative Advantage.* Oxford: Oxford University Press, 2001.

Stackelberg, Heinrich Von. *Market Structure and Equilibrium* [Marktform Und Gleichgewicht]. Heidelberg: J. Springer, 1934.

Stewart, Miranda. "Global Trajectories of Tax Reform: The Discourse of Tax Reform in Developing and Transition Countries." *Harvard International Law Journal* 44, no. 1 (2003): 139–90.

Sullivan, Scott. *From War to Wealth: Fifty Years of Innovation.* Paris: OECD Publishing, 1997.

Swank, Duane. "Tax Policy in an Era of Internationalization: Explaining the Spread of Neoliberalism." *International Organization* 60, no. 4 (October 25, 2006): 847–82. https://doi.org/10.1017/S0020818306060280.

't Riet, Maarten van, and Arjan Lejour. "Optimal Tax Routing: Network Analysis of FDI Diversion." *International Tax and Public Finance* 25, no. 5 (October 2018): 1321–71. https://doi.org/10.1007/s10797-018-9491-6.

Tanzi, Vito. "Globalization, Technological Developments, and the Work of Fiscal Termites." *Brooklyn Journal of International Law* 26 (2000): 1261–85.

Thomas, Alun H., and Juan P. Trevino. *Resource Dependence and Fiscal Effort in Sub-Saharan Africa.* Washington, DC: International Monetary Fund, 2013.

Thuronyi, Victor. "International Tax Cooperation and a Multilateral Treaty." *Brooklyn Journal of International Law* 26 (2000): 1641–81.

——. "Introduction." In *Tax Law Design and Drafting*, edited by Victor Thuronyi, xxi–xxxv. Washington, DC: International Monetary Fund, 1998.

——. "Tax Treaties and Developing Countries." In *Tax Treaties: Building Bridges between Law and Economics*, edited by Michael Lang, Pasquale Pistone, Josef Schuch, Claus Staringer, Alfred Storck, and Martin Zagler, 441–58. Amsterdam: IBFD, 2010.

Tiebout, Charles M. "A Pure Theory of Local Expenditures." *Journal of Political Economy* 64, no. 5 (1956): 416–24.

Tilly, Charles. *Coercion, Capital, and European States, A.D. 990–1990.* Cambridge, MA: Basil Blackwell, 1992.

——. "Extraction and Democracy." In *The New Fiscal Sociology*, edited by Isaac William Martin, Ajay K. Mehrotra, and Monica Prasad, 173–82. Cambridge: Cambridge University Press, 2009. https://doi.org/10.1017/CBO9780511627071.011.

——, ed. *The Formation of National States in Western Europe.* Princeton, NJ: Princeton University Press, 1975.

Towns, Ann E. "Norms and Social Hierarchies: Understanding International Policy Diffusion 'From Below.'" *International Organization* 66, no. 2 (April 5, 2012): 179–209. https://doi.org/10.1017/s0020818312000045.

Tran-Nam, Binh. "Economic Liberalization and Vietnam's Long-Term Growth Prospects." *Journal of the Asia Pacific Economy* 4, no. 2 (January 1999): 233–57. https://doi.org /10.1080/13547869908724681.

———. "Taxation and Economic Development in Vietnam." In *Taxation in ASEAN and China: Local Institutions, Regionalism, Global Systems and Economic Development*, edited by Nolan Cormac Sharkey, 126–46. Abingdon: Routledge, 2012.

Truman, Mike. "Tax Prat of the Year." *Taxation*, February 6, 2013.

Tsebelis, George. *Veto Players: How Political Institutions Work*. New York: Russell Sage Foundation, 2002.

Tsingou, Eleni. "Club Governance and the Making of Global Financial Rules." *Review of International Political Economy* 22, no. 2 (2014): 225–56. https://doi.org/10.1080 /09692290.2014.890952.

UNCTAD. "International Tax and Investment Policy Coherence." In *World Investment Report 2015*, 175–218. Geneva: United Nations Conference on Trade and Development, 2015. http://unctad.org/en/PublicationChapters/wir2015ch5_en .pdf.

UNCTAD and Japan Bank for International Cooperation. *Blue Book on Best Practice in Investment Promotion and Facilitation*. Geneva: United Nations, 2006.

UNICE. "UNICE Comments on US Transfer Pricing Regulations." *Intertax* 21, no. 8 (1993): 380–81.

United Nations. "Economic Committee: Summary Record of the One Hundred and Sixteenth Meeting." United Nations, 1951. IR40/9959. National Archives, London.

———. *Manual for the Negotiation of Bilateral Tax Treaties between Developed and Developing Countries 2918*. New York: United Nations, 20019.

———. *Model Double Taxation Convention between Developed and Developing Countries*. 2011 ed. New York: United Nations, 2011.

———. "Report of the Fiscal Commission (Third Session)." United Nations, 1951. IR40/9959. National Archives, London.

———. *Tax Treaties between Developed and Developing Countries: First Report*. Edited by Ad Hoc Group of Experts on Tax Treaties between Developed and Developing Countries. New York: United Nations, 1969.

———. *Tax Treaties between Developed and Developing Countries: Second Report*. Edited by Ad Hoc Group of Experts on Tax Treaties between Developed and Developing Countries. New York: United Nations, 1970.

Vega, Alberto, and Ilja Rudyk. "Explaining Reservations to the OECD Model Tax Convention: An Empirical Approach." *Indret*, no. 4 (2011): 1–19.

Volden, Craig, Michael M. Ting, and Daniel P. Carpenter. "A Formal Model of Learning and Policy Diffusion." *American Political Science Review* 102, no. 3 (August 25, 2008): 319–32. https://doi.org/10.1017/S0003055408080271.

Vu, Huong. *Several Tax Issues*. Hanoi: Vietnam Business Forum, 2014.

Wade, Robert H. "Emerging World Order? From Multipolarity to Multilateralism in the G20, the World Bank, and the IMF." *Politics & Society* 39, no. 3 (September 2011): 347–78. https://doi.org/10.1177/0032329211415503.

Waltz, Kenneth Neal. *Theory of International Politics*. Boston: McGraw-Hill, 1979.

Webb, Michael C. "Defining the Boundaries of Legitimate State Practice: Norms, Transnational Actors and the OECD's Project on Harmful Tax Competition." *Review of International Political Economy* 11, no. 4 (August 2004): 787–827. https://doi.org/10 .1080/0969229042000279801.

———. "Shaping International Corporate Taxation." In *Global Corporate Power*, edited by Christopher May, 105–26. Boulder: Lynne Rienner, 2006.

Weiss, Linda. "Bringing Domestic Institutions Back In." In *States in the Global Economy: Bringing Domestic Institutions Back In*, edited by Linda Weiss, 1–34. Cambridge: Cambridge University Press, 2007.

Were, Emmanuel. "Kenya: France Telecom Entry Eases Tax Burden." *Business Daily*, December 16, 2007.

Weyland, Kurt. *Bounded Rationality and Policy Diffusion: Social Sector Reform in Latin America*. Princeton, NJ: Princeton University Press, 2007.

———. "Theories of Policy Diffusion - Lessons from Latin American Pension Reform." *World Politics* 57, no. 2 (2005): 262–95. https://doi.org/10.1353/wp.2005.0019.

Weyzig, Francis. "Tax Treaty Shopping: Structural Determinants of Foreign Direct Investment Routed through the Netherlands." *International Tax and Public Finance* 20, no. 6 (December 11, 2013): 910–37. https://doi.org/10.1007/s10797-012-9250-z.

Wigan, Duncan, and Adam Baden. "Professional Activists on Tax Transparency." In *Professional Networks in Transnational Governance*, edited by Leonard Seabrooke and Lasse Folke Henriksen, 130–46. Cambridge: Cambridge University Press, 2017.

Wijnen, Wim, and Jan de Goede. *The UN Model in Practice, 1997–2013*. Amsterdam: International Bureau of Fiscal Documentation, 2013.

Wijnen, Wim, Jan de Goede, and Andrea Alessi. "The Treatment of Services in Tax Treaties." *Bulletin for International Taxation* 66, no. 1 (2012): 27–38.

Wikileaks. "Public Library of US Diplomacy." Accessed June 22, 2015. https://search.wikileaks.org/plusd.

Williamson, John. "What Washington Means by Policy Reform." In *Latin American Adjustment: How Much Has Happened?*, edited by John Williamson, 7–20. Washington, DC: Institute for International Economics, 1990.

Woods, Ngaire. "Global Governance after the Financial Crisis: A New Multilateralism or the Last Gasp of the Great Powers?" *Global Policy* 1, no. 1 (January 2010): 51–63. https://doi.org/10.1111/j.1758-5899.2009.0013.x.

World Bank. *Cambodia Country Economic Memorandum*. Washington, DC: World Bank, 1998.

Ylönen, Matti, and Teivo Teivainen. "Politics of Intra-firm Trade: Corporate Price Planning and the Double Role of the Arm's Length Principle." *New Political Economy*, September 12, 2017, 1–17. https://doi.org/10.1080/13563467.2017.1371124.

Zambia Ministry of Development Planning and National Guidance. *Second National Development Plan, January, 1972–December, 1976*. Lusaka: Zambia Ministry of Development Planning and National Guidance, 1971.

Zimbabwe Investment Authority. "Exploring Investments in Zimbabwe." Accessed November 19, 2012. http://www.zimottawa.com/files/investing_in_zimbabwe.pdf.

Zito, Anthony R. "Epistemic Communities, Collective Entrepreneurship and European Integration." *Journal of European Public Policy* 8, no. 4 (2001): 585–603. https://doi.org/10.1080/13501760110064401.

Zolt, Eric M. "Tax Treaties and Developing Countries." Law-Econ Research Paper 18–10, UCLA School of Law, 2018.

Zürn, Michael, and Jeffrey T. Checkel. "Getting Socialized to Build Bridges: Constructivism and Rationalism, Europe and the Nation-State." *International Organization* 59, no. 4 (2005): 1045–79. https://doi.org/10.1017/S0020818305050356.

Index

Note: Page numbers in *italics* refer to figures and tables.